Sports Agents and Labour

The sports agent has become a highly significant figure in contemporary sport business. The role of the agent is essential to our understanding of labour markets and labour relations in an increasingly globalised sports industry. Drawing on extensive empirical research into football around the world, this book explains what agents do, how their role has changed, and why this is important for future sport business.

Offering analysis from economic, legal, social and historical perspectives, the book explores key topics such as:

- the history of sports agents, including the emergence of the modern agent in US sport
- typologies and demographic profiles of agents in football
- valuations and organisational analysis of leading European agents and agencies
- relations between agents and clubs
- future directions for research into sports agents.

Focusing on the major European leagues, this book goes further than any other in illuminating an important but under-researched aspect of contemporary sport business. It is a valuable resource for any student, researcher or policy-maker with an interest in sport business, sport management, sport policy, the economics of sport or labour economics.

Giambattista Rossi is currently Lecturer in Sport Labour Markets at Birkbeck, University of London, UK.

Anna Semens is currently Head of Analytics at Havas Sports and Entertainment Cake, with a PhD focussing on the economics of football – specifically the role of agents in football labour markets.

Jean Francois Brocard is a Lecturer at the University of Limoges, France, and a researcher at the Centre de Droit et d'Economie du Sport.

Routledge Research in Sport Business and Management

Sports Agents and Labour Markets

Evidence from world football

Giambattista Rossi, Anna Semens and Jean Francois Brocard

Routledge
Taylor & Francis Group

LONDON AND NEW YORK

First published 2016
by Routledge

2 Park Square, Milton Park, Abingdon, Oxfordshire OX14 4RN
711 Third Avenue, New York, NY 10017

Routledge is an imprint of the Taylor & Francis Group, an informa business

First issued in paperback 2017

British Library Cataloguing-in-Publication Data
A catalogue record for this book is available from the British Library

Library of Congress Cataloging in Publication Data
A catalog record for this book has been requested

ISBN: 978-1-138-01522-7 (hbk)
ISBN: 978-0-8153-9477-8 (pbk)

Typeset in Times New Roman
by Wearset Ltd, Boldon, Tyne and Wear

Contents

Figures

Tables

About the authors

Giambattista Rossi is currently Lecturer in Sport Labour Markets at Birkbeck, University of London. Holding a PhD in Management from Birkbeck, his research focuses on the economics of the labour market in football. His expertise is on pay-performance relationships, production functions and players' salaries and transfer fees. In 2011, Giambattista was awarded the CIES-FIFA Joao Havelange Scholarship. He carried out extensive and relevant research on football agents with the big five European football leagues. His expertise on the industry of sports agents was also enriched by his previous working experience for a leading football agency in Italy. This has allowed Giambattista to deepen his knowledge and to create his research network.

Anna Semens is currently Head of Analytics at Havas Sports and Entertainment Cake, with over ten years of experience in the sport and entertainment industry and a PhD focussing on the economics of football – specifically the role of agents in football labour markets. She has consulted for a wide range of football clubs, brands and governing bodies, as well as conducting commissioned research for national governments and the European Commission on various issues relating to commercial and economic aspects of the sports industry.

Jean Francois Brocard is the General Secretary of the International Association of Sports Economists. He has Masters degrees in both Management and Economics from the Ecole Normale Supérieure of Paris. In 2009, he was a member of the research group that conducted the Study on Sports Agents in the European Union on behalf of the European Commission. At the end of 2012, he was awarded a doctoral degree in Economics, conducting an extensive research on the intermediation of professional athletes in Europe and in the United States. He is currently associate researcher for the Centre for Law and Economics of Sport (CDES) in Limoges. Jean Francois has published extensively on various aspects of the role of intermediaries in the industry of sport in both academic and practitioner publications.

Preface

Sports Agents and Labour Markets: Evidence from world football analytically examines the intriguing profession of football agents, and the industry encompassing it, within the context of labour and transfer markets. Our intention is to give an up to date and complete picture of the evolution of the labour market from the perspective of the agent's profession. Despite being a multi-million pound industry, little analysis has been conducted around the role of agents, and what has been published tends to be found in newspaper articles, governing bodies' reports and media investigations. It is not surprising therefore that the focus has tended to be on the shady side of player recruitment and transfer markets. The authors at times agree with these reports but have also seen another side to the profession. Based on our research interests, expertise and publications, this text looks at the business and legal aspects that impact the profession of football agents, using case studies and empirical analysis while also giving a nod to relevant theoretical frameworks.

The first four chapters of this book describe the historical context in which the agency business has developed, as well as the current picture of activities currently occurring in the industry. Chapter 1 examines the development of the football agent's industry in Europe, drawing parallels with that of other sports in the US representation industry. Chapter 2 provides an exhaustive description of the role of football agents today and a brief insight into what the typical agent looks like in terms of their demographic profile. Chapter 3 considers the business structure of agents, paying particular attention to consolidation in the market, before Chapter 4 provides an empirical analysis of what these developments mean for the industry in terms of power in the marketplace. Addressing concerns which may arise relating to this market concentration, the regulatory framework is considered in Chapter 5. The legal evolution of the profession is then charted from the first FIFA licensed system to the most recent intermediary reforms, introduced by FIFA. Throughout the book we refer to power struggles and Chapter 6 takes a closer look at where this power comes from and how it is perpetuated through the lens of network theory. The way in which agents have come to adapt to their environment by being entrepreneurial is presented in Chapter 7, which delivers a case study of the practice of third party entitlement in football, particularly highlighting how agents have been able to exploit this to extend their influence within transfer markets. Chapter 8 draws all of the current debates together and presents what we think may be future challenges to the current football landscape which have an impact directly and indirectly on the function of agents. The final chapter evaluates where we currently stand and where the industry is headed.

It should be noted that the book focuses specifically, although not exclusively, on European football transfer and labour markets. Although the football agent industry does have global dimensions, these markets are the richest, and arguably the best, in the world and as such are central to its operation. They therefore provide a strong lens through which to view the profession.

With the emphasis on European football labour markets, we focus on the big five European leagues. As competition for clients from the non-major football leagues in South and North America and South Asia increases, many of the issues impacting the major leagues will affect these emerging leagues as well.

A point of style should be noted. The legally correct name for the individual who represents the athlete is 'athlete agent', not 'sports agent'. The individual is the agent for the athlete, not the sport. The term 'sports agent', however, has developed, as probably the most commonly recognised and accepted label, so the terms 'athlete agent', 'sports agent', and 'agent' are used liberally and interchangeably throughout. Similarly, recent changes in FIFA's legislation replace the governance of agents with rules on dealing with intermediaries. There are subtle differences between the two which will be explained where relevant. However, these nuances do not materially affect the way these individuals operate.

While we have endeavoured to present the most complete picture possible there are inevitable constraints in terms of words and time. The industry is constantly changing and we have done our best to keep pace with this. The situation when we began to write this book was such that stricter regulations were being called for to make the industry more respectable. Financial fair play and the home grown players' rules were forcing European teams to think twice about spending huge sums of money (even if they were still doing it), while cases of third party ownership were a rarity, in England at least, and didn't really enter the public consciousness aside from the odd scandal in the press. In a relatively short space of time the concept of a licensed agent has been replaced by a free market of intermediaries, financial fair play has been relaxed and TPO in various guises has been banned completely. Various legal challenges have been launched around all of these issues. In such a fast-paced environment it is inevitable that a lot of detail that we could have included has not made it into the final edit of this book. We hope that there is enough that has to sustain the reader's interest!

Abbreviations

ABI	Acquired Brand Income
AEAF	Asociación Española de Agentes de Futbolistas
AEG	Anschutz Entertainment Group
AFA	Association of Football Agents
AFE	Asociación de Futbolistas Españoles
AFIP	Administración Federal de Ingresos Públicos
AIACS	Associazione Italiana Agenti Calciatori e Società
AIM	Alternative Investment Market
ASA	Advertising Standards Authority
ASL	American Soccer League
CAA	Creative Artists Agency
CAS	Court of Arbitration for Sport
CBA	Collective Bargaining Agreement
CBF	Confederação Brasileira de Futebol
CDES	Centre de Droit et d'Economie du Sport
CEO	Chief Executive Officer
CFAS	Commission Fédérale des Agents Sportifs
CFI	Court of First Instance
CIES	Centre International d'Étude du Sport
CNMC	Comisión Nacional de los Mercados y la Competencia
CONCACAF	Confederation of North, Central America or Caribbean Association Football
CONMEBOL	Confederación Sudamerica de Fútbol
COO	Chief Operating Officer
CVM	Comissão de Valores Mobiliários
DDR	Deutsche Demokratische Republik
DFB	Deutsche Fußball-Bund
DNCG	Direction Nationale du Contrôle de Gestion
DTMS	Domestic Transfer Matching System
EBITDA	Earnings Before Interest, Taxes, Depreciation, and Amortization
EC	European Commission
ECA	European Club Association
ECJ	European Court of Justice

EEC	European Economic Community
EFAA	European Football Agents Association
EPFL	European Professional Football Leagues
ERPA	Economic Rights Participation Agreements
EU	European Union
EVP	Executive Vice President
FA	Football Association
FAA	Futbolistas Argentinos Agremiados
FAF	Football Association of Finland
FFF	Fédération Française de Football Association
FFP	Financial Fair Play
FIFA	Fédération Internationale de Football Association
FIFPro	Fédération Internationale des Associations de Footballeurs Professionels
FIGC	Federazione Italiana Giuoco Calcio
FL	Football League
FSA	Full Service Agency
FPF	Federação Portuguesa de Futebol
FPFPF	First Portuguese Football Players Fund
GNCF	Groupement National des Conseillers du Football
GPX	Global Player Exchange
HHI	Herfindahl-Hirschman Index
HMRC	Her Majesty's Revenue and Customs
HOTS	Head of Terms
ILO	International Labour Organization
IMG	International Management Group
IPO	Initial Public Offering
IRT	Intermediary Regulations Tool
ISA	Income Share Agreement
ISL	Indian Super League
ITC	International Transfer Certificate
ITMS	International Transfer Matching System
KNVB	Koninklijke Nederlandse Voetbal Bond
LFP	Liga de Futbol Profesional
LPFP	Liga Portuguesa de Futebol Profissional
MLB	Major League Baseball
MLBPA	Major League Baseball Players Association
MLS	Major League Soccer
MRP	Marginal Revenue Product
NDA	Non-Disclosure Agreements
NASL	North American Soccer League
NFL	National Football League
NFLPA	National Football League Players Association
NGB	National Governing Body
NGO	Non-Governmental Organisation

OFEX	Off Exchange Market
PAR	Players' Agents Regulations
PFA	Professional Footballers Association
PL	Premier League
PMA	Player Management Agency
QSI	Qatar Sports Investment
RBFA	Royal Belgian Football Association
RBV	Resource Based View
RFEF	Real Federación Española de Fútbol
RGA	Regulations Governing the Application
ROE	Return on equity
RSTP	Regulations on the Status and Transfer of Players
RWI	Regulations on Working with Intermediaries
SAJ	Syndicat Agents de Joueurs
SNA	Syndicat National des Agents
SNAS	Syndicat National des Agents Sportifs
TFEU	Treaty on the Functioning of the European Union
TLO	Team Liaison Officer
TPE	Third party entitlement
TPI	Third party investment
TPO	Third party ownership
UASF	Union des Agents Sportifs de Football
UCFP	Union des Clubs Professionnels de Football
UEFA	Union of European Football Associations
UNESCO	United Nations Educational, Scientific and Cultural Organization
UNFP	Union Nationale des Footballeurs Professionnels
VVCS	Vereningng Von Contract Spelers
WADA	World Anti-Doping Agency
WMG	Wasserman Media Group
WWI	World War I
WWII	World War II

1   The history of football agents

Overview

The development of football as an industry has led to the creation of whole new professional categories and roles. Amongst them, football agents have undoubtedly emerged as the most powerful cast of actors on the stage, operating as the negotiating bridge between players and clubs. In controlling players and in some instances controlling clubs, they have been responsible for a significant part of the creation of the modern football landscape. Whether or not they are a blot on that landscape has divided opinion.

Although football agents have been socially recognised as representatives of players since the early twentieth century, their role (and regulation) was not formally crystallised until 1994, when FIFA enacted its first rules to govern them. Ever since, public authorities and governing bodies have sought to identify and control this profession from both legal and economic perspectives. With formal recognition has come a more rigorous classification and definition of the roles, duties and responsibilities assumed by those seeking to look after the interests of professional footballers and, in so doing, look after their own interests and bank balances.

In order to understand how and why the modern day industry developed, we must first set out what is meant by the term 'agent'. While the words agent and intermediary (since the formal creation of the 'profession' of a Football Intermediary after the consignment of 'Authorized Football Agents' to the dustbin of sporting history) are used interchangeably in common parlance, there have traditionally been subtle differences between the two. This distinction can help us to explain the development of the industry (Frenkiel, 2014). In the business context, both terms are defined as professionals who act with or in between two or more trading parties for legitimate economic activities, illegitimate payments, or a combination of both, offered by a supplier to a consumer. However, while agents are legally authorised to act on behalf of one of the two parties concluding a specific contract, intermediaries mainly carry out only material actions (establishing contracts, arranging meetings, etc.) in order to bring the contracting parties together and, as such, tend to have a less formal relationship. That is the strict legal position but a glance at the headlines in the newspapers is enough to convince us that legal positions may have little or nothing to do with the real world of football.

In many ways, without knowing the technicalities of the relationships in place, it is impossible to distinguish between the work of the two and to an extent the terms are therefore used interchangeably. Whatever the position before the creation by FIFA of the football intermediary the roles of the new intermediaries and the old agents cannot be distinguished from each other in practical terms. Only the expertise of those carrying them out is really different as the market has opened up, just in the UK, to some additional untrained and inexpert intermediaries who have paid their subscription to the FA in order to follow their hearts and their fortunes and discover if the streets of the world of football really are paved with gold.

This chapter explores the circumstances through which the football agents industry has developed globally, where appropriate using the US market for sports agents as a comparison. The transition of football agents from a social norm lacking any official status, to a coveted, legally recognised, profession central to the operation of global football markets, can be charted through three periods mirroring the dispersion of the game commercially and in parallel, the liberalisation of the labour and transfer markets (Magee, 2002; Gouget and Primault, 2006):

- From the late nineteenth century to the late 1950s: scouting and intermediation on behalf of clubs;
- From the early 1960s to the mid-1990s: the representation of football players;
- From the mid-1990s to the mid-2010s: the professionalisation of football agents.

In each of these time periods, we draw out the main structural changes in the marketplace which impacted the labour market for players and, as a corollary, the way in which agents operate.

1.1 From the late nineteenth century to the late 1950s: scouting and intermediation on the behalf of clubs

Intermediaries in the football market have existed since the advent of professionalism, performing scouting and recruitment roles for clubs. As clubs developed, they internalised this activity and, by developing their own scouting networks, diminished the role of middlemen. These changes in the market led intermediaries to seek other roles and their position as middlemen, working between players and clubs, started to develop. The first mention of intermediaries in official documents was in 1936 when the twenty-third FIFA Congress banned the use of intermediaries in transfers, believing they might have encouraged illegal moves (Semens, 2008). While middlemen are still known to have operated in the intervening period, it was not until the 1960s that 'agents' as we recognise them today began to emerge when they contracted directly with athletes to work as their representatives.

Agents emerged much earlier in more lucrative US sports. At the time of the Civil War (1861–1865), touring professional baseball teams were established across the country and were promoted by various intermediaries, with their involvement later classified as that of a sports agent (Lamster, 2007). While their role was bespoke to each particular case, they would typically fund the production of a particular tour or event in order to generate future returns from ticket and commercial revenues. Former baseball player Albert Goodwill Spalding, for example, was a pioneer of the World Tour team of all-American baseball stars in 1888, when he offered players $50 per week to join the new tour (Levine, 1986). In contrast to the football market which was developing in Europe, in the US agents were recognised as facilitating these popular new forms of entertainment and, as such, their role was widely accepted. The US government gave sport a certain level of autonomy, choosing not to intervene, and allowed individual promoters and organisers to enjoy considerable independence. This space afforded these entrepreneurs the opportunity to profit through initiatives that were very avant-garde for their time (Lamster, 2007).

At the same time, players typically represented themselves in contract negotiations, meaning that a fundamental imbalance existed in the bargaining process when negotiating with experienced general managers (Gould, 1992). Against the backdrop of increased commercialisation in sport, athletes realised that they could potentially earn more money if they had the help of an experienced negotiator. Charles C. Pyle, commonly known as 'Cash & Carry' Pyle, is credited as the first sports agent in the modern sense of the term (Neff, 1987; Reisler, 2008). In 1925 the theatrical promoter negotiated a $3,000 per game contract for Harold 'Red' Grange with the Chicago Bears, plus $300,000 in movie rights and additional endorsements (Greenberg and Gray, 1998; Berry *et al.*, 1986). Pyle represented other prominent athletes, including French tennis star Suzanne Langlen, during the 1920s and 1930s. When the New York Yankees' baseball player 'Babe' Ruth hired Christy Walsh, a sportswriter-turned-manager, as his financial consultant to help with negotiations, it marked a change in the way agents were viewed as franchises realised that they could lose some of their profits because of this new power dynamic. Until this time, the idea of representing athletes in every aspect of their lives had not existed and would in fact take decades to have an impact on professional sports (Reisler, 2008).

Whereas US sports agents, operating as promoters and intermediaries, were able to exploit the overtly commercial opportunities in setting up leagues and other competitions, the same was not true in the UK where football was the most popular sport and closely controlled by the existing football authorities. The first agents in the UK are not thought to have emerged until around two decades later than in the US and their role was largely confined to advising clubs on sourcing new football talent. Although the first case of professionalism in football dates back to 1876, with the transfer of the player James Lang to Sheffield Wednesday, the English FA sought to curb the use of professional players and it was almost a decade later in 1885 when they eventually reluctantly sanctioned professionalism. In this context, football agents operated only on behalf of clubs to scout and recruit players (Roderick, 2001).

At this time, clubs still tended to recruit based on recommendation; however, this was about to change. J. P. Campbell from Liverpool is thought to have been the first agent to promote some players to clubs through newspaper advertisements in March 1891 (Taylor, 1999). Clubs also began to use intermediaries more often; these middlemen were usually small-time entrepreneurs who, recognising the gap in the market, were able to exploit the lack of organisation in early professional clubs. Middlesbrough Iranopolis, for example, employed a Mr Ferguson, who was paid £5 commission for every player he recommended to them who then went on to play for the club. Nevertheless, the judgements of agents were not infallible and in 1893, the entire Aston Villa committee was compelled to resign after an intermediary recruited some sub-standard players who had not been seen by committee members (Carter, 2006).

1893 was an important year for football in England. The retain and transfer system was introduced which enabled football clubs to exercise a great degree of control over the movement of players (Magee, 2002). In the early years of the twentieth century, clubs began to take responsibility for their own recruitment of players and agents' activity declined. The FA felt that agents were against the ethos of football and did not approve of their profession, to such an extent that the activities of individuals who attempted to profit as go-betweens for clubs and players were officially banned. However, despite clubs being regularly warned not to deal with agents, there was still demand for their services. Agents were clearly operating in various guises – the magazine *Football Chat* published a letter from a London-based agent willing to procure players for any clubs (Taylor, 2005). Despite affirming that he did not act as an agent, but in a private capacity for friends working for clubs, a detailed scale of travelling costs and charges was listed. The FA's suspension of former players H. J. Sims of East Ham and C. F. Caswell of Cardiff, and the ban of Birmingham's Football Player Agency, show that agents were fully operating (Taylor, 2005). Similarly, while players tied to clubs through restrictive contracts were unable to solicit a move, agents were beginning to play a role in working for players that was similar to what we have seen emerging in the US, as they often touted a player around clubs while he was still under contract (Banks, 2002).

Regardless of their disputed image, the growth and increasing openness of the international transfer market offered an opportunity for agents to start to gain both exposure and a prominent position in the development of football. From their inception, all of the professional leagues imported foreign players in accordance with the respective domestic transfer market restrictions (Taylor, 2006). In the 1920s, the football league ASL in the US made no restriction on the grounds of nationality and clubs hired agents to attract players, such as Scotland's Alex Jackson. In Europe, however, limits on importing foreign players were widespread. In 1933, the German federation imposed a blanket ban on foreign players and managers, while in Italy only foreign players with dual citizenship from South America, the so-called 'oriundi', were allowed to play. From 1931, foreign players in England were required to have lived in the country for at least two years before the FA would recognise them as residents. Their number therefore remained limited and they were used to playing with the status of amateurs. In addition, the presence of the maximum wage in England meant that other, less restrictive, leagues were preferred by players and several British players transferred to French clubs. Since the English FA was not a member of FIFA at that time, foreign clubs were not obliged to pay any transfer fees for players. Agents appeared from abroad to collaborate with local intermediaries, who mainly operated domestically, in order to transfer British players overseas (Taylor, 2002). Consequently, agents were not welcome and team managers did not want to deal with them.

French football saw strong growth post WWI, with the diffusion of amateur leagues (Gouget and Primault, 2006). As its popularity increased, so too did match-day revenues. It became standard practice for clubs to reimburse expenses and award match prizes to players. Gradually, football took hold in traditionally working class areas with many players coming from mining regions and with a strong contingent of Polish and Italian migrants. At that time, players were allowed to change clubs at will, hence creating a similar role for agents to that seen in England in supporting clubs' recruitment. In order to control the touting of players, a factor of instability for clubs, the French national association, FFF, also established its own equivalent of the retain and transfer system, called licence A, on 18 April 1925 (Wahl and Lanfranchi, 1995). Seven years later professionalism was introduced in France with the support of the most powerful clubs which sought to control the movement of their best players. Recruitment of players from abroad also started to become widespread (Lanfranchi and Taylor, 2001). In contrast to the English case, after the formation of the French professional league, between 1932 and 1939 approximately 30 per cent of players were foreigners. Since clubs were allowed to field up to five foreign players in every match, they hired intermediaries abroad to scout players who were keen to emigrate (Taylor, 2006). Selling clubs also saw a role for these intermediaries in helping them to profit by transferring the most talented players to other clubs for a fee. This situation did however create problems, with several sub-standard players, from Latin America countries in particular, found to have reputations generated by intermediaries that were far in excess of their actual talent. This asymmetric information between the buying club and the player/ selling club also enabled some intermediaries, acting as merchants of men, to make money by transferring injured players from overseas to French clubs (Wahl and Lanfranchi, 1995). This early trend for opportunistic behaviour has meant that trust, often developed over a long period of time, has become one of the most important features of the relationship between clubs and the agents that they work with.

By the end of WWII, intermediaries were widespread throughout the main football markets. However, the majority of players were still not professionally advised in transfer deals or contract negotiations (Taylor, 1999). In 1948,

Middlesbrough rejected the transfer request of the player Wilf Mannion and, for the next eight months, the club and the player were in dispute over possible moves without reaching any agreement (Varley, 1997). The player has latterly admitted that an agent would have been a useful aid to find a solution that was better for both sides. Players at that time were seen purely as a commodity without the proper labour legislation in place to protect their rights. Nevertheless, influences from other sports were becoming clear – in 1949, the journalist Reg Hayter assisted the cricketer Dennis Compton by arranging lucrative endorsement contracts. When Compton also played for Arsenal as a football player, Hayter introduced him to Bagenal Harvey, who became the first modern sports agent in Britain (Harding, 2004). The opportunity to profit from football, either through activities outside of the game or by capitalising on the fact that their talent could be more valuable to another club, had not escaped some players.

Competition from foreign leagues with the strong desire to sign the most high profile players offered appealing alternatives. This situation was also aggravated by the presence of the maximum wage, which remained in place until 1961. Consequently, the best English players were not able to command fair-market compensation from their clubs. In the 1950s and 1960s the top players frequently moved to Italy through agents who became ever more closely embroiled in negotiations. John Charles' move from Leeds United to Juventus in 1957 was notable for the involvement of Teddy Sommerfield, whose other clients included television celebrities such as Eamonn Andrews. It was the first time a British player himself had employed an agent to facilitate a transfer deal abroad (Harding, 2004). As Somerfield looked after Charles' interests outside the game and was not very familiar with football matters, he asked for input from another of his clients, the BBC football commentator Kenneth Wolstenholme (Risoli, 2012). At that time, the most famous intermediary was Gigi Peronace (Foot, 2006; Maximo, 2011). Described as the *real agent* or *Italian man* in England, he worked part-time as a scout and intermediary in the Anglo-Italian transfer market for several clubs, such as Chelsea, Manchester United, Lazio, Torino, Juventus and Milan. According to Greaves (2003), his knowledge of football and players was deep and complemented by his equivalent financial expertise.

As increasing numbers of players began to take up the opportunity to go to leagues overseas, they also played a role in attracting their former colleagues to follow them (Wahl and Lanfranchi, 1995). When the former Manchester United player Charlie Mitten moved to Colombia to play for Independiente Santa Fe in 1950, he attempted to persuade other British stars to join him. Similarly, the Lincoln player Jack Dodds was banned by the FL for acting as a British-based agent for another Columbian club. As clubs were beginning to see their control diminished, the very idea that players could be represented by an agent was seen as a threat to the fundamental power of club management.

From the early 1940s, intermediaries were organising friendly matches between clubs or tournaments which acted as a showcase for players (Frenkiel, 2014). These matches provided an opportunity for agents to both scout and showcase players to clubs. Any clubs that identified a potential transfer target would then negotiate with the club that held the player's registration to see if they were willing for the player to transfer. As representing players was still prohibited, intermediaries were paid fees in relation to the organisation of the match to hide the commission fees related to any successful player transfer. For this reason, in 1969, the European federation, UEFA, decided to create a licence for match agents and monitor their activity. Facing increasing scrutiny over their actions, the Spanish intermediary Luis Guijarro was banned from being a match agent in 1978 after the president of Boca Juniors, Alberto José Armando, reported him for irregular payments relating to the transfers of Marcelo Trobbiani, from Boca Juniors to Elche, and Heraldo Bezerra from Atletico Madrid to Boca Juniors (Paradinas, 1978). Fernando Torcal, Guijarro's former assistant manager and later a UEFA registered match agent himself through his company Continental Sports, acknowledged that he too worked on behalf of players, stating that 'clubs come for advice and I give it. That does not mean anything shady or sinister. I think that UEFA will lift the ban. The intermediary exists in all markets' (Relaño, 1978).

In Spain, the first generation of football intermediary started operating in the 1940s and 1950s (AEAF, 2012; Corcuera, 2010). Angel Rodriguez 'El feo' was one of the most famous, dealing mainly in domestic transfers. Juanito Cadenas, in contrast focused his attention on Catalan players' moves to Andalusian and North African clubs, advertising the players he represented who wished to transfer in the Spanish daily newspaper *El Mundo Deportivo*. With a surge in the number of players being recruited from oversees other intermediaries, such as the Armenian Arturo Bogossian who exploited his networks in South America with Uruguayan and Paraguayan clubs, also emerged. However, again asymmetric information meant that some intermediaries exploited the transfer market, with scandals such as *el timo de lo orioundos*, emerging wherein South American players were to forge their passports in order to obtain Spanish citizenship and, later, move to Spanish clubs (Corcuera, 2012).

The nature of the transfer market at that time has been criticised as being akin to slavery, wherein players could be transferred to another club on the whim of their club chairman, while intermediaries acted as 'human flesh brokers' (Wahl and Lanfranchi, 1995). From the mid-1950s, conflicts between players and club owners throughout Europe were regular and related both to demands for increased wages and to transfers.

Within the football transfer markets, there was much collusion between clubs' managers and directors (Carter, 2006). Players' transfers were agreed at inflated fees in order to write off money on their tax returns. The actual fee would be recorded as much lower in the buying club's accounts and those parties involved in the deal would then split the extra cash and, sometimes, give a small portion to the player. In Italy the so-called *Calciomercato*, the official football transfer market founded by the Prince of Trabia, Raimondo Lanza who, at that time, was the chairman of Palermo Calcio, began in the 1950s. It has developed into an annual meeting where club owners, club directors and intermediaries come together to hold meetings about buying and selling players at the Gallia Hotel in Milan (Sorgi, 2011). While, in England, club managers were the main drivers of the transfer market, in the rest of Europe club directors became prominent. In Italy and Spain, club directors such as Giuseppe Viani, Italo Allodi, Romeo Anconetani, Raimundo Saporta, Pablo Hernandez Coronado and Luis Culina were the *Domini* of football transfers and deals using their unique knowledge of transfer networks and players' characteristics and attitudes (Esposito, 2011; Tamburini, 2012; Vasco, 2012).

1.2 From the early 1960s to the mid-1990s: the representation of football players

The structure of football was such that entrepreneurial individuals were able to recognise commercial opportunities to generate revenue from value chains, be that through setting up matches that would not have otherwise been played, seeing potential for players to gain sponsorship and promotion deals or recognising discrepancies between the value of players and what they are paid. By 1960, in England it had become apparent that the restrictions in the labour market were not conducive to keeping the best players, and the players' union, the PFA chaired by Jimmy Hill, was using its influence to campaign against the maximum wage and the retain and transfer system. These campaigns not only led to the rules being relaxed, but also cemented the position of the unions. Alan Hardacket, secretary of the English FA, claimed that the situation had been engineered by the agent Bagenal Harvey who saw the opportunity to increase players' wages and transfer fees and, as a corollary, his own commissions (Harding, 2004).

The decision in 1961 to abolish the maximum wage balanced the bargaining power between players and clubs to the point where most athletes started negotiating their contracts with the assistance of personal representatives (Magee, 2002). Between 1960 and 1964, the wages of First Division players increased by 61 per cent[1] (Szymanski and Kuypers, 1999). Labour market liberalisation continued in 1963 when the High Court ruled in the George Eastham case[2] that the 'retain and transfer' system was illegal, on the basis that it constituted an unjustifiable restraint of trade (Banks, 2002). Through this liberalisation, players began to redress the imbalance of power that had been a feature of their relationships with clubs. In making the transfers of players more flexible, leagues and football associations legitimised the use of intermediaries. Nevertheless, there were still restrictions on the movement of players as clubs could unilaterally extend players' registrations so long as terms equal to their previous contract were offered; in essence, it meant tying a player to the club for as long as the club was willing to pay for his services, irrespective of whether the player wished to remain at that club.

In France, a similar process of reform was underway, led by Just Fontaine who realised the need to organise in order to take on the powerful clubs (Gouget and Primault, 2006). Following the examples of their English colleagues, French players founded their own union, the UNFP, in 1961 and immediately initiated

negotiations with club representatives which led to the signing of the first collective agreement, including reform of the pension system in November 1964.
By 1969, the UNFP had challenged the legal framework of the labour market
and the possibility for players and clubs to negotiate 'fixed-term' contracts was
finally realised. Under this system a player could only be contracted to a club for
a limited period of time, which would be subject to negotiation, and which could
not be less than three years for an amateur player signing his first professional
contract, and not less than one year in any other case.

In the US too, the 1960s was a defining period, with three major changes
underway across American sports (Shropshire and Davis, 2008):

1   The demise of the extensive use of reserve and option clauses in standard
    player contracts;
2   The competition from newly formed leagues offering an appealing altern-
    ative to athletes who played in the established ones;
3   The commercialisation of sport through broadcasting and sponsorship deals.

Similar to the retain and transfer system, the reserve clause was standard in
playing contracts in the US. It effectively meant that, at the end of a contract,
although there were no obligations either for a player to play for his team or for
the franchise to pay him, the player was not free to enter into a contract with
another franchise unless the club previously holding his registration agreed. This
could tie a player to a franchise indefinitely. Legal challenges to this system
resulted in the abolition of the reserve clause and the players' unions subsequently negotiated a collective bargaining agreement, with an impartial arbitra-
tor to assist in resolving disputes.

This situation, combined with the expansion of the leagues' opening of new
franchises in other cities and the ease with which people could now travel long
distances, afforded players the opportunity to ply their trade elsewhere. Consequently, athletes were able to tell owners that they would command fair-market
compensation or they would take their services to rival leagues. This demand led
to higher salaries, which were simultaneously enlarged by the strong desire of the
newly formed leagues to sign well known players (Miller *et al.*, 1992). In contrast
to the European system, where players negotiate contractual conditions directly
with clubs, in the US player associations bargain as a single unit with leagues
over basic working conditions, leaving players to negotiate their own salaries.
This meant that the same information asymmetries and power imbalances recognised in Europe were also a feature of the US market. As revenues rose for
franchises throughout the 1960s, experienced managers of clubs were able to
keep salaries low, since players had little business or financial experience and no
knowledge of what other athletes were earning and their own potential worth to
their club (Mason and Slack, 2003; Mason and Duquette, 2005).

Up to this period many franchises had shown an unwillingness to negotiate
with agents; in the now infamous case of NFL player Jim Ringo, who arrived
with an advisor to renegotiate his contract with Green Bay Packers of the NFL in

1963, the player found himself summarily transferred to Philadelphia, without discussion, by the general manager, Vince Lombardi (Greenberg and Gray, 1998). While this was not an isolated case, the role of agents at this time was beginning to be recognised as useful in the negotiation process, with franchises realising that agents with business savvy could actually have a positive effect in speeding up the process (Sobel, 1987).

Across the American sports, the unions had played a key role in solidifying the agents' business by not getting involved in salary negotiation as unions traditionally do (Shropshire and Davis, 2008). Despite the fact that the baseball players' association, the MLBPA, did not allow players to have an agent according to their CBAs, the former Yankees' official Frank Scott became the first player agent sui generis (Ruxin, 1993). Respecting the MLBPA regulations, in the 1950s and 1960s he assisted players such as Joe DiMaggio, Mickey Mantle, Yogi Berra, Whitey Ford, Casey Stengel, Willie Mays, Frank Gilford and other top professional athletes with their off-the-field earnings in order to increase their endorsement and promotional deals (Litsky, 1998; Madden, 1998). Similarly, while technically not acting as an agent, in 1964, the lawyer Bob Woolf assisted pitcher Earl Wilson with contractual matters in a legal capacity before formally negotiating his contract with the Boston Red Sox in 1966 (King, 1994). In 1967, after his trade to Detroit Tigers, Wilson again sought Woolf's help in his negotiations to renew his contract; whenever Wilson had a question, he excused himself from the room and called Woolf for more advice (Woolf, 1976). Around this time, other representatives were also becoming more prominent. In 1965 Los Angeles Dodgers star baseball pitchers, Sandy Koufax and Don Drysdale, appointed the Hollywood agent Bill Hayes to help with their contract renewals (Helyar, 1994). Although the two players had immense talent, the MLB rules forbade them from negotiating with other teams. Hayes suggested that, together, the players could launch a holdout, thus forcing the Dodgers to meet their demands. The amount of money the two players demanded and the threat of using the same tactic for other players outraged the Dodgers. While the negotiations resulted in less money than they originally sought, they received far more than they would have achieved had they bargained individually and without an agent. Against this backdrop, players across the major American sports leagues were recognising their own value to clubs and sought to use this power to improve their conditions. Finally, in 1970 the MLBPA negotiated with the MLB for the player's right to be represented by an agent (Masteralexis, 2005). In the NFL too this was a period of negotiated power wherein, in response to the owners' lockout, the NFLPA, the American football players' association, went on strike in July 1970 to force through an increase in pre-season pay and their pension fund. The dispute ended with the acceptance of these requests by the league and players were also given the right to have agents for the first time (NFLPA, 2014).

By the late 1960s, influenced by the general political climate as well as debates going on within sport in general and football in particular, football players in Europe also continued to readdress the power balance. In France, by 1969, the fixed term contract reform was approved, meaning that at the end of his contract, a player could negotiate with any club without his former club's opposition or the payment of any transfer fee. French football was experiencing a reversal of the power balance in favour of players and for the next 20 years France became the only country without a formal transfer system (Lanfranchi and Taylor, 2001). Two regulations partially limited the free movement of players (Faure and Suaud, 1999). First, a player who had been an apprentice at his club for three years was bound to sign his first professional contract with his training club. Second, in order to recompense the investment and time spent on training, clubs received compensation for the first transfer of players that they had trained. This meant that players' conditions had improved considerably with the majority experiencing a relatively free market in France, to the point that this was having an impact on clubs' budgets. As might be expected, this negotiating power heralded the arrival of intermediaries on a large scale (Azhar, 1996; Frenkiel, 2014).

This period of reform and liberalisation was replicated across many major footballing nations, often with governmental support (Marzola, 1981). In Argentina, the players' union, FAA, was successful in its request to abolish the retain and transfer clause with the approval of the statute of the professional football players by law n. 20160 on 23 February 1973. In Portugal too, on 15 May 1975 the government enacted a law that established players' rights and duties in relation to their labour contracts. Similarly, in Brazil, on 2 September 1976, the approval of law n. 6354 radically reformed the transfer market.

However, while these reforms facilitated the movement of players domestically, their movement between national federations remained highly regulated. According to Marzola (1990), by the end of the 1970s there were three main transfer systems governing domestic transfers in Europe:

- The 'retain and transfer' system which was still active in Belgium, the Netherlands and Germany.
- The parametric system, present in Italy, which allowed a player to transfer under the payment of predetermined fees based on various parameters.
- The free agency system, operating in France, Spain and Portugal, which enabled any out of contract player to move freely to a different club without the payment of any fee.

With the increasing integration of Europe politically and as a trading market, it was necessary to create a homogenous and standard transfer system, approved by football governing bodies, which could allow the free movement of players at national and international levels, leading to a fourth overarching system to address this:

- The UEFA system which fixed a maximum transfer fee limit.

On 23 February 1978, in Brussels, football associations from several European countries and the Executive Committee of the EEC met to establish the principle of free movement of football players within the borders of EEC member states (Marzola, 1990). Nevertheless, it was agreed that a period of transition was needed before the football associations could determine the specific regulation for a common transfer system to be implemented within European football.

Concurrently, media interest in sports as part of regular television programming expanded very rapidly, bringing enormous amounts of revenue into the leagues. First in the US, then spreading to the rest of the world, increased media exposure for athletes meant that their popularity soared, resulting in a boom in the value of commercial endorsement for players (Shropshire and Davis, 2008). While sports governing bodies were very keen to restrict the role of agents in all matters relating to the relationships between players and clubs, they did not seek to regulate their activity with third parties and therefore a role in arranging for players to benefit from sponsorship and endorsements has thrived with little or no interference. Recognising these commercial opportunities, the use of agents by players first flourished throughout the 1960s and 1970s. Mark McCormack is credited as the pioneer of the modern representation industry. He was the first to recognise the commercial potential of sports stars, representing a generation of leading golfers in the 1960s, including the so-called Big-Three, initially Arnold Palmer and then Jack Nicklaus, with Gary Player (Katz, 1994). Through his company IMG, he utilised the image and skills of his clients to generate commercial value through endorsement contracts and advertisement campaigns. At that time, other prominent agents were Steve Arnold and Marty Blackman, who in 1963 founded Pro Sports Inc., still one of the longest established active sport agencies (Woolf, 1976; Davis, 2007; Wolohan, 2007). A similar trend followed in the UK when George Best, who was represented by Ken Stanley, also Denis Law's agent, was involved in the advertisement campaign for Irish sausages and modelling assignments for the Great Universal Stories catalogue (Harding, 2004).

As the activities of sports agents became more widely acknowledged, their number increased and individuals from diverse backgrounds and professions entered the industry (Holt *et al.*, 2006). Likewise, the increased revenues available to players meant that the type of advice they required also changed as legal and financial support became necessary. These new services, which tended to be available only through consultants, became a necessity, which favoured the arrival of professionals from different business sectors who had not previously been involved in sport. In some cases, agents became involved as they were simply friends of players (Rosner, 2004). For instance, Bobby Moore and Geoff Hurst, England's 1966 World Cup Champions, shunned offers to join IMG, preferring the service of a loyal West Ham United servant and real estate agent, Jack Turner. Hurst was frightened off by the American agency's 20 per cent fee. Although Turner formed Bobby Moore Ltd. with himself as a director, he later admitted that Moore should have been managed by Mark McCormack (Harding, 2004). In Germany, Franz Beckenbauer was guided during his entire football career as a footballer, coach and later football director by his mentor Robert Schwan (Spiegel, 2002). Known as 'Mister 20 per cent', Schwan was considered a football visionary, having held various roles within German football as a coach and later board member of Bayern Munich and Hertha Berlin. As a personal manager and consultant for Beckenbauer, he was able to recognise commercial opportunities and support and provide all the necessary assistance and ability to exploit them.

By the late 1970s, with clubs increasingly looking at global markets, players were marketable beyond their national associations, and agents were playing an ever more important role in this internationalisation. With different transfer regulations and labour market systems country by country, various information asymmetries arose; for clubs, it was still markedly difficult to obtain reliable information on the quality of players at both national and international levels and, even when this was available, their likely future performance was extremely difficult to assess. As McGovern (2002) outlines, patterns of migration within the football industry were mainly socially embedded along regional lines and appropriate economic evaluations of players were infeasible. In this environment, football agents slowly strengthened their position in the transfer market, establishing migration channels favoured by the loosening of transfer limitations on foreign players in different countries, such as England in 1978 and Italy in 1980, and the emergence of new markets following the fall of the Soviet Union block. Within the top five European leagues, the first wave of player migration occurred from the mid-1970s until the mid-1990s and the percentage of expatriate players increased from 8.1 per cent to 18.6 per cent (Poli, 2010a).

The dual factors of increased internationalisation and the related growth in media coverage, combined with the reforms of the transfer market regulations, meant that players could begin to exploit their talent in various ways. While the abolition of the maximum wage meant they could negotiate higher salaries with their existing clubs, the relaxing of transfer restrictions implied that players could move at the end of their contract if another club made them a better offer. This position was accentuated by competition from foreign leagues seeking to attract the best talent and with technological advancements athletes were establishing themselves as entertainers and not just players. These combined factors led to wage increases throughout the world of football (Marzola, 1990). In Italy, the highest players' salary exceeded €0.37 million in 1981. In Germany, the average earnings of professional players increased tenfold in the two decades following the start of the Bundesliga. In 1963, the highest paid player was Hans Novak of Schalke 04, who earned €0.17 million. By 1981 Franz Beckenbauer, earned €1.05 billion, partly paid by his club, Hamburg SV, but mostly by the sponsors, BP and Adidas. In England, the best players earned between €0.25 million and €0.37 million, with the biggest players able to considerably increase their earnings through commercial deals. Kevin Keegan, for example, earned a basic salary of €0.33 million from Southampton but a further €1.1 million in endorsement deals. In France too, Michel Platini, the highest remunerated player, earned around €0.5 million per year. In Belgium, the average salary of a player was about €70,000 per year. The most popular players, such as Vincent Van den Berghe and Jan Ceulemans, earned no more than €0.22 million. In the Netherlands, in the post-Cruijff era, salaries were drastically reduced, with most players receiving salaries of €70,000 to €220,000 per year from their clubs.[3] In Spain, clubs favoured uncontrolled increasing wage inflation. Barcelona paid Bernd Schuster a salary of €1.23 million. Finally, in the Swiss league the levels of remuneration were relatively low, with peaks between €0.13 million and €0.15 million, respectively for the Swiss national Claudio Sulser and the Yugoslavian Drazan Jerkovic (Marzola, 1990).

As the value of contracts increased, the profession of football agents became more lucrative and a new generation of agents emerged, mainly to assist players with their endorsement contracts so they provided legal advice to players (Minguella, 2008; Canovi and Mazzocchi, 2011; Caliendo, 2012): this new generation of agents included Dario Canovi and Antonio Caliendo in Italy; Norbert Pflippens and Wolfgang Fahrian in Germany; Dennis Roach and Mel Stein in England; Jose Minguella, Alberto Toldra and Roberto Dale in Spain; and Bernard Généstar in France.

Trevor Francis' agent, Dennis Roach, explained that the first occasion on which a player transferred for £1 million opened up avenues not previously available to footballers, who began to realise how much they could exploit the transfer market in their favour (Harding, 2004). In 1977, Kevin Keegan became the wealthiest football player in Europe by signing for Hamburg SV. He also sold his image rights to his agent and club to promote whatever products they deemed fit and he quickly became the most recognisable player in the world (Bradford, 2006).

By the 1980s, agents in the UK transfer market were relatively commonplace, yet without official recognition from any football governing bodies, their activity was unregulated. Moreover, the absence of any supervision in transfer negotiations led to an opportunity for inappropriate behaviours to be undertaken by some agents, managers and football directors. The lack of accountability in the transfer market left it exposed to an unwritten code of conduct based on the 'bungs' culture within the football industry. In the early 1990s the involvement of some football managers, such as Brian Clough and Graham Taylor, in illicit payments received from agents in player transfers confirmed that the activity of football agents needed to be officially regulated by football governing bodies at national and international levels (Bower, 2007). In Italy too there were various active agents, whose presence was acknowledged in February 1990, when the Italian football association, FIGC, was the first to formally accept the activity of football agents followed by the formation of Assoprocuratori, the first representative body of football agents (Stagi, 1990). Likewise, in France in the same period, the first agents' association, GNCF, was founded on the initiative of some agents, Pape Diouf, Dominique Rocheteau, Bruno Satin and Jeannot Werth, later followed by another association, SNA, renamed as SAJ (Frenkiel, 2014). On 3 July 1995, Spanish football agents, following their European colleagues, formed their association, AEAF, to express their voice and to protect their interests within Spanish football (AEAF, 2011).

In 1994, FIFA formally recognised and regulated the activity of football agents with the first licensing system accepted by all football federations, signalling the transformation of the activity of football agents into a profession. Finally, this formal recognition implied a more rigorous definition and regulation of the role, duties and responsibility of the agents whose licence was officially issued by their national football association. This official recognition meant that some important figures who had long been involved in the football business in various guises could now be classified legitimately as stakeholders.

1.3 From the mid-1990s to the present: the professionalisation of football agents

While the combination of commercialisation and labour market liberalisation from the 1950s to 1980s provided the perfect platform for agents to firmly establish themselves in American sports, it was not until much later that their role in football became widespread in Europe. The Bosman ruling[4] in 1995 fundamentally changed the way that football in Europe had operated, bringing the contracts of athletes into line with those of other workers within Europe and establishing that out of contract international transfer payments are incompatible with Article 39 of the EC Treaty (Dubey, 2000). Any amendments to the transfer system operating in Europe therefore, of necessity, had to comply with EU law. Following much debate between key stakeholders, a new transfer system was eventually agreed in March 2001, with agreements put in place to maintain contract stability, ensure that clubs were rewarded for the investment made in training players and guarantee the redistribution of income to improve competitive balance between clubs (Parrish, 2003; Dimitrakopoulos, 2006). The latest set of transfer regulations came into force in September 2001. The system of transfer windows was enacted in which there are two time periods each season when players are allowed to move. Each player is permitted to move once per season, excluding loans. Unilateral breaches of contract are permitted at the end of the season but result in the payment of a fee so as to protect the interests of the training clubs (Dimitrakopoulos, 2006). A system of training compensation is enforced for players under the age of 24 and international transfers of players under 18 must be authorised subject to agreed conditions, with solidarity mechanisms introduced to redistribute transfer fees between clubs. Players over 24 are permitted to move at the end of their contract on a free transfer. A player can move in the final year of a four or five year contract if he hands in a request to the club no more than 15 days after the end of the previous season (FIFA, 2005). Under these circumstances the club would be entitled to compensation. This new market scenario was favoured by the exponential revenue growth in the football industry resulting from greater competition and de-regulation in the broadcasting market, which meant that pay-TV incumbents were willing to pay a premium for rights to broadcast live premier league matches. This revenue filtered through to clubs, which in turn sought to employ the best players. Agents found themselves in a market that allowed them to fully exploit players' bargaining power and their transfer freedom across EU borders.

Clubs had to start dealing fully with players' representatives, who negotiated the best possible contracts for their clients as well as for themselves (Banks, 2002). With players able to move without a fee at the end of their contracts, the only way that clubs could recoup their investment in players was to sell them while they were still under contract. Conversely, if clubs wanted to retain players, whose contracts were due to expire, they would need to offer new contracts with improved terms before the current terms expired. Both situations represented lucrative bargaining positions for players and their agents. In the 2001/2002 season, English PL clubs spent £475 million on players' wages and £323 million on transfers, according to Deloitte (2003). In that season, agents would have earned about £46 million. Citing one PL financial director, 'there is nothing atypical about the amounts that English clubs pay agents. Every club has its own policies and indeed the levels would vary depending on the agent and the club's desperation for a player' (Wild, 2003).

Recognising the opportunity to profit in the game, a new wave of agents entered the football industry from various business sectors. In England, for example, Jon Holmes used to be a life-insurance salesman; Eric Hall and Athole Still moved into football after representing performing artists; and Cyril Regis, Jasper Olson and Barry Silkman were former professional players (Harding, 2004). By February 2001, there were 631 licensed agents worldwide and this number increased in the following years, when, under pressure from the EU Competition Commission, FIFA modified the rules governing the acquisition of an official licence. From 1994 to 2009, in Europe alone, the number of football agents increased by about 1,000 per year, equating to around 300 per cent (Poli, 2010a). In December 2009, there were 5,193 officially licensed agents worldwide. Although 133 countries had at least one licensed agent by 2015, there are still significant disparities between continents. These differences reflect the transfer market and where the big leagues tend to be signing players from. From 2003 to 2009, when the number of African players in England and France was increasing, and those from Latin America were also switching to the English and Spanish Leagues, the number of agents registered in Africa rose by 6.3 per cent and in Latin America by 3.4 per cent. Amongst non-EU countries, Brazil, Argentina and Nigeria have the most agents, which is unsurprising given that they are leading exporters of players worldwide. The number of licensed agents in UEFA member countries increased from 1,211 in 2003 to 4,001 in 2011 (Poli, 2010a). While the vast majority of these have licences issued by European football federations, the percentage of agents based in Europe declined from 81 per cent to 70 per cent during the same period.

The Bosman judgement also prohibited domestic and European leagues from imposing quotas on foreign players. Previously, clubs in the EU were only authorised to use five foreign players, three of whom had to be EU citizens. This was adjudged to be contrary to Article 39 of the EU Treaty (Asser, 2005; Feess and Mühlheußer, 2003). Essentially a pan-European market for players was created (Holt *et al.*, 2006). This judgement was extended in 2000 when Maros Kolpak, a Slovakian handball player, argued that, as a third country national, he should be entitled to the same freedom as EU nationals. Since Slovakia had entered into an association agreement with the EU entitling Slovakian nationals to treatment equal to that of EU citizens, it was held that freedom of movement be extended to those citizens of the other 23 countries with association agreements with the EU (Asser, 2005). A similar decision had been reached in the Malaja and Simutenkov cases.

Besides contract negotiations, the role played by agents encompasses the development of transnational networks which scout and train players. Once a talented player is identified, intermediaries organise short term trials in clubs with which they have existing relationships. European based agents often collaborate with 'tipsters' living in particularly fertile markets who, in exchange for a regular salary or periodical commissions, scout local talent and organise tournaments, which their European-based partners then attend in order to finalise a deal (Poli, 2010b). Between 1995 and 2009, the percentage of expatriates had increased by at least 15 per cent across the big five European leagues. The lowest increases were in Spain (15.4 per cent) and France (15.8 per cent) (Poli, 2010a). However, between 2005 and 2008, France was the only country in which the proportion of expatriates had not increased. The strongest growth was registered in England by 43.4 per cent, where almost 60 per cent of players in the English PL were recruited from abroad.

In response, and possibly to combat the effects of the Bosman ruling, in April 2005 UEFA's 52 member federations approved the imposition of specific quotas on clubs for locally trained players in Champions League and UEFA Cup matches. The intention of the rule is to enhance the training and development of young talent (UEFA, 2007). The implication of the rulings in the Bosman, Kolpak, Malaja and Simutenkov cases is that EU law prevails over association law and when sport is classed as an economic activity, a sports governing body cannot enforce restrictions on the participation of non-nationals of the specific member state (Asser, 2005). While it is questionable whether the home-grown players rule would be legally enforceable, there is scope for sport to be treated as a special case with the rule passed on the basis of preserving a level playing field (as with transfer windows). In an effort to circumvent potential conflicts with EU law, the rule does not refer to a player's nationality, but to where a player was trained and educated between the ages of 15 to 21 (Asser, 2005). This too has created a role for agents in recruiting players at younger and younger ages.

In the US, sports agents have now become an integral part of the sports industry and, as contracts and endorsement agreements become more complex and economically valuable, the need for representation has increased. While the advent of sports agents certainly helped some players to improve the outcome of their contract negotiations, there was also concern that middlemen were earning huge amounts of money from these deals. Some agents were able to bring in commissions that rival those of the athletes they represent, with approximately $230 million paid to agents annually. Indeed, the agents' total fees kept growing each year as salaries in the four major American sports increased, with a 125 per cent rise from 1996 to 2005 (Karcher, 2007). Despite this huge earning potential, people did not necessarily need any qualifications to become an agent, but had a significant impact on the lives of those involved. The first legal framework to regulate the profession of sports agents was introduced in the 1990s, mainly focusing on the recruitment of university athletes.

From a comparative perspective, sports agents in the US are genuine player representatives – acting solely for the player in the negotiation of their final package, rather than being involved with clubs as scouts or initiators of transfers (KEA *et al.*, 2009). In the MLS, players' contracts are negotiated with the league as it owns the players' transfer rights. Football players are under contract with the league and not with the football franchise. The transfer market in the US is based on the strategic trade of contracts or signing players at the end of their current contract in order to respect the different mechanisms of revenue distributions. In addition to representing players in the negotiation of their employment contract, agents in the US lead the way in managing their clients' commercial interests.

In an increasingly global world, massive investments in football networks are essential in order to recognise and attract the best players (Poli, 2010c). This requires that football agents have a deep and selective knowledge of professional football worldwide, so as to be able to scout players on behalf of clubs (Pinna, 2006). Semens (2012) explains that, while clubs have their own networks, well-connected agents can act as a link when club networks do not otherwise overlap. Agents are also responsible for the structure of migration channels conceived as information systems that guide labour migrations and govern entry into the foreign labour market. In the transfer market, they control the entry into the migration system and the flow dynamics by motivating players to migrate. In this context, as Poli (2010c) highlights, agents play a key role in manipulating the different steps of players' career trajectories and they can influence clubs' football strategies through their role in recruiting and buying players on the transfer market. These arrangements have been known to include a commission for the identifying agent, should the player be sold on for a higher amount in future. This issue is increasingly important to the extent that, in recent years, there has been a proliferation of companies and investment funds whose main business is to invest in football players by buying and selling shares of their economic rights in exchange for financial profit. An established practice in South America, so-called third party entitlement, TPE, has also been deployed in Africa and Europe, particularly when clubs cannot afford to invest in the recruitment of new players. Either setting up or actively taking part in TPE investments, the professional activity of football agents has now acquired an entrepreneurial dimension that goes beyond their historical roles and functions within football labour markets.

In 2009, the FIFA Congress announced its intention to undertake an in-depth review of its licensing system for players' agents. Its proposal was to require clubs and players to record the use of any intermediary in a player transfer and to regulate how such intermediaries were used (FIFA, 2015a). However, new regulations came into force on 1 April 2015 and no longer attempt to regulate access to the activity, but instead control the activity itself. With no direct link between football's governing bodies and the agents, any sanctions can only be enforced on players or clubs, whose responsibility it is to ensure that their selected intermediary is behaving in an appropriate way. Simultaneously, on 22 December 2014, the FIFA Executive Committee officially banned the practice of TPE in football, amending its RSTP (FIFA, 2015b).

1.4 Conclusions

The historical evolution of football agents is largely explained by the reforms of the football labour market that provided players and clubs with the opportunity to use agents' expertise and expanded the transfer markets on a global scale, with foreign players now viewed as almost essential to any of the best teams. Facilitating these movements has been a crucial factor in increasing the number of active agents. This market scenario, in conjunction with additional revenue sources from the commercialisation of the football industry, has resulted in spiralling players' salaries and transfer fees. In this context, football agents have been able to maintain multiple roles, scouting on clubs' behalf, representing players in their negotiations and facilitating transfer deals on behalf of clubs.

The activity of agents can therefore be explained in terms of players' mobility, their transfer fees and wages, and clubs' competitive balance in the market. Agents benefited from an increase in the number of players hired by clubs in relation to the growing transfer budgets. Indeed, in maximising the number of contracts signed, and thus their income, agents affected players' mobility. The interest of agents in the mobility of players then generated competition between clubs, encouraging clubs' conflicts, media pressure and player manipulation. The biggest clubs increased their power in the transfer market at the expense of middle and low ranking clubs. However, despite these issues, which seem to reflect a balance of power in favour of players, the supply and demand sides of the labour and transfer markets became highly fragmented. Beyond the primary market for star players, the secondary market rewards less well-known players with a relatively weak status. The market for players at youth academy level conquered a relevant importance for clubs. Unemployment also became a reality for players excluded from these markets. In this context, football intermediaries adapted in order to position themselves in a market characterised by a high degree of specialisation.

Relatively obscure until the early 1980s, football agents are nowadays integral and influential stakeholders, having moved from being a passive and marginal member of the football family to an active and influential protagonist in the football industry. However, this evolution was mainly based on the need for their expertise of other football stakeholders, i.e. players and clubs; and it has never seen their direct involvement in the reforms of labour markets in football, leaving them in a marginalised but influential position.

Latterly, football agents' activity has developed an entrepreneurial dimension, controlling players' transfers and manoeuvring financial flows for their benefit.

This has been driven by identifying gaps in the market which their services and networks can fill. Agents predominantly occupy a position whereby their knowledge of the market affords them the role of gate-keeper through which clubs can gain access to the best players, but without which clubs will struggle to attract and maintain the best assets. From being merely scouts on behalf of clubs to clubs' consultants and players' representatives, nowadays agents operate in the legislative and financial vacuums of the transfer markets, directly investing and supporting financial and speculative projects in the football industry.

Being in contact with managers, football directors and players, agents act as genuine mediators, intermediaries and brokers and in this role they are often unauthorised or unqualified. The significance of agents working for clubs has been noted since the nineteenth century; however, their position has been cemented due to the complexities of the transfer markets and regulatory contexts requiring higher levels of specialisation and influence in transfer negotiations. According to Jon Holmes, former chairman of SFX Sports, there are two types of agents (Bygrave and Johnson, 2004): the American model, where agents represent players and advise players on all aspects of their careers; and the European model where agents are traditionally brokers of deals, middlemen. In Europe, in order to overcome the political, legal and economic barriers, agents are employed to facilitate deals which clubs acting alone might not have been able to achieve. Such tasks require that agents also understand the value of a player with respect to his club and to other teams and the player's position in terms of his career trajectory.

Acting simultaneously as intermediaries for clubs and for players is a dual role that could raise important issues regarding conflicts of interests. Additionally, there is concern regarding the manner in which agents are able to utilise the control they have over a player for their own financial gain (Weir, 2008). This 'gate-keeping' role, according to former FA CEO Graham Kelly, has given agents a 'licence to print money' (Gross, 2006: 72). Similarly, Magee (2002) suggests that the agent has become the most important figure in the football market and consequently more have become involved, fuelled by the large commission fees available for negotiating multi-million pound contracts. Agents are able to manoeuvre and act by inhabiting the space that occurs between player and club, coming to occupy a key role in player trading. In a survey conducted in 2002 with the financial directors of English PL, Championship and Scottish PL clubs, 78 per cent stated that agents were becoming too powerful and influential. At the same time, the same financial directors admitted that agents were a 'necessary evil' because they add costs and hinder contract negotiation, but could be useful when clubs need to sell and buy players (PFK, 2002). It was only in 2005 that agents in England decided to form a united representative body, the AFA, which furthered their interests. Two years later, in 2007, there followed the creation of the EFAA, currently the international voice of players' agents that is recognised by the EC and football stakeholders as an official organisation (Martins, 2008).

Notes

1 The average increase across all four English leagues was 54 per cent (Szymanski and Kuypers, 1999).
2 In 1956, George Eastham signed for Newcastle United on a rolling one-year contract. With his contract due to expire soon, in 1959 Eastham refused to sign a new one and requested a transfer to Arsenal. Unfortunately for Eastham, Newcastle United refused to let him go. The FA's draconian retain and transfer system allowed the club to prevent him from moving. The rules allowed clubs to retain players as long as they were offered terms that were reasonable, effectively tying a player to one club until it agreed to release him while refusing to pay them if they had requested a transfer. As he was unable to leave, Eastham decided to go on strike at the end of the 1959–1960 season. Finally, in October 1960 Newcastle United relented and decided to sell Eastham to Arsenal for £47,500. This could have been the end of the matter but Eastham considered the issue worth standing up and fighting for. Backed by the PFA, who provided £15,000 to pay for Eastham's legal fees, he took Newcastle United to the High Court in 1963. In the High Court, Eastham argued that this was an unfair restraint of trade, and that Newcastle United owed him £400 in unpaid wages and £650 in unpaid bonuses. The judge, Mr Justice Wilberforce, ruled partly in the player's favour, stating that the retain and transfer system used by clubs was unreasonable. At the conclusion of the case, although Eastham did not gain personally, he succeeded in reforming the British transfer market. The retain element of the transfer system was greatly reduced, providing fairer terms for players looking to re-sign for their clubs and setting up a transfer tribunal for disputes.
3 Only Kist and the Van de Kerkhof brothers exceeded €0.22 million.
4 Jean-Marc Bosman, football player in the Jupiter league in Belgium for RFC Liege, wanted to move to France and play for Dunkerque. However, using the cross-border transfer ruling, Liege wanted a payment. Dunkerque was not willing to pay the sum of money RFC Liege wanted so the deal fell through and, subsequently, Bosman took court action against the European football authorities, RFC Liege and the Belgian Football authorities; he argued that payment of transfer fees for free agents conflicted with EU citizen's right to free movement within employment. The case took five years to be settled as each ruling was appealed; finally, it reached the ECJ in Luxemburg. Bosman sued on grounds of restraint of trade and argued that FIFA's Article 17 breached this and was in fact illegal. On 15 December 1995, the court ruled in favour of Bosman as the system, as it was constituted, placed a restraint on freedom of movement of workers and was prohibited by Article 39 of the EU treaty of Rome. The same considerations apply in relation to Article 48 of the Treaty, with regard to rules which impede the freedom of movement of nationals of one member state wishing to engage in gainful employment in another member state. As a result, the EU demanded that regulations concerning players' transfers and limitations on foreign players be amended almost immediately. This ruling meant Bosman and every other EU footballer were free to negotiate deals to any other EU based team after their current contracts expired. They were also allowed to sign pre-contract deals with other clubs if they had six months remaining on their current deals. This ruling also stopped UEFA imposing quotas on how many foreign players are allowed to play in a team at any one time. At the time UEFA were imposing a quota on their European competitions that only allowed three non-nationals in a team on match days. While these quotas were not fully outlawed, they could not be used to restrict the number of non EU players in a match day team.

Bibliography

AEAF (2011) Historia de nuestra asociación. *Boletin de la AEAF.* 1, pp. 5–7. Available from: www.agentesdefutbolistas.com/boletines/Boletin-de-la-AEAF-N%201-Julio-2011.pdf [accessed 17 April 2012].

AEAF (2012) Entrevista a Roberto Dale, presidente honorífico de la AEAF. *Boletin de la AEAF* [online] 2, pp. 32–34. Available from: www.agentesdefutbolistas.com/boletines/boletin-de-la-AEAF-2.pdf [accessed 7 March 2012].

Asser (2005) *Professional sport in the internal market, Working Paper.* Brussels: European Parliament's Committee on Internal Market and Consumer Protection.

Azhar, A. (1996) *Agent du foot: Histoires secretes.* Paris: Éditions Solar.

Banks, S. (2002) *Going down: Football in crisis.* Edinburgh: Mainstream Publishing.

Berry, R. C., Gould, W. B. and Staudohar, P. D. (1986) *Labor relations in professional sports.* Dover, MA: Auburn House Publishing.

Bower, T. (2007) *Broken dreams: The definitive exposé of British football corruption (updated version).* London: Pocket Books.

Bradford, T. (2006) *When Saturday comes: The half decent football book.* London: Penguin Books.

Bygrave, M. and Johnson, A. (2004), Reform disgraceful fees, MPs tell soccer clubs. *Independent on Sunday*, 1 February 2004. Available from: www.independent.co.uk/news/uk/politics/reform-disgraceful-agent-fees-mps-tell-soccer-clubs-78548.html [accessed 15 January 2014].

Caliendo, A. (2012) *Nessuno prima di me. L'evoluzione del calcio e del procuratore sportivo.* Milan: Libreria dello Sport.

Canovi, D. and Mazzocchi, G. (2011) *Lo Stalliere del re. Fatti e misfatti di 30 anni di calcio.* Milano: Dalai Editore.

Carter, N. (2006) *The football manager: A history.* London: Routledge.

Corcuera, J. I. (2010) Intermediarios: un negocio viejo. *Cuadernos de Fútbol.* 10. Available from: www.cihefe.es/cuadernosdefutbol/2010/06/intermediarios-un-negocio-viejo/ [accessed 15 July 2015].

Corcuera, J. I. (2012) El timo de los paraguayos. *Cuadernos de Fútbol.* 36. Available from: www.cihefe.es/cuadernosdefutbol/2012/10/el-timo-de-los-paraguayos/ [accessed 15 July 2015].

Davis, T. (2007) United States. In: Siekman, R. C. R., Parrish, R., Martins, R. B. and Soek, J. (eds) *Players' agents worldwide: Legal aspects.* The Hague: T. M. C. Asser Press, pp. 655–692.

Deloitte (2003) *Deloitte annual review of football finance, 13th Edition.* Manchester: Deloitte.

Dimitrakopoulos, D. G. (2006) More than a market? The regulation of sport in the European Union. *Government and Opposition. An International Journal of Comparative Politics.* 41(4), pp. 561–580.

Dubey, J. P. (2000) *La libre circulation des sportifs en Europe.* Bern: Staempfli.

Esposito, E. (2011) *Testa alta, due piedi.* Roma: Absolutely Free Editore.

Faure, J. M. and Suaud, C. (1999) *Le football professionnel à la française.* Paris: Puf.

Feess, E. and Mühlheußer, G. (2003) Transfer fee regulations in European football. *European Economic Review.* 47(4), pp. 645–68.

FIFA (2005) *Players' agents regulations.* Zurich: FIFA.

FIFA (2015a) Working with intermediaries – reform of the players' agents system. *FIFA [online].* Available from: www.fifa.com/governance/news/y=2015/m=4/news=

working-with-intermediaries-reform-of-fifa-s-players-agents-system-2583543.html [accessed 19 November 2015].

FIFA (2015b) Third-party ownership of players' economic rights. *FIFA [online]*. Available from: www.fifa.com/mm/document/affederation/footballgovernance/02/59/55/80/third-partyownershipofplayerseconomicrights-backgroundinformation_neutral.pdf [accessed 19 November 2015].

Foot, J. (2006) *Calcio: A history of Italian football*. London: Fourth Estate.

Frenkiel, S. (2014) *Une histoire des agents sportifs en France: Les imprésarios du football (1979–2014)*. Neuchâtel: Editions CIES.

Gouget, J. J. and Primault, D. (2006) Les agents dans le sport professionnel: analyse économique. *Revue Juridique et Économique du Sport*. 81, pp. 7–44.

Gould, M. T. (1992) Further trials and tribulations of sports agents. *Entertainment & Sports Lawyer*. 10, pp. 9–14.

Greaves, J. (2003) *Greavsie: The autobiography*. London: Time Warner.

Greenberg, M. J. and Gray, J. T. (1998) Agents. In: Greenberg, M. J. (eds) *Sport law practice*. 2nd edn. Charlottesville, VA: Lexis Law Publishing.

Gross, J. (2006) We'll sue: bung whistleblower Newell threatened with court action by angry agents. *Mirror*. 13 January 2006.

Harding, J. (2004) It was my agent's idea. *WSC When Saturday Comes* [online]. 4 February 2004. Available from: www.wsc.co.uk/the-archive/102-Agents/2193-it-was-my-agents-idea [accessed 1 May 2014].

Helyar, J. (1994) *Lords of the realm: The real history of baseball*. New York: Villard.

Holt, M., Michie, J. and Oughton, C. (2006) *The role and regulations of agents in football*. London: The Sport Nexus.

Karcher, R. T. (2007) Fundamental fairness in union regulation of sports agents. *Connecticut Law Review*. 40(2), pp. 355–408.

Katz, D. (1994) *Just do it: The Nike spirit in the corporate world*. New York: Random House.

KEA, CDES and EOSE (2009) *Study on sport agents in the European Union*. Brussels: Sport EC.

King, L. (1994) Remembrances of Bob Woolf, America's first sport agent. *Jeffrey S. Moorad Sports Law Journal*. 1(1), pp. 3–5.

Lamster, M. (2007) *Spalding's world tour: The epic adventure that took baseball around the globe and made it America's game*. New York: The Perseus Group.

Lanfranchi, P. and Taylor, M. (2001) *Moving with the ball: The migration of professional footballers*. Oxford: Berg.

Levine, P. (1986) *A. G. Spalding and the rise of baseball: The promise of American sport*. Oxford: Oxford University Press.

Litsky, F. (1998) Frank Scott, 80, baseball's first player agent. *New York Times*. 30 June 1998.

Madden, B. (1998) Frank Scott, pal of players, dies. *New York Daily News*. 30 June 1998.

Magee, J. (2002) Shifting power balances of power in the new football economy. In: Sugden, J. and Tomlinson, A. (eds) *Power games: A critical sociology of sport*. London: Routledge, pp. 216–239.

Martins, R. B. (2008) European Football Agents Association wants to end malpractice in the international transfer of players. *The International Sports Law Journal*. 1–2, pp. 96–99.

Marzola, P. (1981) *Il Mercato del lavoro negli sports professionistici di squadra*. Ferrara: Editrice Universitaria.

Marzola, P. (1990) *L'industria del calcio*. Roma: La Nuova Italia Scientifica.

Mason, D. S. and Duquette, G. H. (2005) Globalisation and the evolving player-agent relationship in professional sport. *International Journal of Sport Management and Marketing*. 1(1–2), pp. 93–109.

Mason, D. S. and Slack, T. (2003) Understanding principal-agent relationship: evidence from professional hockey. *Journal of Sport Management*. 17(1), pp. 37–61.

Masteralexis, L. P. (2005) Sports agency. In: Masteralexis, L. P., Barr, C. and Hums, M. (eds) *Principle and practice of sport management*. 2nd edn Sudbury: Jones and Bartlett Publishers, pp. 221–252.

Maximo, C. O. (2011) *Gigi Peronace*, Jett Press.

McGovern, P. (2002) Globalization or internationalization? Foreign footballers in the English League, 1946–95. *Sociology*. 36(1), pp. 23–42.

Miller, L. K., Fielding, L. W. and Pitts, B. G. (1992) A uniform code to regulate athlete's agents. *Journal of Sport and Social Issues*. 16(2), pp. 93–102.

Minguella, J. M. (2008) *Quasi tota la veritat*. Barcelona: Base.

Neff, C. (1987) Den of vipers, a sports scourge: Bad agents. *Sport Illustrated*. 19 October 1987.

NFLPA (2014) History. *NFLPA* [online]. Available from: www.nflplayers.com/About-us/History/ [accessed 23 September 2014].

Paradinas, J. J. (1978) La UEFA veta a Guijarro como intermediario. *El País*. 28 June 1978.

Parrish, R. (2003) The politics of sports regulations in the European Union. *Journal of European Public Policy*. 10(2), pp. 246–262.

PFK (2002) *The Annual Survey of Football Clubs Finance Directors*. London: PFK.

Pinna, A. (2006) The international supply of sport agent services. *International Sports Law Journal*. 1–2, pp. 20–27.

Poli, R. (2010a) *Le marché des footballeurs: Reseaux et circuitsdans l'économie globale*. Bern: Peter Lang.

Poli, R. (2010b) Agents and intermediaries. In: Hamil, S. and Chadwick, S. (eds) *Managing football: An international perspective*. Oxford: Elsevier Butterworth-Heinemann, pp. 201–216.

Poli, R. (2010c) Understanding globalisation through football: The new international division of labour, migratory channels and transnational trade circuits. *International Review for the Sociology of Sport*. 45(4), pp. 491–506.

Reisler, J. (2008) *Cash and carry: The spectacular rise and hard fall of C. C. Pyle, America's first sport agent*. Jefferson NC: McFarland & Co. Inc.

Relaño, A. (1978) Fernando Torcal, monopolizador del negocio futbolistico. *El País*. 19 August 1979.

Risoli, M. (2012) *John Charles: Gentle giant*. Edinburgh: Mainstream Sport.

Roderick, M. (2001) The role of agents in professional football, *Singer and Friedlander's Review 2000–01 Season*. The Centre for Research into Sport and Society: University of Leicester. Available from: www.le.ac.uk/crss/of-review/001-01/01article3.html [accessed 20 January 2012].

Rosner, S. R. (2004) Conflicts of interests and the shifting paradigm of athlete representation. *UCLA Entertainment Law Review*. 11(2), pp. 193–245.

Ruxin, R. (1993) *An athlete's guide to agents*. Sudbury: Jones & Bartlett Publishers.

Semens, A. (2008) *Player representation in the English football industry*. PhD University of Central Lancashire.

Semens, A. (2012) Bridge, gate keepers, negotiator: The sport agent as entrepreneur. In: Ciletti, D and Chadwick, S. (eds) *Sports entrepreneurship: Theory and practice*. Morgantown: Fitness Information Technology, pp. 81–95.

Shropshire, K. L. and Davis, T. (2008) *The business of sports agents*. 2nd edn. Philadelphia: University of Pennsylvania Press.

Sobel, L. (1987) The regulation of sports agents: An analytical primer. *Baylor Law Review*. 39, pp. 701–786.

Sorgi, M. (2011) *Il grande dandy. Vita spericolata di Raimondo Lanza di Trabia, l'ultimo principe siciliano*. Milano: Rizzoli Editore.

Spiegel (2002) Robert Schwan gestorben: Beckenbauer verliert seinen 'besten Freund'. *Spiegel* [online], 14 July 2002. Available from: www.spiegel.de/sport/fussball/robert-schwan-gestorben-beckenbauer-verliert-seinen-besten-freund-a-205191.html [accessed 3 September 2015].

Stagi, P. (1990) 007 a Milanofiori Missione Procuratori. *L'Unitá*. 13 July 1990.

Szymanski, S. and Kuypers, T. (1999) *Winners and losers*. London: Penguin Books.

Tamburini, A. (2012) *Italo Allodi: Ascesa e caduta di un principe del calcio*. Ancona: Italic Editore.

Taylor, M. (1999) No big deal. *WSC When Saturday Comes* [online], 14 November 1999. Available from: www.wsc.co.uk/the-archive/102-Agents/4042-no-big-deal [accessed 18 June 2013].

Taylor, M. (2002) Work and play: The professional footballer in England c.1900–1950. *The Sports Historian*. 22(1), pp. 16–43.

Taylor, M. (2005) *The leaguers – the making of professional football in England, 1900–1939*. Liverpool: Liverpool University Press.

Taylor, M. (2006) Global players? Football migration and globalization, c.1930–2000. *Historical Social Research*. 31(6), pp. 7–30.

UEFA (2007) News from Brussels. *UEFA Direct*. 58, p. 5.

Varley (1997) *Golden boy: A biography of Wilf Mannion*. London: Aurum Press.

Vasco, M. A. (2012) Luis Guijarro: El primer representante modern. *AS Color*. July 2013, pp. 16–19.

Wahl, A. and Lanfranchi, P. (1995) *Les footballeurs français des années trente à nos jours*. Paris: La Vie Quotidienne Actuelle, Hachette.

Weir, M. J. (2008) The ugly side of the beautiful game: 'Bungs' and the corruption of players' agents in European football. *Southwestern Journal of Law & Trade in the Americas*. 14, pp. 145–170.

Wild, D. (2003) Agents net £50m from football. Accountancy Age (online), 20 November 2003. Available from: www.accountancyage.com/aa/news/1752064/agents-net-gbp50m-football [accessed 8 April 2013].

Wolohan, J. T. (2007) United States. In: Siekman, R. C. R., Parrish, R., Martins, R. B. and Soek, J. (eds) *Players' agents worldwide: Legal aspects*. The Hague: T. M. C. Asser Press, pp. 637–653.

Woolf, B. (1976) *Behind closed doors*. New York: The New American Library.

2 The activity of football agents

Overview

Despite more than a century of activity, empirical research on football agents is sparse, with the majority of insights revealed through media enquiries and institutional reports, which have almost inevitably focused on misconduct and corruption. Recently, several agents' biographies and autobiographies have been published, adding more interesting information on their profession and their working experience. However, a more detailed and generic description of their activities and their profile is necessary to understand the development and evolution of this profession in the sport industry. Empirical data collected by one of the authors as part of a research study on football agents conducted for the CIES[1] is relied upon in the next two chapters to establish an overview of the marketplace.

This chapter begins by looking at the agents market in terms of its size and scale as well as who these people are and why they have come to perform this role, before looking at the specifics of what duties an agent is likely to perform. The practicalities of the tasks undertaken by agents often relate directly to their pre-agency careers. We therefore consider the typical profile of an agent, what they need to be able to do as a minimum, and the scope of the profession. Focussing on the big five European leagues, we identify trends in the socio-demographic profile of agents, including their education background and previous professional experience. This background often has an impact on the type of agent they become. Various typologies are therefore presented, highlighting the vast differences between how agents operate and the players that they represent.

2.1 Players' labour market and football agents

While Chapter 1 highlighted that, technically, the term agent refers to a person who contracts with either the club or the player, whereas an intermediary does not necessarily have that official mandate yet plays the same role, the diversity of scale and scope of those involved as football intermediaries mean that the difference between the two in practice is often very difficult to identify. In reality the work performed is often indistinguishable at the level of actions. The primary definition of an 'agent' in a football context is from Article 14 of the RGA of the FIFA Statutes (FIFA, 2008), which states that:

> the players' agent is a natural person, who, for a fee, on a regular basis introduces a player to a club with a view to employment or introduces a club to another with a view to concluding a transfer contract.

In theory, this definition provides a very simple description of the agency relationship whereby an agent is merely an intermediary ensuring that the supply and demand for labour within the football market is met. For a fee, the agent assists players in finding clubs, or vice-versa. A contractual relationship exists between the player and his or her representative, which enables the agent to control and manage their clients' careers for a specific period of time. Brokering a deal is often supplemented by management services, whose nature depends upon the needs of the player (Hendrickx, 2007).

As commercial activities have become more important to some players, those with the highest profile have transitioned towards becoming entertainers instead of athletes, which opens up myriad opportunities which agents can help them to exploit. Nevertheless, for lower league players, these opportunities usually do not exist and therefore their agents must perform a different role. Similarly, the market structure is different for the top players compared to average players. These factors mean that the balance of power in negotiations between clubs and players and, where relevant, other commercial stakeholders is fluid. In order to better understand the role of agents it is therefore worth briefly considering the structure of the player labour market.

The market for playing talent can be thought of as operating in the same way as any other labour market and analysed in terms of the interaction of supply and demand. Players are allocated to teams through a process of matching bids and offers for the player's services. Under perfect competition, the maximum clubs will be willing to pay a player in wages is the amount his signing and performance would add to the revenue of the club through additional support and broadcast revenue – known as his marginal revenue product, MRP. Paying any more than a player's MRP would decrease club profits, while anything below his MRP would increase profits (Dobson and Goddard, 2001). However, the assumptions of the perfectly competitive model may not be appropriate for the sporting labour market. As shown in Table 2.1, Downward and Dawson (2000) propose three main alternatives to perfect competition in understanding wage determination.

Traditionally, labour markets in sport have been thought of as monopsonies, (Scully, 1974; Medoff, 1976) in which the club occupies a strong position relative to the many equally talented players who wish to play. This may be because the number of clubs is small or there are a large number of clubs but certain teams are more attractive than the others so players want to play for them. Since there will always be an oversupply of footballers, clubs have a certain amount of bargaining power. This power that the clubs are able to exert over the players has led

Table 2.1 Structure of the players' labour market

Player power/club power	Low	High
Low	Perfect competition: 'just wage'	Monopsony: exploitation of players
High	Monopoly: 'star model'	Bilateral monopoly: 'bargaining over rents'

Source: Downward and Dawson (2000).

to monopsony exploitation in which they are paid salaries below their MRP. This is often thought to be a more realistic model for professional team sports, wherein the product market teams may have a local monopoly (Rottenberg, 1956; Sandy *et al.*, 2004). While, in a competitive market, a player being paid less than his MRP would simply move to another club who were willing to pay him his full value, under the retain and transfer system in England, and the reserve clause in the US players were tied to just one employer.[2]

In contrast, if the number of clubs implies more economic competition but there is high player power, then circumstances akin to a monopoly occur in which certain players have rare talent and have monopoly power as there is no substitute for their skill (Downward and Dawson, 2000). If this is the case, clubs will compete to sign the player; wages become demand driven and players are able to earn economic rents (Neale, 1964). This is often thought of in the context of the best players being superstars, where the ability for players to attain monopoly power is related to the notion of scarcity. Real stars are few in number and their talent is not easily replicated by an average player. Rosen (1981) referred to this as the superstar phenomenon and illustrated how human capital interacts with production technology to magnify small differences in talent, resulting in large differences in earnings. Technological developments mean that the product can be reproduced at a low cost. Stadia enable thousands of people to consume the product at the same time and broadcasting widens the market still further.

When both clubs and players have high market power, a bilateral monopoly exists in which the equilibrium wage is indeterminate. There is a range of possible wages and the value of the contract depends on the relative bargaining power of the parties involved (Downward and Dawson, 2000). In sum, under perfect competition, wages would equate to marginal revenue product. In the case of monopsony, players will receive salaries below their MRP. With bargaining, wages will lie somewhere between the two as each party bargains over the available economic rents. Dawson and Downward (2000: 189) identify an 'evolutionary path that has moved from monopsonistic labour markets to bargaining structures and then competitive outcomes'. With increased player power, wage bargaining approximates to perfect competition as outcomes of bargaining, on average, now reflect a player's marginal revenue product.

It is predicted that as bargaining power for a player increases, such as after the Bosman ruling, salaries will rise beyond the levels experienced under monopsony. Downward and Dawson (2000) suggest that particularly talented players will have even greater bargaining power and hence receive even higher salaries. Frick (2007) identifies that, in contrast to the US, European football clubs try to maximise utility instead of profit (Sloane, 1969; Kesenne, 2007); therefore 'increasing revenues from ticket sales, merchandising activities and especially the sale of broadcast rights have induced a massive increase in player salaries' (Frick, 2007: 426).

Under the monopsony conditions of the retain and transfer system, clubs effectively held a unilateral long term contract over the player, 'though a particular contract might be 'nominally specified for a set number of years' (Downward and Dawson, 2000: 210). Clubs faced no financial loss from losing a player to another team. However, in moving towards a more competitive market, there was a real economic threat to clubs who had to face the risk of losing their best players without being compensated. In this respect, clubs sought to retain their own power by tying players to long term contracts.

Coinciding with improved broadcasting contracts, players were renegotiating contracts in the knowledge that great financial riches were available. In an effort to reduce the impact of the Bosman ruling clubs offered higher salaries to players reaching the end of their contracts, and also tried to renegotiate improved terms with players so they would not wish to move. Longer contracts were also introduced and transfer fees for in-contract players increased as clubs tried to prise them away from their current clubs, and the number of foreign players making a living in the English leagues increased (Magee, 2002; Magee, 2006; Greenfield and Osborn, 2001). A combination of these effects has meant that the top players in particular were able to assume much control in the market as clubs could not afford to lose them on a free transfer and were therefore willing to offer improved contractual terms. As Magee (2002: 221) identifies 'the evolution of the modern-day footballer into a high earning superstar saw the pendulum of power over labour rights shift away from the clubs/authorities and rest with the player'. With this, player representatives became central to the negotiation process, assisting players to acquire a powerful position over clubs.

However, at the lower end of the market, the Bosman ruling has meant increased uncertainty for players. Clubs have been able to offer reduced packages to players who are out of contract elsewhere, with increased numbers of players being released at the end of their contract (Magee, 2006). It is therefore suggested that lower league clubs have been able to regain some of their power over contractual conditions, whereas star players have been able to use the Bosman ruling to their advantage, essentially holding clubs to ransom (Magee, 2002).

2.2 The functions of football agents

As a consequence of increased sums of money being available to the elite players, the number of people seeking to be involved in the agents industry has also grown. According to KEA *et al.* (2009), we could count around 2,920 licensed agents in 2009 in Europe. This number falls far short of the true total if we consider the involvement of unlicensed agents, as well as agents not listed by federations, and of family members and lawyers acting as agents.

Power has an important role to play in the football market and at times it is necessary for agents to take different roles according to who they represent. Typically, agents work either for players or for clubs; however, their role can become blurred, particularly when considering who the agent is paid by. Modern agents play a mediating role between the parties involved in a transaction, but without the impartiality that distinguishes a mediator from other professionals (KEA *et al.*, 2009). This is due to the commercial nature of the relationship between the player and the agent – the agent acts on behalf of the player to get him the best possible contract, but it is not unusual for the agent to also act in the interests of the club, once the player has signed for it, in order to make sure that the player acts appropriately in order to achieve the highest possible playing standard. We will first consider the roles an agent performs on behalf of a player, before looking at their role in acting for clubs.

Players tend to delegate authority to their agent for seven main functions as shown in Table 2.2 (Sobel, 1987; Magee, 2002; Masteralexis, 2005).

The first and most implicit function is the negotiation of a player's contract. As discussed in the previous chapter, the changing conditions in the football industry, allied to labour market liberalisation, led to salary increases for players throughout the 1980s. However, occupational freedom was still restricted since clubs were still able to demand a transfer fee for out of contract players they had offered terms to (Magee, 2002). The Bosman ruling changed the landscape of the football market completely, with players post Bosman able to move to any club with whom they could agree personal terms. Another implication of the Bosman ruling allowed increased mobility of players across Europe, leading to 'increased traffic of football labour across European borders … as players utilised their new freedom to criss-cross the continent in search of inflated salaries in the wealthy core leagues' (Magee, 2002: 222). Coinciding with improved broadcasting contracts, players were renegotiating contracts in the knowledge that great financial riches were available. Entering into a contract with a club without third party advice can therefore be disadvantageous as the negotiation often tends to be unbalanced, with the relative naivety of the player being pitted

Table 2.2 Percentage of agents performing a specific task, per type of service provided

Services provided	%
Negotiating players' contracts	98
Negotiating players' marketing and endorsement contracts	65
Legal counselling and dispute resolution	51
Career and post career planning	48
Personal care	46
Financial planning	38
Marketing planning	31

against the club who have entered into various agreements of this sort before and have a much wider knowledge of the market – bargaining power would therefore likely be stacked in favour of the club (Smienk, 2009). As the player is unlikely to be familiar with the inner workings of a club, including its existing pay structures, he is more likely to succumb to potential pressure tactics used by the club and accept 'take it or leave it' contract offers (Roderick, 2006).

An agent, equipped with the relevant skills and knowledge, can significantly improve a player's pay and conditions as well as providing valuable career advice. Even players who may be competent negotiators can benefit from the help of agent in order that they can focus on their playing career without becoming distracted by business matters which may affect their on the pitch performance. In this context, an agent acts as a buffer between the player and the club (possibly the manager), allowing the player to concentrate on his profession (Shropshire and Davis, 2008). However, power imbalances can also emerge between the player and his agent who have a complex principal–agent relationship. This occurs when a player heavily relies on his agent to negotiate on his behalf. In this situation, conflicts of interests can arise in the long term if the player does not adequately supervise the actions of the agent.[3] Consequently, it was reasonable that a player's mandate to an agent lasted a maximum of two years and then became renewable in accordance with FIFA PAR (FIFA, 2008).

While FIFA regulations apply only to transfer negotiations, almost two thirds of agents are also involved with procuring sponsorship and image-rights deals for their clients. When these contracts expire, the agent is responsible for renewing them or obtaining other, alternative contracts from third parties. From a financial perspective, these have increased in importance for all top players in recent years. Image rights have become a key factor to be negotiated between clubs and agents. For example, following Real Madrid's example, the Italian Serie A club Napoli always includes the acquisition of players' image rights in its contract deals. In 2011, the club was estimated to have earned €7 million from the exploitation of this revenue source, which represented 7 per cent of its turnover (Ilaria, 2011).

In England, the FA standard contract for players implies that the player would give away most of his image rights to the club. According to the tax authority, HMRC, wealthy PL players often set up private businesses through which to receive income related to endorsements and the use of their image rights (Wilson, 2011). This allows corporation tax of 28 per cent to be levied instead of the higher rate of income tax of 50 per cent. While this procedure is legal, issues arise if clubs are suspected of using image rights as a way of unjustifiably inflating players' salaries. In June 2010 Paris Saint-Germain and Nike France were found guilty of hiding payments to players within the image rights contract by the 11th Chamber du Tribunal Correctionel de Paris. This tax fraud system allowed the French club to lessen the cost of players' recruitment (Brown, 2010a, 2010b). In this context, at the end of 2012, the British island of Guernsey introduced the world's first image rights register that offers the opportunity of

registering them in a tax neutral jurisdiction, with specific legislation that protects them from unauthorised use (Wilson, 2013).

Since a player's career is relatively short but the remuneration is high, it is
complicated for a player to make proper investment decisions due to a lack of
knowledge, expertise and time. The complex, but short career path in which they
become wealthy at a young age, when they may not be fully aware of all likely
expenses and financial liabilities, makes it essential to have good advice. Nevertheless, providing these services can be a complex matter for agents if they do
not have the proper in-house competence and expertise. Consequently, only 38
per cent of agents provide this kind of consultancy. It is likely that agents – and
probably players themselves – prefer to subcontract this service to other professionals. In the business of football representation, scandals of incompetence,
fraud and breaches of fiduciary duties often derive from cases of financial mis-
management by agents. The level of dependency which develops between some
players and their agents can make the former vulnerable to exploitation by the
latter. For example, Ian Elliott, the former agent of England winger Stewart
Downing, was charged for fraud (Collins, 2011). The player earned almost half a
million pounds by endorsing a sports wear brand from 2005 to 2008. The agent,
who made the deal on the player's behalf, was accused of siphoning hundreds of
thousands of pounds of Downing's money into his own failed business interests.

Related to this is legal and tax counselling with approximately half of the
licensed agents offering this service. Nevertheless, some players prefer to
involve sports lawyers, who do not usually act as agents but are considered more
competent than 'simple' intermediaries. In Germany, legal advice may only be
provided by legally authorised persons. Theoretically, unless they are lawyers,
German agents are not allowed to negotiate the content of an employment contract with a club. Thus, their activity is limited to the role of intermediaries. In
practice, the law on legal advice (RBerG) is largely ignored by the parties concerned (KEA *et al.*, 2009). Solicitors or legal advisors therefore often work in
collaboration with solo agents to perform these roles. Agents who provide these
services are likely to work for an agency or company who provide the services
to a relevant list of clients in the entertainment business (Magee, 2002).

Some agents also invest time, money and effort in planning the career of their
clients while they are playing at youth academy level, in minor leagues, and
abroad. Career planning also concerns the players' involvement in charitable
events, football schools and community club projects as well as helping players
to prepare for life after their playing careers. The fierce competition for recruiting players and the instability of player-agent relationships explain why fewer
than half of all agents are involved in this.

Finally, agents are identified as providing general ancillary services for their
clients, this is particularly important when players are relocating, and may
include finding houses and schools and ensuring that the player and his family
can settle in a new area without having to worry about anything that could dis-
tract him from playing football. Often related to this is the role of agents in
ensuring that the players they represent behave in the manner expected of an

elite athlete who is also a role model. While, stereotypically, agents are thought to assist players with their day to day activities, such as finding housing, transportation, health, tax advice, etc., one-fifth of agents never get involved with these tasks, while only 16.9 per cent carry out these tasks for their clients on a daily basis, as illustrated by Figure 2.1. According to the FA licensed agent Alex Levack,

> some agents are happy to just do the football deal and some others literally manage everything off the pitch whether it is finances, buying a house, car, mobile phone, going on holiday. I think it also depends on the player's preference: some players want to do all and others don't.

(Gill, 2010)

The nature of the football market means that the activities conducted by agents will alter according to the time of year – particularly after the introduction of transfer windows – and the number and type of players they represent. However, there are some commonalities: 61 per cent of agents are involved in building relational networks on a daily basis. Scouting players and staying up to date on relevant information such as regulatory issues or club needs are also popular activities, with around 40 per cent of agents doing these tasks every day. This is to be expected as agents fill a key role in brokering deals.

As well as providing services to players, an estimated 70 per cent of agents also assist clubs, as seen in Table 2.3. The majority are engaged in helping clubs

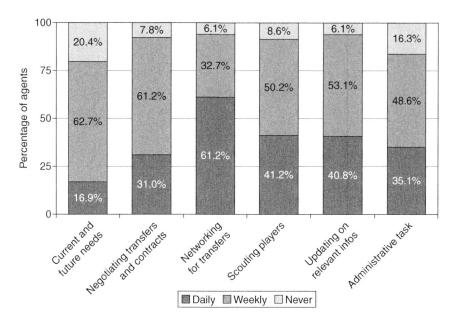

Figure 2.1 Percentage of agents according to task frequency.

Table 2.3 Percentage of agents according to the type of service provided to clubs

Services provided	%
Transferring players	71
Scouting professional players	65
Scouting youth players	50
Organising events	23

to recruit professional players, while half are involved in finding talent for clubs at the youth level. In addition, around a quarter of agents also support clubs in the organisation of events such as friendly matches and tours.

These differences in the roles that agents play are often related to their backgrounds and careers prior to entering the football industry.

2.3 The profile of football agents

This increase in the number of agents operating has created a cluttered market whereby the choice of representation increases for an athlete, but the competition between agents to represent the best talent becomes fierce and many fail to make a living purely in this field. As the agent's network is usually key to effective operation in the industry, it often requires a long period of apprenticeship and occasional involvement in order to gain the required experience and competence and, most importantly, contacts. Since the basic manner of doing business in this sector is always based on trust and face-to-face interaction (Roderick, 2006; Shropshire and Davis, 2008; Poli, 2010), the centrality and the relevance of the individual agent is still crucial in the representation of football players.

Given the close networks involved in the football market and the necessity of having a wide range of contacts, it is unsurprising that more than one third of licensed agents have worked in the sports industry before becoming an agent, as shown in Chapter 6. Nevertheless, since the vast majority of players, during their own playing careers, rely on third parties to represent them, it is interesting to note that almost a quarter of agents were previously professional footballers themselves.

In Figure 2.2, various trends can also be seen in terms of previous non-football related work experience, with experience in the financial and legal sectors proving particularly popular. The complexities of deals mean that the ability to provide financial and legal guidance through contracts, taxes, budgeting, investments and insurance is a solid base, essential in many situations. This can be particularly useful when assisting clients at the start of their careers who, given their progression through the ranks of a football club, are likely to be largely unaware of the legal and financial stakes related to their profession. Moreover, these professionals are used to operating as problem solvers in business sectors which require the careful balancing of multiple clients

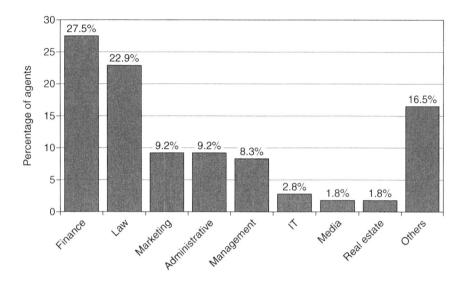

Figure 2.2 Percentage of agents with previous non-football work experience, per sector of experience.

and parties to transactions, affording them sensitivity to understanding clients' needs.

While lawyers are subject to stringent professional regulations and training to govern their conduct, eliminating the need for any additional licensing under the previous system of regulation, it has been argued that those who also act as agents to broker deals on behalf of players or clubs do not know enough about football matters and are not able to provide the best services to their clients. Being conscious of this possible competitive disadvantage, some law firms have formed partnerships with or employed former professional players and managers who can provide the necessary football expertise. For example, the former English PL players John Hendrie, Brian Deane and Robbie Savage have worked as consultants to the Leeds law firm Blacks, while former England national team player and 1995 English PL champion Stuart Ripley retired in 2000 and retrained as a lawyer, offering legal consultancy to several clubs for their transfer deals at Brabners Chaffe Street (Rose, 2010; Sport Business International, 2011).

The switch from marketer to agent is also relatively common. As the best players have come to earn more money from their activities off the pitch than from those on it, many footballers seek the guidance of a former marketing professional with proven experience in sponsorship and endorsement deals, as well as PR campaigns and links to big brands. Modern players are fully aware that the combination of playing talent and the right image portrayed in the best possible light can create a highly marketable brand, providing an income which can be sustained beyond their playing careers.

While representing the top players is hugely rewarding financially, it can be difficult for those with lower level clients to make a living purely from being an agent. Overall, only 41 per cent of licensed agents are estimated to work full-time. As shown in Table 2.4, this proportion varies by country, with the figure rising to above 50 per cent only in France, whereas in England it is less than one third. On average, full-time agents represent 16 players; six more than part-time agents.

Those who do not work as full time agents tend to work in different business sectors, which heavily overlap with the background of full time agents outlined above, though they operate at various levels from business owners through to managerial and administrative levels.

A small minority of part time agents, 4.3 per cent, also have a parallel career in the football industry, working as football managers, technical directors, PR and club marketing managers at the same time. FIFA has sought to stop these conflicts of interest from occurring and in November 2011 the former Italian player Claudio Sclosa resigned as a licensed agent for the football agency IFA Bonetto before being named as Juventus' chief scout (Alaimo, 2011). However, this is not always the case: in 2011, at the English league club Doncaster Rovers, Willie McKay had exclusive control over the transfers of the club for two years, but remained licensed as an agent with the FA (Sinnott, 2011). Formally, McKay had the final say over every player that either joined or left the club. The agreement was verified by the English FA after the agent contacted the governing body with the details of his contract.

The agent must be immersed in the sport in which he operates in order to develop his network and contacts. Therefore, the vast majority of agents, 90 per cent, only represent football players. For those who do have cross disciplinary interests, alternative disciplines tend to depend on the popularity of other sports in the market in which they operate. In Germany, for example, where handball is very popular, some agents represent both handball and football players while in Spain, agents are more likely to also represent professional futsal and basketball players. The differences in the needs of athletes between different sports mean that it is rare to see these crossovers. Representing an individual athlete differs significantly from a team-sport sportsperson. Individual athletes' earnings depend much more on consistent performance in key events and the ability to promote and market their image. Their agents are thus more involved in managing the individual player's career, much like the business managers hired by

Table 2.4 Percentage of agents working full-time per country

Country	% of agents working full-time as agents
France	55.1
Italy	42.1
Germany	38.2
Spain	33.9
England	31.0

entertainers. Despite football being a key component of the entertainment industry overall, the cross over between representing athletes and artists is not widespread, with only about 7 per cent operating in both sectors. The English based agent Athole Still is a notable exception – as well as being responsible for the career of Sven Goran Eriksson, amongst others, he is also highly regarded for his company Athole Still Opera, which represents singers, musicians and conductors (Inside Croydon, 2012).

The global nature of the football market, particularly post Bosman has meant that multilingual agents, often with experience of having lived abroad, are at an advantage through being able to create networks internationally. Silvano Martina, a well-known Italian agent representing Gianluigi Buffon, for example, also works on behalf of some Serbian players, such as Nemanja Vidić, Bosko Janković, and Milan Milanović (Perrone, 2013). Over 70 per cent of agents speak at least one foreign language with 21 per cent and 7.5 per cent speaking respectively two and three foreign languages and a small minority, 1 per cent, speaking four foreign languages. The fact that agent Mino Raiola speaks seven languages certainly helped him at the beginning of his career when he signed an agreement with the Dutch professional players' union, VVCS, to become the main representative of Dutch players abroad.

Just under two-thirds of agents are thought to have spent up to six months abroad, with one-third of these having lived in two countries at least. Confirming the extraordinary international nature of this profession, only a small minority of agents, 7 per cent, have never lived abroad. French and English agents tend to have lived abroad much more than their German and Spanish colleagues. Those who do not have the relevant skills and experience to adequately manage the issues that players face when they move to a foreign country must look for external guidance, leading to a role for third party advisors. Even though there is no professional qualification for agents, more than two-thirds hold a bachelor's degree, with a further 7 per cent holding postgraduate qualifications.

According to FIFA lists of licensed agents, 97 per cent of football agents in Europe are male. Rachel Anderson, who has represented several English PL players and clubs, was the first female to be licensed by FIFA. However, despite being well respected in the industry, her career path has not been straightforward. In 1998, after having been banned from the men-only Annual PFA awards dinner for two years in a row, she sued the English PFA (BBC, 1999). Anderson won the case at the Central London County Court and the PFA were fined £200,000. Despite this victory it is clear that when a union of this size can operate in such an old fashioned manner the opportunities for female stakeholders to be involved in professional football are going to be limited and it is little wonder that so few females are involved. In other markets, while Italian agent Patrizia Pighini obtained her licence in 1994 and works mainly with fellow agent Antonio Caliendo, one year earlier Silvia Patruno became the first Italian female licensed agent (Repubblica, 2001; Ripamonti, 2006). Soukeyna Ba Bengelloun became an agent to represent her sons, Youness and Samir (Frenkiel, 2014). Nowadays, other high profile female agents do operate throughout

Europe: Margarita Pilar Gary-Bret, for example, is general director of Bahia Internacional and plays a key role in the management of various Spanish national team players. In France, Daphnée Bravard and Sonia Souid from the agency Essentially and Jennifer Mendelewitsch, the daughter of the former agent Patrick Mendelewitsch, are the most active female agents. Perhaps the largest sub-group of female agents are those with a direct relationship to the player, which in some ways is viewed as legitimising their position in the market: Dani Santa Ana, the former wife of the Barcelona player Dani Alves, for example, acts on his behalf and became a licensed agent in 2010, allowing her to represent other players through her company Flash-Forward.

2.4 The development of football agencies

As the industry has developed, different types of representatives have emerged. Agents tended to work alone in the early days and were often part time agents and full time stockbrokers, lawyers, accountants or members of any other profession (Shropshire and Davis, 2008). Magee (2002) identifies four types of agents operating in football. Essentially, the traditional agent present since the 1960s is still identified by Magee as the most popular type in England, the 'solo agent', who usually deals mainly with transfers and contracts. A second type of representative may be a 'solicitor/legal advisor' who provides a legal service. In addition, 'the sports agency' is described as providing a 'wider support service beyond contracts' and there is also the 'promotions agency' which usually provides 'career management and promotion opportunities' as opposed to contract negotiation (Magee, 2002: 231). It is notable that despite the need for agents to be registered from 1994–2015, many people operated without having that status (Magee, 2002).

With a limited number of players/clients available, it is essential for agents to have a basic portfolio of players that they work for to negotiate contracts and provide related services. As such, careers are built on the formation and the consolidation of, often transnational, networks which require investment of time and financial resources. Thus, many intermediaries started working as unlicensed agents in collaboration with established professionals in order to understand the dynamics of the football transfer market and to build their own networks within it.

Though it is no longer necessary for agents to be licensed, it is still instructive to see how many were operating outside of the rules under the previous system. According to the English FA (2011), during the 2010/2011 season transfer windows, clubs engaged 2,910 players but only committed to pay an agent in 570 of these transactions. Undoubtedly, unlicensed individuals might have been involved in several transactions. Given the competition for the best players, clubs tended to find ways round the rules in order to use unregistered agents if they were operating as the player's gate-keeper. This of course made the system even less transparent and sits at the heart of FIFA's reasoning for stopping the licensing system and instead regulating the actions of players and clubs. The fact that only around 30 per cent of international transfers are thought to involve a registered agent, despite very few players being unrepresented, calls into question the efficacy of the licensing system (Sinnott, 2010). The accepted involvement of unauthorised personnel has resulted in a gradual weakening of the football authorities themselves (Magee, 2002). One of the most famous unlicensed agents is the Serbian Vlado Lemic who became influential through his strong connection within PSV Eindhoven in the 2000s. Over the years Lemic developed business links with Frank Arnesen and Pedrag Mijatovic, respectively the former Chelsea and Real Madrid technical directors. In August 2011, Lemic and Mijatovic, as business partners, worked actively behind the transfer negotiations of Samuel Eto'o's transfer from Inter Milan to Anzhi Makhachkala.

Within the big five European leagues, 23 per cent of licensed agents are believed to have been active in the football representation business before getting their licence. In markets that are thought to be well policed, such as Germany, England and Spain, the number is much lower. However, in Italy and France the proportion of unlicensed agents is much higher. On the other hand, many aspiring agents decide to pass the exam without having a clear business plan for how they can make a living from this new activity. As a consequence, few people obtaining a licence are able to launch their careers as agents straight away. Interestingly, almost 11 per cent of agents registered in 2012 were thought not to represent any players. In contrast, some represent up to 100. Almost half of licensed agents had between one and ten players in their portfolios.

In Figure 2.3, of all the footballers represented, 42 per cent were professional while 10 per cent of the respondents represented only youth academy players. A further 10 per cent of the licensed agents exclusively focus on professional players. This implies that the pressure exerted by intermediaries on young players is probably great and some agents have become illegally involved in representing players under the age of 16, thereby breaking licence regulations.

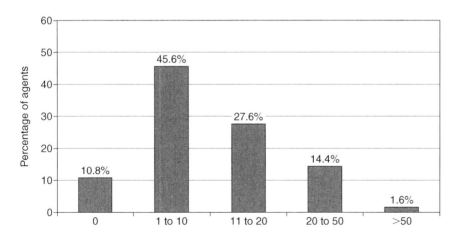

Figure 2.3 Percentage of individual agents per number of players directly represented.

The English FA has worked with clubs to ensure youth academy players are not left vulnerable to illegal approaches by agents (White, 2011). Chelsea, for example, has taken a proactive role in educating their players about agents. The club does not let agents attend most academy matches. It is very common for agents to approach youth academy players through social media. As a consequence, for instance, Manchester United discourages its players from holding Facebook accounts.

Top agents tend to represent the best international and national players. These players are most likely to gravitate towards an agent who can offer the best network through which to arrange future transfers, as well as to those able to offer career and financial advice. Their networks go beyond football and their involvement in the sport is driven mainly by the ability to drive revenues from this source. For them, intermediation on behalf of clubs is more relevant than scouting as their strategic market position allows them to be involved in the most profitable deals. This in turn means they have a strong record of being involved in high profile deals, which in turn makes them attractive to players. At a lower level are agents who normally work on behalf of mid-level players and have their transfer network connected to specific clubs. For these agents, scouting players is a key activity and they develop specialised knowledge which enables them to target football market segments according to a player's age, nationality, position and league level. Their main objective is to discover promising players in order to eventually be involved in the biggest transfers through these players. If this does become a reality, these agents may become connected to 'super' agents for some specific transfer situations in which big clubs are involved.

Across the main European leagues, the majority of agents have founded their own company (Spain 60 per cent; Germany 59 per cent; England and France 58 per cent). In almost eight cases out of ten, a formerly licensed agent is the main shareholder. The exception to this is in Italy, where only 36 per cent of agents have founded their own companies. This is partly due to rules created in the aftermath of the Calciopoli scandal, which aim to avoid any form of market concentration. Article 4 of FIGC PAR specifies that licensed agents can operate through companies only if they are authorised by their clients to do so when they sign an official mandate (FIGC, 2011). Agents have to be the main shareholders, with a maximum of three licensed agents in the same company. Moreover, it is forbidden for agents' companies to sell their shares to other agencies.

The categories of representative presented by Magee (2002) all still exist in the current market, but the addition of ex-players as a discrete sub group is also important. These roles have developed in response to the needs of players and to structural changes. Increases in players' salaries have made the agents' industry much more lucrative as a career. Applying standard neoclassical economic theory, an increase in the number of agents should, ceteris paribus, increase quality and reduce the price of the service they provide. Additionally, the agent would be expected to be less inclined to behave opportunistically because, if the player found out that the agent had acted in self-interest, he could choose to be represented by any one of a lot of other agents. Bad agents would therefore, theoretically, be driven out of the market. It would therefore be in the agent's interest to ensure that he was well qualified and capable of performing a range of services for his client.

2.5 Conclusions

Chapter 1 identified that structural changes have made the players' labour market increasingly liberalised. Coinciding with these developments, improvements in technology and deregulation of the broadcast markets have enabled football clubs to earn much higher revenues. As players have sought to extract a greater share of this revenue from clubs, in line with the liberalisation of the labour market, agents have been able to play a key role. Their role has been varied, seemingly adapting to the market conditions at work between clubs and players.

Labour market liberalisation has enabled players to obtain a greater share of their MRPs; hence wages have increased. As the negotiation process moved towards a more competitive bargaining structure, the economic rents available to players have soared, making it increasingly important for them to have good advisors and negotiators. Consistent with predictions of Rosen's (1981) super-stars model, the elite players have most bargaining power and differences in talent become exaggerated in terms of income because of the joint consumption of the media and a mass audience, combined with the fact that nothing can substitute for a star, given consumer preferences. While bargaining is more realistic for the best players in the PL for example, the competition between a large number of equally talented players in lower leagues means that clubs are regaining their power and the market is more competitive.

There is a clear difference in the roles the agent occupies at different levels and there are therefore very different justifications for why an agent may be paid by the club. While the clubs who use agents as scouts can justify paying a finder's fee for the service provided, in other situations the agent appears to be paid for doing relatively little. The elite players have power over clubs since they are thought of as a scarce commodity and, as such, are irreplaceable. Through agents, strategies are devised to effectively 'hold clubs to ransom' and the market is such that the top clubs who compete to sign such players appear to be willing to give in to the demands of the player and agent. By acting as a gate keeper – denying access to the player apart from through him/herself, the agent is able to hold power over the club. Cultural differences across countries and a win at all costs mentality for some clubs make it possible for players to make demands which clubs feel forced into meeting.

Power centres on the capacity of actors to redefine the parameters of what is socially, politically and economically possible for others (Hay, 1997). While the agents mainly gain their power through the close relationships they have been able to develop with players and clubs, industry norms, which appear to have developed and are mediated by regulations, are not necessarily constrained by those regulations. While dual representation, for example, has traditionally been an issue which authorities sought to regulate against, in reality market forces suggest that if clubs are willing to pay agents on behalf of players then they will find a way to do that. industry norms, which appear to have developed and are mediated by regulations, are not necessarily constrained to keep within regulations.

The nature of the football industry is such that it is a closely networked environment in which individual actions tend to be known by most of the people involved. This has created the opportunity for a disproportionate number of agents to be involved who had prior experience within the network through either working in the football industry previously or in roles which need similar skills. It is important for agents to be trusted by their clients, both players and clubs, so that they continue to work together. Networks are important in identifying talent and agents are integral to this. Since they often have knowledge of the international market or access to information from different sources, relationships are built up between individuals who continue to work together.

There are a number of roles an agent performs and specialist types of agent have arisen to fill these, with big differences in their specialisms, the services they provide to clients, and the way they are paid. Different types of agents tend to represent different levels of players, reflecting the split market for players which has emerged. While the most lucrative clients for agents will be the elite players, the lower level players often need them to help them find a club and then negotiate a fair salary. In this way football agents act in a very similar way to other recruitment professionals in other industries, providing a matching service between those seeking and those providing talent. Recognising all of the various activities that agents can be involved in, full service agencies, FSAs, have emerged as leading the market in order to meet the needs of modern players and clubs – the implications of this development are considered in more detail in Chapter 3.

Notes

1 The research report was written by Poli and Rossi (2012) as part of the João Havelange Scholarship awarded to Dr Giambattista Rossi by CIES.
2 The core behavioural assumptions are the same in economic literature for each of these approaches, with only the peripheral assumptions that characterise the market structures changing.
3 The principle agent relationship is discussed in more detail in Chapter 5.

Bibliography

Alaimo, A. (2011) Sclosa alla Juve, Bonetto: 'Ottima scelta'. *Tuttomercatoweb* [online]. Available from: www.tuttomercatoweb.com/serie-a/esclusiva-tmw-sclosa-alla-juve-bonetto-ottima-scelta-302091 [accessed 14 February 2012].
BBC (1999) Female football agent attacks PFA 'sexism'. *BBC News* [online]. Available from: http://news.bbc.co.uk/1/hi/uk/410983.stm [accessed 30 March 2012].
Brown, A. (2010a) French court accuses PSG and Nike of hiding salaries. *World Sports Law Report*. 8(3). Available from: www.e-comlaw.com/world-sports-law-report/article_template.asp?Contents=Yes&from=wslr&ID=1209 [accessed 11 May 2011].

Brown, A. (2010b) PSG & Nike used image rights deals to hide player payments. *World Sports Law Report*. 8(7). Available from: www.e-comlaw.com/world-sports-law-report/article_template.asp?Contents=Yes&from=wslr&ID=1241 [accessed 11 May 2011].

Collins, N. (2011) Football agent 'siphoned hundreds of thousands' from England star's account. *Telegraph* [online]. Available from: www.telegraph.co.uk/news/uknews/crime/8367170/Football-agent-siphoned-hundreds-of-thousands-from-England-stars-account.html [accessed 21 July 2012].

Dobson, S. and Goddard, J. (2001) *The economics of football*. Cambridge: Cambridge University Press.

Downward, P. and Dawson, A. (2000) *The economics of professional team sports*. London: Routledge.

FA (2011) *Agents' fees report*. London: FA.

FIFA (2008) *FIFA players' agents regulation*. Zurich: FIFA.

FIGC (2011) *Regolamento agenti 2011*. Roma: FIGC.

Frenkiel, S. (2014) *Une histoire des agents sportifs en France: Les imprésarios du football (1979–2014)*. Neuchâtel: Editions CIES.

Frick, B. (2007) The football players' labour market: Empirical evidence from the major European leagues. *Scottish Journal of Political Economy*. 54(3), pp. 442–446.

Gill, N. (2010) Sport.Co.Uk meets … football agent Alex Levack. *Sport.co.uk* [online]. Available from: www.sport.co.uk/features/Football/971/Sportcouk_meetsfootball_agent_Alex_Levack.aspx [accessed 20 December 2011].

Greenfield, S. and Osborn, G. (2001) *Regulating football: Commodification, consumption and the law*. London: Pluto Press.

Hay, C. (1997) Divided by a common language: Political theory and the concept of power. *Politics*. 17(1), pp. 45–52.

Hendrickx, F. (2007) Belgium. In: Siekman, R. C. R., Parrish, R., Martins, R. B. and Soek, J. (eds) *Players' agents worldwide: Legal aspects*. The Hague: T. M. C. Asser Press, pp. 105–115.

Ilaria, M. (2011) Bilanci piú sani con la flessibilitá. Quella vera. *La Gazzetta dello Sport*. 8 September 2011, pp. 14–15.

Inside Croydon (2012) All singing sports agent will transfer attention to Olympic pool. Inside Croydon [online]. Available from: http://insidecroydon.com/2012/07/22/all-singing-sports-agent-will-transfer-attention-to-olympic-pool/ [accessed 13 April 2013].

KEA, CDES and EOSE (2009) *Study on sport agents in the European Union*. Brussels: Sport EC.

Késenne, S. (2007) Player labour market. In: Késenne, S. (ed.) *The economic theory of professional team sports: An analytical treatment*. Cheltenham: Edward Elgar, pp. 30–37.

Magee, J. (2002) Shifting power balances of power in the new football economy. In: Sugden, J. and Tomlinson, A. (eds) *Power games: A critical sociology of sport*. London: Routledge, pp. 216–239.

Magee, J. (2006) When is a contract more than a contract? Professional football contracts and the pendulum of power. *Entertainment & Sports Law* [online]. 4(2). Available from: www2.warwick.ac.uk/fac/soc/law/elj/eslj/issues/volume4/number2/magee/magee.pdf [accessed 25 March 2012].

Masteralexis, L. P. (2005) Sports agency. In: Masteralexis, L. P., Barr, C. and Hums, M. (eds) *Principle and practice of sport management*. 2nd edn. Sudbury: Jones and Bartlett Publishers, pp. 221–252.

Medoff, M. H. (1976) On monopolistic exploitation in professional baseball. *Quarterly Review of Economics and Business*. 16(2), pp. 113–121.

Neale, W. (1964) The peculiar economics of professional sports. *Quarterly Journal of Economics*. 78, pp. 1–14.

Perrone, R. (2013) Martina, il portiere di Cecco Beppe. *Corriere della Sera* [online]. Available from: http://milano.corriere.it/milano/notizie/cronaca/13_marzo_5/martina-portiere-cecco-beppe-perrone-21228373801.shtml [accessed 15 April 2014].

Poli, R. (2010) Understanding globalisation through football: The new international division of labour, migratory channels and transnational trade circuits. *International Review for the Sociology of Sport*. 45(4), pp. 491–506.

Poli, R. and Rossi, G. (2012) *Football agents in the biggest five European markets. An empirical research report*. Neuchâtel: CIES.

Repubblica (2001) Io, donna e procuratrice in un mondo al maschile. *Repubblica* [online]. Available from: www.repubblica.it/online/calciomercato/donna/donna/donna.html?ref=search [accessed 15 July 2012].

Ripamonti, D. (2006) Patrizia Pighini la signora del calcio. *Viasarfatti 25* [online]. Available from: www.viasarfatti25.unibocconi.it/stampa.php?idArt=2447 [accessed 21 January 2015].

Roderick, M. (2006) *The work of professional football: A labour of love?* London: Routledge.

Rose, N. (2010) Lawyers struggle to get in the game as substitute for football agent. *Guardian* [online]. Available from: www.theguardian.com/law/2010/oct/26/law-football-agents [accessed 12 May 2012].

Rosen, S. (1981) The economics of superstars. *American Economic Review*. 71(5), pp. 845–858.

Rottenberg, S. (1956) The baseball players' market. *Journal of Political Economy*. 64(3), pp. 915–930.

Sandy, R., Sloane, J. P. and Rosentraub, M. S. (2004) *The economics of sport: An international perspective*. Basingstoke: Palgrave MacMillan.

Scully, G. (1974) Pay and performance in Major League Baseball. *American Economic Review*. 64(6), pp. 915–930.

Shropshire, K. L. and Davis, T. (2008) *The business of sports agents*. 2nd edn. Philadelphia: University of Pennsylvania Press.

Sinnott, J. (2010) FIFA 'to axe licensed agent rule'. *BBC Sport* [online]. Available from: http://news.bbc.co.uk/sport1/hi/football/9049037.stm [accessed 20 March 2012].

Sinnott, J. (2011) Agent Willie McKay's plan to keep Doncaster in the Championship. *BBC Sport* [online]. Available from: www.bbc.co.uk/sport/0/football/15755659 [accessed 20 March 2012].

Sloane, P. J. (1969) The labour market in professional football. *British Journal of Industrial Relations*. 7(2), pp. 181–199.

Smienk, M. (2009) Regulation in the market of sport agents. Or not at all? *The International Sport Law Journal*. 3(4), pp. 70–78.

Sobel, L. (1987) The regulation of sports agents: An analytical primer. *Baylor Law Review*. 39, pp. 701–86.

Sport Business International (2011) Talented Mr. Ripley. *Sport Business International*. 171, p. 72.

White, D. (2011) Chelsea and Manchester United among clubs working to stop agents targeting young players on Facebook. *Telegraph* [online]. Available from: www.telegraph.co.uk/sport/football/teams/manchester-united/8335849/Chelsea-and-Manchester-United-among-clubs-working-to-stop-agents-targeting-young-players-on-Facebook.html [accessed 24 April 2012].

Wilson, B. (2013) Altered images for top sport earners. *BBC* [online]. Available from: www.bbc.co.uk/news/business-23928760 [accessed 4 April 2014].

Wilson, J. (2011) Premier League and HMRC in talks over payments for players' image rights. *Telegraph* [online]. Available from: www.telegraph.co.uk/sport/football/com-petitions/premier-league/8265218/Premier-League-and-HMRC-in-talks-over-payments-for-players-image-rights.html [accessed 4 April 2014].

3 Football agencies' structure and market consolidation

Overview

The market place for agencies today is a far cry from how it looked just 20 years ago. While, traditionally, solo agents operated to improve the contractual terms of a limited number of players, in the post Bosman era an agent is almost essential to ensure that players are able to achieve their value in the labour market as well as maximise their return on investment in other areas. The internationalisation of the market place has also helped to create more opportunities for agents to perform scouting and recruitment roles for clubs as detailed in Chapter 2. As a consequence, the traditional solo agent, who operated alone and dominated the market in the 1990s, has been overtaken in terms of activity by other types of agent with greater access to skills and resources.

This chapter intends to look in greater detail at the structure of the agents market. Building on the roles outlined in Chapter 2, we first consider why some companies are based around solo agents, who tend to operate alone and represent very few players, while others are large multi-national corporations who are likely to have various in-house services also available to their clients. Drawing on evidence from the big five European leagues we begin by mapping the agency landscape, highlighting the trends in its development.

3.1 Football agencies and their organisational structure

Given the developments in the football industry which have meant that different types of players and clubs require different services from agents, it is unsurprising that different specialisms have emerged. In parallel, the sheer number of people purporting to be a football agent has also increased. In 2012, around 2,500 agents were licensed in the big five leagues alone, with many others known to exist in other markets. The necessity of having links to the industry in order to successfully acquire clients, means it is not surprising that success appears to breed success, with agents typically able to acquire more clients and have access to more clubs once they have successfully placed and managed a player and hence proved their worth in the market place. While the categories of representative, proposed by Magee (2002) and detailed in the previous chapter, all still exist in the current market, additional sub groups, such as former players who have become agents, have gained greater importance in the current climate. These roles have all developed in response to the needs of players and to structural changes in the labour and product markets outlined in Chapter 1. As a consequence, there has been a shift in the distribution of clients between different types of agents.

In terms of numbers, the solo agent, who operated alone and tended to represent few clients was the most popular type in 2002 according to Magee (2002). As displayed in Figure 3.1, our evidence suggests that this is still the case a decade later in terms of numbers of agents, with more than 40 per cent of agents in Europe working alone in 2012.

A similar percentage of firms only have one or two employees, 36.9 per cent. Traditionally, these smaller agencies have sought to offer a wide range of services to players. However, these services are usually offered by other small companies with which the football agents have strategic alliances, as opposed to the agents offering the full range of services themselves. However, where agents have united under a wider agency umbrella they have been able to capitalise on economies of scale and scope, bringing these activities in house. Due to the high level of competition, the majority of agents' companies adopt flexible and informal structures, which easily allow them to adapt to the dynamics of a transfer market based on changing relational networks. Individual agents have a greater flexibility to decide which project to focus on. This allows them 'to dedicate full concentration to one or two deals without the distraction of deciding upon larger company policy' (Trimboli, 2011). Conversely, only the biggest agencies, holding dominant market positions, can afford complex and stable business structures.

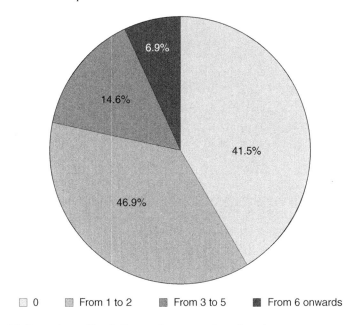

Figure 3.1 Percentage of football agencies per number of employees.

That is not to say that smaller agencies, like the two thirds of the sector shown in Figure 3.2, are not supported by other staff; on average, there are two licensed agents for every three paid employees in agency companies. Technically, employees of agencies were only allowed to carry out administrative tasks or those related to a player's commercial agreements. According to Article 3 of FIFA PAR 'a player's agent may organise his occupation as a business as long as his employees' work is restricted to administrative duties' and 'only the players' agent himself is entitled to represent and promote the interests of players and/or clubs in connection with other players and/or clubs' (FIFA, 2008). However, this rule no longer applies and anybody who wishes can now act as an intermediary. In practice, this was often the case even when the regulations said otherwise as many licensed agents made use of their employees to carry out a variety of tasks within the competence of licensed agents, such as scouting players or negotiating minor aspects of transfer deals (Roderick, 2006). In 2011, for example, the Italian Football Federation, FIGC, suspended the agent Andrea D'Amico for two months and fined him €20,000 when it was proved that his brother Alessandro D'Amico acted as an unlicensed agent on his behalf in various player transfers (FIGC, 2011a).

Throughout Europe, as shown by Figure 3.3, over half of all agents' companies have other shareholders aside from the agent. Traditionally, these partners can offer support in other relevant business sectors and are often lawyers, marketing managers, PR or financial consultants. However, companies do tend to be relatively small with 68 per cent having two shareholders or fewer.

This shift towards providing more services has occurred largely in line with the increase in the scope of services that a footballer needs. Financial investment

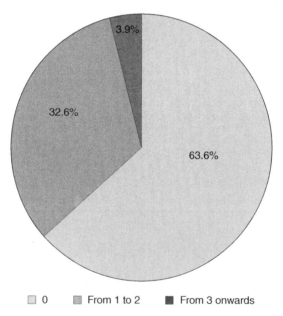

| □ 0 | ▨ From 1 to 2 | ■ From 3 onwards |

Figure 3.2 Percentage of agencies per number of licensed agents employed.

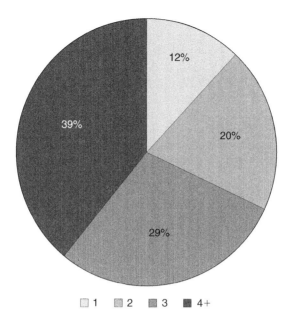

Figure 3.3 Percentage of football agencies according to the number of shareholders.

and tax planning advice, for example, has become a necessity for players who, after negotiating a lucrative compensation package, have to ensure that their money is protected. Similarly, the propensity for footballers to gain endorsement and sponsorship deals away from their club has also created a gap for skilled marketers to help shape a football star's career trajectory. One way of managing all of these roles has been to form an FSA, following the trend in the US over the last 20 years (Shropshire and Davis, 2008). FSAs and collaboration between agents in different markets have changed the nature of the business, with some companies becoming very powerful in the process.

These free-standing sport management firms may be further divided into two categories: those that represent players only and those that combine player representation and event management. Shropshire (1992) notes that the benefits to a free-standing sport management firm are twofold: the player receives high quality services without needing to find various relevant experts; and the firm's agents manage all of the business aspects of their clients, thus minimising the chances of them going elsewhere for help.

The move toward consolidation of different aspects of the industry has been influenced by the impact of global technological development which has made information available at the touch of a button and increased the global profile and opportunities available to athletes worldwide (Shropshire and Davis, 2008). Following the increase in the number of foreign players in the top European Leagues, and the English PL in particular, the profile of football has risen exponentially worldwide. To exploit this potential, large corporations with little experience in the sports agent industry have established themselves as credible service providers by purchasing top sports agency firms or solo operators. Shropshire and Davis (2008) describe this as a key feature of the US agencies in the 1990s. A series of mergers in the UK occurred in the early 2000s, with agents joining forces with entertainment enterprises and marketing specialists to exploit the broad range of commercial opportunities available to clients.

While there is little difference in the negotiation process according to the type of agent a player decides to use, with their style being personal to the individual and not necessarily the company they work for, there are distinct differences in the way that different types of representative are remunerated. While agents tend to work on a commission basis, lawyers tend to charge an hourly fee, irrespective of the value of the contract itself, which in many cases can be much more cost effective for a player. However, being a solicitor and being an agent are not necessarily mutually exclusive and many players employ both to do their contract negotiation, particularly in higher leagues where contracts may contain complex terms.

Sports law has been a growing area over the last 20 years and it is not unusual for major law firms to have a specialist team focussing on representing sportsmen and women. In many cases, players feel more comfortable being represented by lawyers who, by the nature of their profession and the rules that they are bound by, are perceived as more trustworthy than an agent. These sports lawyers often practice as external consultants to a football management agency. Sports lawyers are typically not involved in financial management, marketing, or investing the athlete's money, but oversee the player's needs in relation to contract negotiation, legal representation in arbitration or other proceedings, legal counselling, dispute resolution, and the preparation of tax forms. Other independent specialists would be brought in to provide specialist advice on other matters when needed.

As lawyers develop a specialism for player representation, they may decide to expand their offer beyond legal services. Some have transformed their law practices into a free-standing sports management firm, but others have maintained a law practice next to a sports management subsidiary to provide those services not traditionally offered by lawyers. For example, the Italian law firm PDP mainly operates in football, whereas in England Mel Stein has been recognised as the main solicitor acting as an agent with football players, later partnering with the sports agency First Artist.

While most of the types of representative have been born of the ability to profit from providing much needed services to players, it is also worth considering the unique position in the representation market that is held by a player's union. Like lawyers, they do not work on a commission basis. Across the course of a contract this can save players millions of pounds.

Nevertheless, the vast majority of players choose not to be represented by their union, instead seeing them as a forum to go to in the case of a dispute.

Likewise, as part of the football establishment, there is a general feeling amongst some footballers that their union would not be able to get them as good a deal as an agent as they would not, for example, be willing to engage in promoting the player before the end of his contract.

Any agency set up by a player's union should theoretically have access to much more knowledge in the domestic market place than any individual agent or lawyer. However, players do not seem to recognise that they could use this knowledge to their benefit. While in the early 1990s in England the PFA would automatically be given an opportunity to meet all players at professional clubs with a view to representing them, this is no longer the case. As the market has become saturated with agents and agencies, few top players have chosen to be represented by union agencies (James, 2009). There is also a certain credibility attached to some high profile agents so that if a player is represented by one of them then he is perceived by others to be of a certain quality, and is therefore willing to pay a premium to be recognised in this way. In contrast, the perception of working for a player union is that they look after young players and those in lower leagues. The fact that this type of agency is part of a union that is very much in touch with the governing bodies should provide it with a unique position in the market. It would be in the interests of the unions to have regulations on transfer activities enforced since they already comply with them. Nevertheless, agents in England argue that the PFA role in representation is a conflict of interest since they are not thought to be fully independent. This is considered in more detail in the case study below.

Case study: the English PMA

In 1989, as a response to complaints about agents' unscrupulous ways and lack of accountability, the English PFA introduced a service of representation to players for their contract negotiations. In September 2004, they formally created an internal player management agency, known as PMA, with a staff of 11 fully qualified agents. The services provided include individual contract negotiation and legal, financial, and commercial services, as well as media training, post-football career advice and lifestyle management courses. According to a survey conducted by the English newspaper the *Independent* in 2006, 73 per cent of English professional players were in favour of the PFA proving this service and were interested to know more about it (Harris and Moore, 2006). Likewise, in 2002, the French player association, UNFP, opened up its agency, Europ Sport Management, based on a team of three agents (UNFP, 2002).

Despite interest from players, the challenge facing the unions in actually providing an agency service however is three-fold (Karcher, 2007). First, it completely changes the way unions operate. Second, players might doubt whether the union agency would be as good a negotiator as third-party agents. Finally, the union agency might be perceived as favouring certain players over others in the representation process. Hence, the players' association needs to convince players that its player management agency is a valid alternative option for them. Such a process would first entail educating players about: the economics of the current player representation system, the incentives created thereby, and the overall impact on players resulting from both.

In 2010, the Australian PFA (2010) also established its own agency in response to an overwhelming demand by the elite professional players. The move followed extensive research by the PFA into the quality of player agency services available to Australian players and what they want from a management agency. The research highlighted that:

> 98 per cent of A-League players and 100 per cent of scholars in the Australian Institute of Sport believed that the PFA should establish a player management agency;
>
> 29 per cent of A-League players were very likely to join the PFA's services, with another 55 per cent indicating they were likely to do so;
>
> 88 per cent of scholars in the Australian Institute of Sport were very interested or interested in joining the PFA's service; of those who were very interested, 37 per cent are presently with another agent.

A significant increase in the number of disputes between players and their agents also contributed to the decision of the Australian PFA. In the previous three years, the association represented players in 53 disputes against their agents. Of greater concern was the large number of overseas based players in dispute with clubs that refused to honour basic contractual commitments which could have affected the careers of some promising players. The PFA research showed that, for 80 per cent of players, their first overseas move was to the best ranked club of their career. Furthermore, one in six players joined a top tier club, with only half of them playing there for more than one season. While many agents encourage players to leave Australia as soon as possible and work their way up leagues overseas, the PFA suggests that players should adopt a more strategic approach. For this reason, the PFA is determined to maximise the international competitiveness of Australian football through the Players Management Services.

For players, being represented by their union can be a cost-effective alternative to using an agent (Karcher, 2007). Unions have all pertinent data and information necessary to effectively negotiate player contracts as well as being able to monitor the competency of their agents, thus avoiding the types of disputes that they have traditionally intervened in. When the English PFA relaunched its agency arm in 2005, it increased its client list by around 30 players in the first eight months. However, it has proved difficult to maintain this growth and in particular they have struggled to attract the very best players after the departure of leading agents such as Alex Black in 2002 and Phil Sproson in 2009 (James, 2009).

One of the main benefits of using a players' union over a management agency is that its agents are salaried employees and, as such, there is no benefit for them to act in any way other than in the interests of the players they represent (Karcher, 2007). Due to their compensation scheme, union-hired agents do not have the incentive of soliciting prospective clients or engaging in client stealing from other agents. Thus, the harmful effects to the players, the teams and the league that flow from this intense competition are substantially reduced. Similarly, complaints that agents make too much in commission from contracts and transfers would also be addressed. For example, in 1989 Nigel Martyn, the first £1 million goalkeeper in English football, paid just £200 to the English PFA to arrange for his move from Bristol Rovers to Crystal Palace (Harding, 2004). The revenue generated by the activity of the PMA usually supports initiatives at the PFA, including helping former professionals who are experiencing financial difficulties.

3.2 Football agencies and their market expansion

While there are various options available to players in terms of who represents them, there has been a clear trend in recent years for agents to collaborate either formally or informally to expand their networks and as a consequence their business potential. The complexity and international dimension of transfer markets have favoured the collaboration and aggregation of agents through the formation of new companies (Roderick, 2006). Football agencies can therefore be classified according to the services they provide to their clients and the markets in which they operate, as well as the number of players they represent. Following Coe *et al.*'s (2007) classification of transnational staffing agencies, Poli (2010) adopted a similar classification system for sports agencies based on their geographical coverage and the range of professional settings in which they deal, with four different categories identified:

The first category, 'global generalist', emerged in the last two decades as a result of consolidations. The biggest of these companies have come to dominate the entertainment market place, with activities and offices worldwide operating across various sectors of the entertainment industry, from talent management to events and anything in between. However, these companies have largely failed to replicate their success in other fields in the lucrative football industry, though there are some exceptions. The most well-known global generalist to have succeeded in football is undoubtedly IMG, which has a long history of working with athletes globally and has managed to focussed on this as well as marketing its global fashion and entertainment credentials to attract footballers. Other less well known global generalists include James Grant Group which also manages the career of TV commentators, presenters, comedians and actors in the UK; while in the Netherlands, SEG Group has a music branch in artist management, label services and music supervision.

The second category takes the form of 'global specialist' whereby companies of agents which have transnational networks operate across several continents, but their activities are mainly focused on the scouting and transfer of football players. Each national transfer market is characterised by the presence of at least one or two agencies of this type, which mainly work on exporting domestic talent to markets overseas. Typically, the network of offices would be arranged around the main markets in which players are scouted as well as the leagues which they are likely to transfer into. Examples of global specialists include Bahia International and Groupe USM.

'Regional generalist' agencies consist of multiservice companies that have progressively developed their spectrum of activities in the sport and entertainment business. This category comprises the characteristics of global generalist companies except that they work mainly at national level. Due to the increasing global dimension of the sports market, these agencies tend to expand quickly and either diversify into new markets or are the subject of horizontal integration with other regional generalists in other markets.

In contrast to regional generalists, a large number of agencies may be considered in the regional specialist category. Although international transfers continue to increase, the vast majority of moves still occur within national borders. These agencies therefore are by definition very targeted to operate in one market, or in some cases with neighbouring countries, and one sport, usually football, and their specialist knowledge and contacts within that market enable them to take advantage of their close relationships with club officials. With a relatively low turnover, their business is typically based on the work of a few agents who patiently build their network focusing on young talent players from minor divisions. As Frenkiel (2014) highlights, though these agencies are less renowned, their role is very relevant as the majority of licensed agents progress in their career through the flexible and dynamic networks of these agencies. At the same time, their role within the transfer market is also important for small clubs whose recruitment and scouting is limited to specific types of players and geographical areas.

While each of these agency types have grown in different ways over the past two decades it has become clear that they have developed in order to serve the needs of the football market, and in particular to respond to its globalisation. In the same way that the market for players has segmented into an elite set of players who between them earn the most money and command the most column inches, so too can the types of agency be segmented. Nevertheless, that is not to say that solo agents have become irrelevant – in fact they tend to continue to own the relationships with the best players and therefore consolidations are typically built around them and for the players there will be little difference in the service they receive.

3.3 Consolidation in the football agent industry

Processes of consolidation are prevalent in almost every industry through mergers and acquisitions that enable companies to combine resources and to use each other's strengths for their own benefit. In general, companies hope that any potential harm created by a merger will be outweighed by the benefit the surviving entity will bring, usually in the form of financial gain and market power. As sports and entertainment companies converged, both corporate customers and professional athletes have demonstrated a demand for a streamlined service (Maguire, 1999). As a result of the entertainment industry's influence on the sports industry, powerful agencies merged their practices and became super agencies with multiple agents that represented athletes' varying interests and concerns. In 2006, Wasserman Media Group, WMG, struck a deal with Clear Channel to buy the SFX European subsidiary, making WMG one of the most dominant groups in football and significantly expanding its presence in Europe (Garrahan, 2006). Newly consolidated conglomerates are in many ways better equipped from both a financial and personnel standpoint to service the modern professional athlete.

In the sports industry, firms receive new clients in large part based on their existing client list. To establish their presence as credible service providers in the athlete management industry, these large corporations quickly needed to accumulate a well-known list of clients. Without any athlete clients to speak of, the principal way to quickly attain an all-star client list has been to purchase top sport business agencies from high-profile agents. Thus, these large corporations obtained immediate credibility by acquiring the business of reputable agents; however, this has come at a price and the acquisition expenditures have been staggering – and probably above the real market value of the companies targeted. We have therefore seen a process of both vertical and horizontal integration across the last two decades as, recognising their appeal, large corporations acquired sports agencies to enable them to integrate athletes into other areas of their business for promotional and commercial purposes. In this regard, sports event and marketing agencies, as well as other sport-related businesses, were part of this consolidation process. This strategy was, for example, adopted by the American marketing company Marquee Group that, in 1998, acquired Park Associates, at that time the biggest player representative agency in the English football market, with a client list including David Beckham, Alan Shearer, Dwight Yorke and David Platt (SBJ SBD, 1998).

Similarly, horizontal integration has occurred with the merger of agents with shared characteristics but covering different markets: in 2000, under the name of MT&V Sports International, Alex Kroes and Kees Vos joined forces with the agency Kees Ploegsma Management BV to form SEG, which has now expanded into basketball, cycling and the music industry (SEG, 2000). A more recent example is the Swiss media Group Kentaro, that in 2007 became the major shareholder of Northern Sky, one of the leading player representation agencies in Scandinavia. Two years later, Kentaro also agreed a corporate partnership deal with English agent Jerome Anderson's SEM (Kentaro, 2009). These acquisitions enabled Kentaro to offer a comprehensive set of services worldwide. Similarly, in 2009, CAA Sports, the sport division of leading American media agency CAA, and Gestifute, the European-Portuguese football management company, formed a global partnership to represent elite soccer players and managers (Business Wire, 2008). The two agencies agreed to work together to provide global opportunities for current and future clients in the areas of endorsement, speaking engagements, licensing and merchandising. At the time of the deal Gestifute Director Luis Correia said:

> We wanted a partner who could create the best opportunities for our clients across a wide spectrum of possibilities.... With CAA, our clients will benefit from an unmatched spectrum of services and expertise that capitalizes on the global scale of soccer.

Michael Levine, co-head of CAA Sports added 'We know they will be a powerful ally in forcing exciting opportunities for our current combined roster of soccer clients and in growing our partnership to include new players and coaches.' 'CAA and Gestifute working together can only mean great things for players', said Cristiano Ronaldo, the Real Madrid star player and one of the most important clients of Gestifute. 'I wanted to be surrounded by the best advisors possible to help me on the pitch and off. CAA knows how to elevate and expanded careers, and I am thrilled by any new combined representation' (Business Wire, 2008).

The consolidation process in the sports agent industry certainly increased the level of competition amongst agents to sign and retain athletes (Couch, 2000). It became more and more difficult for small firms and independent agents to attract and keep clients because they cannot offer the same range of services as large agencies and they hardly have corporate customers as clients.

Although there tends not to be a formal process of acquisition, partnership agreements often spring from a willingness to create a stronger single entity than two separate ones. Many smaller sports agencies have entered into relationships with external consultants in order to broaden their offering to keep pace with this ever changing marketplace (Rothstein, 2009). These sorts of agreement became common after the Bosman ruling and they facilitated the creation and expansion of football agents' networks. In 1995, when he started his career as football agent, Federico Pastorello, through his company P&P Sport Management, had a formal agreement with Athole Still International. By exploiting this transnational relationship and with it, its various networking opportunities, this partnership facilitated the transfer of players like Carlo Cudicini, Patrice Evra, Tino Asprilla and Gianfranco Zola to English PL clubs.

While the horizontal integration of agencies was able to widen the network of clubs and players for agents, vertical integration throughout the media world can benefit corporate customers who appreciate the ability to deal with only one company for all of their sports–related needs; the diversified sports agency could package the various steps in the distribution chain – the athlete, marketing, event management, and media. For the top athletes there is often the belief that they could earn more income from endorsements and crossover into the entertainment industry with the help of the larger agencies' contacts with potential sponsors and involvement in multimedia projects. At the end of 2003 David Beckham decided to leave his sports agency, SFX, to be represented by the duo Terry Byrne and Simon Fuller, co-founders of the Hollywood agency 1966 Entertainment (BBC, 2003). While Fuller was known as manager of Beckham's wife and former Spice Girl, Victoria, as well as several other entertainers, Byrne directed many football related companies. Beckham's decision was the prologue to his move to Los Angeles to play for Los Angeles Galaxy in 2007. Since then, Beckham's commercial image and career in the US has been managed by the multinational company AEG, owner of LA Galaxy and other sport franchises and media events and venues around the world.

Consolidation offers existing sports agencies enhanced opportunities for longevity. The agencies purchased by large corporations reap significant benefits;

they receive tremendous amounts of money, maintaining their ability to compete in the marketplace. The individual agents also benefit from the greater financial security that a merger of this sort can bring but also because the merger grants the individual agents entry into other business services, such as marketing, financial planning and entertainment, which can also lead to increased revenue streams. In 2003, First Artist hired the MLS licensed agent Patrick McCabb as director of US operation to lead its effort to expand into North America (Mullen, 2003). The American agent merged his agency, Ladruma Sports Group, into First Artist with the ambition of attracting more top American players and broadening his opportunities to placer players with clubs across Europe.

However, there are also some drawbacks associated with the strategy of consolidation. The small-firm agents become less autonomous; their future earnings power may be somewhat limited, as the fees owed to them accrue to the larger agency rather than to the individual agent; and their ability to work in the industry can be restricted should they decide to leave the company and set up as a solo agent again (Karcher, 2007).

A final strategic aspect of the consolidation process is the flotation of football agencies on the stock exchange (Lea, 2009). The early 2000s saw a stream of company flotations in this sector, with relatively small companies recognising the opportunity to capitalise on reputation and client list. In July 2001 the agents Barry Gold and Bill Jennings took their company, Premier Management, to the stock market, raising just over £4 million through quoted bonds. The agency's intention was to expand its business, advancing cash to smaller clubs so that they could buy new players. This strategy meant investing in players from whom it expected to earn short term fees and then, in the long term, make profits on player sales. Moreover, the agency planned to buy other football agencies, expanding the number of players represented. At the same time, Proactive Sport Management joined the stock market with a total market capitalisation of £32 million. With 200 players on its books the company expected to negotiate 100 transfers or contract deals a year. In real terms, this meant that each player was expected to move or negotiate a new deal with his existing club every two years. Given that contracts were getting longer and four-year deals were becoming the norm, it was clear that, in order for Proactive and its shareholders to prosper, there would have to be a lot of players expressing a desire to move while under contract, or agents advising their players to move irrespective of whether it was the best option for them. The one-club player, who spends his career at the same club and is willing to accept what the club offers, is of little value to today's corporate agencies. In the case of Proactive, this strategy was even supported by the presence of managers and players as clients and shareholders who could possibly have favoured some transfer deals.

Another drawback of the consolidation and the development of sports agency groups that hold substantial portfolios might be an increasing risk of the conflicts of interest that usually characterise all the results of vertical and horizontal acquisitions. In 2003, having acquired Kingsbridge Asset Management, Proactive could provide financial services and advice to a client base which included over 600 UK based professional footballers, managers and football stars (Proactive, 2003). In the same year, it was reported that PL club managers like Martin O'Neil, Sam Allardyce, Graeme Souness, Kevin Keegan and Peter Reid were Formation shareholders. This situation clearly revealed conflicts of interests with the football industry which were manifest at that time. Given that not all people with an interest in an agency have to be named, and with the added complication that many agency companies were backed by people who were closely related to football managers, potential conflicts of interest were rife. Specifically, these could relate to agents recommending that players move when it is in the agent's interest, but also this process could be facilitated by 'friendly' managers who could push transfers through, often in exchange for a cut of the profits. In an attempt to improve this, in Italy, Article 4 of the FIGC PAR was introduced, stating that licensed agents have to list the names of all employees and people involved in the company (FIGC, 2011a).

Finally, the agency First Artist also moved from the OFEX to the AIM in December 2001 (First Artist, 2001). In the following case study, the entire process and strategy First Artist has pursued over the last decade is revealed. This case provides a clear illustration of how the strategy of an agency can change according to its business ambitions and in relation to the specific market conditions in the entertainment industry.

Case study: First Artist

Founded in 1986 by Jon Smith, First Artist had, from its launch, represented the England Football Team for a decade with the development of the commercial structure known as 'Team England' (First Artist, 2005). In 1992, the company was involved in the formation of the Premier League and was instrumental in assisting the launch of Sky TV. It had also acted as the commercial agents for the England Cricket Team for ten years, as well as the Welsh Rugby Team. As their primary business activity was to represent the commercial and sporting interests of leading English football personalities worldwide, despite their involvement in other sports, First Artist's reputation was principally one of being a football agency.

After being listed on the stock exchange in 2001, the agency looked to export its full-service model to new markets. With the ambition of becoming the UK's leading integrated media, events and entertainment management group, its key challenge was to maintain its pivotal position in the football market while also generating new business in other areas (First Artist, 2001). Despite a diverse revenue stream, the majority of First Artist's revenue was restricted to the two periods of the football transfer windows. It was necessary therefore for the business to increase ongoing revenue ordinarily paid over the period of a represented player's contract. Accordingly, the company decided to implement a consolidation strategy with three main aims: pursuing synergy and enhancing acquisitions, disposing of non-core areas within the group, and boosting organic growth by pursuing internal synergies between the business divisions through cross targeted selling opportunities.

Table 3.1 First Artist acquisitions

Company	Date	Cost	Main activity
FIMO	January 2002	£3 million	Athletes' representation in Italy.
Team Sport Management	2005	£50,000	Athletes' representation in UK.
ABG Financial Management	July 2005	£3 million	Offering a comprehensive range of services on areas such as investment strategy, tax and inheritance planning, offshore investments and pensions, taxation and financial consultancy to corporate entities, sportsmen and media personalities.
Finishing Touch	September 2005	£3.36 million	Market leader in the organisation of conferences and other events for corporate and public sector clients in the UK and Europe.
Proactive Scandinavia	July 2006	£2.25 million	Athletes' representation in Scandinavia.
NCI Management	July 2006	£1.75 million	Celebrity and media agency, representing sport and TV presenters and other media personalities.
Sponsorship Consulting	August 2006	£0.75 million	Advising sponsors, developing their strategy and negotiating sponsorship arrangements selected by their clients and undertaking strategic works on behalf of major rights holders, assisting them in re-positioning themselves to be more attractive as a sponsorship opportunity for brands.
Dewynters	December 2006	£15.5 million	Providing marketing, design, advertising, promotions, digital media services, publishing and merchandising to its theatre cinema, tourism, arts and culture clients.
Yell Communications	April 2007	£1 million	Event and delegate management business specializing in the financial services industry.
SpotCo	August 2008	£16.4 million	Live entertainment advertising agency.

In 2002, First Artist acquired the Italian football agency FIMO and its subsidiary Promosport. Founded in August 1997 by the agents Vinicio Fioranelli and Vicenzo Morabito, the agency represented, directly and through its partners, over 200 professional players (First Artist, 2005). It also offered a wide range of services to the industry, including sponsorship and marketing services and legal and financial consultancy as well as having co-operation agreements in place with other football agencies in Norway, Sweden, England, Croatia and South America.

In November 2005, First Artist Entertainment Management was launched after the integration of the following three companies in the group: Team Sport Management, ABG Financial Management, and Finishing Touch (Objective Capital, 2007). Team Sport Management was created by the solicitor Mel Stein, who had previously represented Paul Gascoigne, Glenn Hoddle and Alan Shearer. The agreement included the contracts of representation for 20 players, the business assets and the company staff. Founded in 1987, ABG Financial Management was also already well established with a consistent portfolio of clients and strong management credentials, in both direct property investment and property funds. The company was bought as a means of providing wealth management advice to existing First Artist clients and potentially expanding the services offered to some of ABG's clients in the sports world. It subsequently changed its name to Optimal Wealth Management. Established in 1989, Finishing Touch was bought in order to provide additional management services.

In 2006, First Artist signed two joint ventures between Finishing Touch and Sport Event, and between Optimal Wealth Management and Fisher Family Office (Objective Capital, 2007). Additionally, three other acquisitions were concluded: Proactive Scandinavia, NCI Management and Sponsorship Consulting. First Artist Scandinavia was created through the consolidation of Proactive Scandinavia from Formation Group. This integration completed the foundation of a truly pan-European network covering Northern and Southern Europe as well as the UK. The acquisitions of NCI Management and Sponsorship Consulting followed the logic of increasing the possibility of multiple revenue streams for their clients, including product endorsement. Founded in 1997, NCI had a strong track record of talent development based on finding experts in a particular field who are photogenic and then creating a pitch to a broadcaster, ideally with a programme and a sponsor already in place and, following on from that, a book deal. Sponsorship Consulting worked across the spectrum of sports, arts, entertainment, community, environment and education to ensure that sponsorship played an effective part of their clients' integrated marketing and communication strategy.

After having taken over Dewynters, the group launched First Artist Rights in January 2007 (Objective Capital, 2007). Since its foundation in 1924, Dewynters has been one of the UK's leading full service agencies. The company also owns Newman Displays, a subsidiary agency, which designs, manufactures and installs signage, from fascia display and theatre and cinema front-of-house design to retail outlet refurbishment, exhibitions and outdoor advertising. The intention was to develop sponsorship strategies for rights owners with a focus on providing business opportunities. The consolidation process continued with the acquisition of Yell Communications which was intended to expand the corporate events business and to enhance the delivery of multi-site delegate and conference management services.

At the end of 2007, First Artist finances were displaying strong and stable growth (First Artist, 2007). Their turnover increased from £9.5 million in 2006 to

£48.6 million in 2007 (+511 per cent), mainly driven by the media division. These results corresponded to £3.6 million profit (+118 per cent compared to 2006). The consolidation strategy to grow organically in its core business areas led the group to expand in the North American markets for the first time (First Artist, 2008). First Artist acquired SpotCo, a leading US-based agency, to reinforce the group position in the marketing of live entertainment by increasing the market share and improving the quality of the service offered to its client. As summed up in Figure 3.4, after this long and elaborated process of consolidation, First Artist was structured across the three business divisions: marketing, events, and entertainment and sport.

At this point, the consolidating process radically transformed First Artist from a mere football agency to a media, events and entertainment corporation. All the acquisitions created an operating model with attractive underlying earnings, offsetting the more volatile and seasonal revenues generated by its incumbent operations (Crux, 2008). While, in 2003, the impact of revenues generated by football services contributed to 95 per cent of the turnover, this percentage decreased to 12 per cent four years later. In 2008, 90 per cent of the sales were generated by media, non-football entertainment services.

However, from the beginning of 2009, during the financial crisis, the group had to review its non-core business strategy and decided on a series of disposals in order to reduce its debt (First Artist, 2010a). When, in March 2009, Sponsorship Consulting was put into liquidation, the group was in breach of its banking covenants. In June 2009, all its bank borrowings had to be renegotiated through a debt restructuring programme. First Artist decided to refocus its attention on the core activity of its media division (First Artist, 2010b). This meant selling off the other parts of the business.

Following this new strategy, on 2 February 2010, the group sold Optima Wealth Management to Conforto Financial Management for £1.5 million. Eight days later, First Artist Management was acquired by James Grant Group for £0.175 million. On July 2010, the sale of First Artist Scandinavia was also completed for £0.6 million. In the same period, Promosport ceased trading and it was being held in

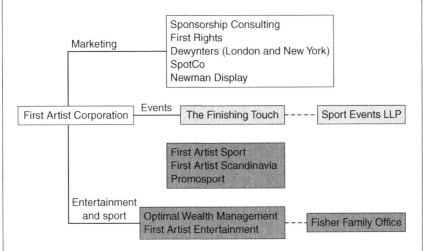

Figure 3.4 First Artist's group structure (source: adapted from First Artist (2007)).

run-off whilst all debtors and accrued income are recouped. At the end of 2010, the total revenue dropped from £90.6 million to £73.8 million with an EBITDA[1] that fell from £3.5 million to £0.55 million. Pre-tax losses increased from 1.4 million to 5.5 million and net debt amounted to £14.67 million. In December 2010, Pivot Entertainment, a US entertainment marketing company, invested £2.5 million in First Artist through share acquisitions and a long term loan with a consequential restructure of the Board (First Artist, 2011).

In February 2011, Finishing Touch was sold to ExEvents for £0.1 million and one month later First Artist raised £4 million after having placed 18 million shares on the market. On 1 May 2011, after having left the board, the former founders of First Artist, John and Paul Smith, acquired First Artist Sport for £1 with a debt of £0.4 million. Floating at 50p ten years ago, First Artist shares were trading around 115p four years ago, before collapsing to 7p during 2010. On Friday 27 May 2011, the Board of First Artist Corporation resolved to change the company name to Pivot Entertainment Group. Jon Smith frankly admitted that they should not have joined the stock market (English, 2010). According to him, the business of football representation is a great industry for small, tightly managed agencies but not for the stock market. Investors look for constant and secure returns from their investments and if earnings are unstable, a business like this one is not attractive anymore.

After ten years, the process of consolidation managed by First Artist collapsed. It is difficult to evaluate how the general financial and economic situation in the last decade affected the final result. Nevertheless, the original core business of football was radically dismantled in the name of a growing ambition in parallel businesses across the entertainment industry. For First Artist, the aspiration of emulating other successful sport and entertainment business models such as Octagon, IMG and Wasserman was not sufficient to justify all of the mergers.

3.4 The benefits of FSAs over the corporate forms

While concern has been expressed over the dominance of FSAs, there are undoubtedly benefits for both them, and some of their clients. Players have instant access to specialist knowledge in any area on which they may need advice, while the agent does not risk losing any of his business from the client looking elsewhere for particular services. Competition is fierce in the market to represent the best players so, often, large firms buy up smaller firms to achieve the status attached to representing the associated clients. Larger firms are often willing to waive fees for younger players in the hope that they will gain more than their initial outlays when the player signs a lucrative deal in the future; again, this competition is difficult for a solo agent to sustain. Companies with greater financial resources available to them hold a competitive advantage as, with larger numbers of clients, they are able to spread the risk of one player losing form or becoming injured and effectively cutting off the agent's pay.

The most popular payment structure for agents is commission based on a percentage of the player's salary successfully negotiated for the client. This is typically between 3 and 5 per cent, though in some cases it is known to be a lot higher. FSAs again can have an advantage since they charge additional fees for any service outwith the standard contract negotiation which is usually charged at a higher rate. An endorsement, for example, can cost the athlete as much as 30 per cent of the value of the contract negotiated and there may be an extra 1 per cent of the portfolio for investment management services, with a separate hourly rate for legal and tax services. Players who are likely to attract the most attention from commercial and endorsement deals may be charged a reduced fee for contract negotiation, with agents instead preferring a larger share of commercial revenues. This has led to a shift away from traditional employment contract negotiations for some companies to a focus on the more profitable and unregulated commercial endorsements. FSAs have segmented their operations with specialised agents in charge of specific areas of representation across different sports and entertainment sectors. For example, the extent to which WMG represents clients differs in relation to agency activity as defined by the FA agents' regulations; commercial activities; broadcasting activities; and a combination of all these activities (WMG, 2013). In some cases this seems to be simply another way to avoid the licensing system. In the transfer of Harry Kewell, for example, the unlicensed Bernie Mandic said he was only responsible for the commercial concerns of the player. This was not uncommon under the previous system of licensing for agents, with many unlicensed agents who appear to represent their clients in all aspects of their career management justifying their lack of a licence by stating that they were mainly commercial and someone else signed off the deals they made. Third parties who are registered agents have in the past become involved in transfers purely as a way to circumvent regulations, particularly those which forbid the dual representation of players.

The introduction of transfer windows has made it even more important for agents to be involved in commercial deals; otherwise their cash flow is restricted to two time periods each year. Since the potential to make a profit for an agent is greater for a 'superstar' who has a greater propensity to generate revenue from endorsement deals than from wages, representatives may seek to represent only those elite players with the highest potential for ancillary earnings, thus reducing the ability of less marketable players to get good representation. This causes concern as younger, lower league players who are arguably most in need of agent support, are often left with bad representation. It is suggested that a hierarchy of agents exists in which the best players are represented by the best agents.

However, as FSAs become increasingly popular the potential for conflicts of interest increases, particularly when one company represents a number of clients and there is a possibility that serving the interests of one client may be detrimental to another. This is a departure from the initial necessity for players who, in the past, felt the need to have an agent who was 'always there' (Mason and Slack, 2003). The market share of FSAs has enabled them to increase their power and influence over both clubs and commercial partners and it has been suggested that they use players as bargaining tools in creating more lucrative deals for themselves. In some instances, a disproportionately high number of players at one club are represented by the same agent, though this can potentially be explained by players recommending their agents to colleagues. However, some agents, by making agreements with club personnel to either split the proceeds of deals or guarantee players' signatures have managed to obtain a powerful position within clubs. This is considered in more detail in Chapter 5.

Agents have been able to negotiate positions of power by virtue of the players they represent. The industry is such that the networks in which agents act are very close knit and without the right contacts agents struggle to get clubs to listen to them. Though clubs argue that the talent of the player is the only important factor in whether or not he earns a contract, agents understand that there are ways to negotiate with clubs and that, particularly for an unproven player, the agent needs to have a good relationship with clubs before the clubs will even consider the player. This tends to benefit FSAs, who, by virtue of the number of players they represent are likely to have had more contact with club personnel and are therefore likely to have built up good relationships. At times, established agents with greater financial backing have been thought to hijack transfers by promising players additional benefits which solo agents are not able to match. Former England footballer Gary Neville has been quite vociferous in his stance on agents, stating that in his time at Manchester United, before they were banned by the club, agents would 'hang around youth football matches, offering cash inducements to parents and promises to boys to gain an influence over them' (Neville, 2013).

3.5 Conclusions

There is no unique modus operandi in the sports agency business and several agencies survive, develop and prosper following the peculiarities of the market in which they operate. According to scholars such Poli (2010) and Roderick (2006), the transfers of athletes and football players in particular are still characterised by the presence of niche markets that allow a variety of intermediaries to operate irrespective of their financial strength or their ability to cover several geographical markets. This situation allows the presence of multiple types of agencies within the market as the next chapter illustrates.

Taking into consideration this market heterogeneity in the representation industry, consolidations have been present but the newly created companies have not tended to be long lasting. Football agencies tend to grow and to expand their businesses but their expansion is often vulnerable if they step away from their core competencies. There have been mixed fortunes for consolidated enterprises depending on their approach, while the agencies that started as specialists in other areas, away from football, but acquired a roster of clients by buying existing agency businesses tend to have done well. However, when specialist agencies have tried to diversify into other related fields they have tended to struggle. The reasons for this centre around what is important in an agency context – the people who succeed as agents tend to have both a lot of contacts and strong relationships with key individuals who trust them and continue to work with them irrespective of the name of the company. Therefore, when bought out by bigger companies, these relationships continue and can be strengthened by providing clients with access to other non-core products. However, when the integration is reversed and an agency diversifies into other sectors there is a risk that they dilute their core strengths and are not strong enough in other areas to drive the business forward.

It is unsurprising then that solo agents are still relevant today. The individual relationships that they have are the most important part of being an agent and it would be difficult for any individual to represent more than three or four elite players yet still provide a personal service.

Note

1 It stands for earnings before interest, taxes, depreciation and amortisation. This accounting measure is a proxy for a company's current profitability as well as cash flow.

Bibliography

BBC (2003) SFX faces Beckham battle. *BBC Sport* [online]. Available from: http://news.bbc.co.uk/sport1/hi/football/europe/3192150.stm [accessed 12 October 2012].

Business Wire (2008) CAA Sports and international soccer agency Gestifute create global partnership to represent top talent, including player of the year Cristiano Ronaldo and head coach José Mourinho. *Business Wire* [online]. Available from: www.business-wire.com/news/home/20080709005068/en#.UuUntBDFLIU [accessed 18 April 2012].

Coe, N, Johns, J. and Ward, K. (2007) Mapping the globalization of the temporary staffing industry. *The Professional Geographer*. 59(4), pp. 503–520.

Couch, B. (2000) How agent competition and corruption affects sports and the athlete-agent relationship and what can be done to control it. *Seton Hall Journal of Sport and Entertainment Law*. (1), pp. 111–138.

Crux, J. (2008) First Artist: Sure to win new forms. *Grow Company Investor* [online]. Available from: www.growthcompany.co.uk/rss/blocks/334491/first-artist-sure-to-win-new-fans.thtml [accessed 13 May 2013].

English, S. (2010) Blackday for football as 'good agent' Jon Smith sells. *London Evening Standard* [online]. Available from: www.standard.co.uk/business/markets/black-day-for-football-as-good-agent-jon-smith-sells-6740453.html [accessed 13 May 2013].

FIFA (2008) *Players' agents regulations*. Zurich: FIFA.

FIGC (2011) *Comunicato Ufficiale N.73/CDN (2010–11)*. FIGC, 4 April, 2011. Available at: www.figc.it/Assets/contentresources_2/ContenutoGenerico16.$plit/C_2_Contenuto/Generico_27818_StrilloComunicatoUfficiale_lstAllegati_Allegato_0_upfAllegato.pdf. [accessed 18 August 2011].

First Artist (2001) *First Artist Corporation plc: Proposed acquisition of FIMO Sport Promotion AG*. First Artist: London.

First Artist (2005) *First Artist Corporation plc: Annual report 2005*. First Artist: London.

First Artist (2007) *First Artist Corporation plc: Preliminary results for the year end 31 August 2007*, Investor presentation November 2007. First Artist: London.

First Artist (2008) *First Artist Corporation plc: Interim Report six months end 29 February 2008*. First Artist: London.

First Artist (2010a) *First Artist Corporation plc: Report and financial statements for the 15 months period ended 30 November 2009.* First Artist: London.

First Artist (2010b) *First Artist Corporation plc: Unaudited interim results for the six months ended 31 May 2010.* First Artist: London.

First Artist (2011) *First Artist Corporation plc: Final results for the year ended 30 November 2010.* First Artist: London.

Frenkiel, S. (2014) *Une histoire des agents sportifs en France: Les imprésarios du football (1979–2014).* Neuchâtel: Editions CIES.

Garrahan, M. (2006) Wasserman Media to buy SFX Sports. *Financial Times* [online]. Available from: www.ft.com/cms/s/2/ff18701e-6f8a-11db-ab7b-0000779e2340.html#axzz2rW0w5Qj1 [accessed 17 October 2013].

Harding, J. (2004), It was my agent's idea. *WSC When Saturday Comes* [online]. 4 February 2004. Available from: www.wsc.co.uk/the-archive/102-Agents/2193-it-was-my-agents-idea [accessed 1 May 2014].

Harris, N. and Moore, G. (2006) Agents take £125m out of football every season. *Independent* [online]. Available from: www.independent.co.uk/sport/football/news-and-comment/agents-take-163125m-out-of-football-every-season-474021.html [accessed 29 November 2013].

James (2009) PFA fears player drain after agent Phil Sproson decides to go it alone. *Guardian* [online]. Available from: www.theguardian.com/football/2009/mar/24/phil-sproson-pfa-gordon-taylor-mick-mcquire [accessed 22 October 2013].

Karcher, R. T. (2007) United States. In: Siekman, R. C. R., Parrish, R., Martins, R. B. and Soek, J. (eds) *Players' agents worldwide: Legal aspects.* The Hague: T. M. C. Asser Press, pp. 693–727.

Kentaro (2009) Kentaro seals partnership deal with Jerome Anderson's Sport Entertainment Media Group, 12 November 2009. Available from: www.kentarogroup.com/uploads/media/Press_Release_SEM_Kentaro.pdf. [accessed 10 November 2011].

Lea, R. (2009) Premier agency draws a blank. *London Evening Standard* [online]. Available from: www.standard.co.uk/business/premier-agency-draws-a-blank-6770695.html [accessed 12 November 2013].

Magee, J. (2002) Shifting power balances of power in the new football economy. In: Sugden, J. and Tomlinson, A. (eds) *Power games: A critical sociology of sport.* London: Routledge, pp. 216–39.

Maguire, J. (1999) *Global sport: Identities, societies, civilizations.* Cambridge: Polity Press.

Mason, D. S. and Slack, T. (2003) Understanding principal-agent relationship: evidence from professional hockey. *Journal of Sport Management.* 17(1), pp. 37–61.

Mullen, L. (2003) First Artist hires MLS agent McCabe for North American push. *Street & Smith's Sportsbusiness Daily Global Journal* [online]: Available from; http://m.sportsbusinessdaily.com/Journal/Issues/2003/07/20030721/Labor-Agents/First-Artist-Hires-MLS-Agent-Mccabe-For-North-American-Push.aspx [accessed 15 May 2012].

Neville, G. (2013) Football needs to act now. The game is sleeping towards a crisis over agents. *Mail* [online]. Available from: www.dailymail.co.uk/sport/football/article-2279744/Football-sleepwalking-crisis-agents-It-act-Gary-Neville.html [accessed 1 December 2014].

Objective Capital (2007) *First Artist: Initiation report.* London: Objective Capital.

PFA (2010) PFA launches Player Management Agency. *Professional Footballers Australian* [online]. Available from: www.pfa.net.au/index.php?id=5&tx_ttnews%5Bpointer%5D=16&tx_ttnews%5Btt_news%5D=170&tx_ttnews%5BbackPid%5D=4&cHash=3f6823414d [accessed 17 October 2012].

Poli, R. (2010) Agents and intermediaries. In: Hamil, S. and Chadwick, S. (eds) *Managing football: An international perspective*. Oxford: Elsevier Butterworth-Heinemann, pp. 201–216.

Proactive (2003) Acquisitions and board changes. *Proactive* [online] Available from: www.formationgroupplc.com/investor/article.php?id=Mg== [Accessed 10 May 2012].

Roderick, M. (2006) *The work of professional football: A labour of love?* London: Routledge.

Rothstein, W. (2009) The business of sports representation: Agent evolution in the 'industry'. *Virginia Sports and Entertainment Law Journal*. 9, pp. 19–46.

SBJ SBD (1998) The Marquee Group acquires U.K. firms, starts web site. *SBJ SBD* [online]. Available from: http://m.sportsbusinessdaily.com/Daily/Issues/1998/04/2/Finance/THE-MARQUEE-GROUP-ACQUIRES-UK-FIRM-STARTS-WEB-SITE.aspx [accessed 20 February 2011].

SEG (2000) About SEG: History. *SEG* [online]. Available from: www.seginternational.com/corporate/page=site.treenode/tree=about [accessed 13 May 2013].

Shropshire, K. L. (1992) *Agents of opportunity: Sports agents and corruption in collegiate sports*. Philadelphia: University of Pennsylvania Press.

Shropshire, K. L. and Davis, T. (2008) *The business of sports agents*. 2nd edn. Philadelphia: University of Pennsylvania Press.

Trimboli, F. (2011) *Base soccer*. Conference at Wyscout Forum 2011. [accessed 28 November 2011].

UNFP (2002) Création d'Europ Sports Management. *UNFP* [online]. Available from: www.unfp.org/unfp/le-syndicat-des-joueurs-pro/notre-histoire.html [accessed 15 November 2015].

WMG (2013) *Wasserman client list*. London: Wasserman.

4 Concentration and key actors in the representation market for players in the big five European leagues

Overview

As the role of agents has developed, it has become common for different companies to unite under the same umbrella. While the process of consolidation was described in Chapter 3, we have yet to see the outcomes of this process in terms of whether these companies dominate the market. While research by KEA *et al.* (2009) suggested that a small number of companies are representing a disproportionately large number of players in some markets, there has been little research to see whether this situation has existed across longer time periods. Since the profession of football agents and intermediaries is most developed in terms of both volume and value in the big five European markets, we use data from their respective leagues, England, Spain, France, Italy and Germany, across the 2010–2015 seasons as a case study. In so doing, this chapter provides a detailed empirical analysis of the representation market. The first part of the chapter gives a descriptive overview of the representation market across these leagues, before the second part analyses the peculiarities of each in order to explain why the market is organised as it is. We begin by demonstrating the level of concentration across market segments, before providing more detail on the most influential agents and agencies.

From a theoretical perspective we use agency theory to address concerns around potential conflicts of interest which could occur as a consequence of this consolidation process. The main factors which influence the representation market in each league in terms of competitiveness for clients are considered, including: environmental conditions; market conditions that affect agents' contracts by changing the discretionary resources available; and the level and quality of monitoring mechanisms implemented.

4.1 Football intermediaries' turnover in Europe

In 2015, the big five European leagues together generated €11.3 billion in cumulative revenue, and spent €6.7 billion in wage costs and in estimated transfer fees in the region (Deloitte, 2015). With such fees being spent, the most relevant and influential football intermediaries are domiciled in these countries and operate within their professional leagues. The opaque nature of the agents' business, however, whereby individual fees tend not to be disclosed, means that measuring the turnover of football intermediaries has always been a difficult task. The English leagues have led the way in terms of transparency, with both the PL and the FL producing an annual report on the fees that clubs pay to agents, which shows that since the 2008/2009 football season roughly £760 million[1] has been paid by the 92 professional English football clubs to football agents. This is aside from the huge sums estimated to be paid by players themselves.

Given the international nature of the industry, various other reports have sought to demonstrate the size of the market across Europe: in 2014 the ECA published a study on the transfer system which stated that, over the 2011/2012 and 2012/2013 football seasons, UEFA clubs spent $254 million on club agents'[2] commissions, equating to 14.6 per cent of the total value of transfers in which the same clubs were involved (ECA, 2014). Unsurprisingly, clubs from the top European leagues committed to paying the largest commissions to club agents, accounting for $197 million – 78 per cent – of the total. This report considers only the use of licensed agents by clubs in the 865 international transfers with UEFA clubs – 5.5 per cent of total transfers, which generated a turnover of $1,740 million. The amount of club agent commissions was calculated to represent 4.9 per cent of the total value of transfers made by European clubs. Eighty-seven per cent of the commissions paid to clubs' agents, $221 million, referred to transfers within the UEFA territory. Given that the fees paid to players' agents were not included within the analysis, the study argues that agents are receiving a considerable portion of the transfer fees paid by clubs and both their role and levels of compensation need to be reviewed and monitored carefully.

Since October 2010, the FIFA TMS has tracked all international football transfers and its Global Transfer Report states that between 2011 and 2014 $754 million was spent by clubs to pay intermediaries commission for their roles in international transfers (FIFA TMS, 2015). Using these figures from the FIFA TMS (2015) and ECA (2014) and extrapolating across the current season we have been able to model the likely transfer commissions paid to agents by clubs in the big five leagues from the 2009 summer transfer window to the 2015 winter transfer window.

Our calculations suggest that agents received approximately 6 per cent in commission fees per transfer and with transfer spending increasing year on year, agents' commissions are estimated to equal around €370 million per league over the five year period. As Table 4.1 shows, the dominance of the English PL in the transfer market means that around €118 million is spent per year on agents' fee by those clubs alone.

Table 4.1 Estimated football intermediaries' turnover in the big five

League	Total commissions €	Average yearly commissions €
Premier League	710	118
Serie A	433	72
Primera Liga	382	63
Bundesliga 1	355	59
Ligue 1	306	51

4.2 Market concentration in the representation market across the big five leagues

The fees paid to agents are clearly significant sums of money. By investigating the level of market concentration in the representation market, we are able to look at two main concepts, market share and market power, in order to ascertain how the representation of players is distributed and how their market transfer evaluations are apportioned between agents. While market share is defined by the total percentage of professional players represented by an agent or an agency within the big five European leagues, the concept of market power is based on the total sum of the potential transfer market value[3] of the players involved. This in turn gives us an indication of competitiveness within the market for agents and intermediaries. The Herfindahl-Hirschman Index, referred to as HHI,[4] and the Gini Index[5] are commonly used to assess the competitiveness, or otherwise, of markets and we follow the same process here.

In order to complete this analysis data was collected on the main agent for every player registered to a club in the big five European leagues and, where applicable, also on the second named agent. Agents who work for the same agency were grouped under the name of a single entity. Aside from licensed agents, lawyers, players' relatives and unlicensed intermediaries[6] have also been included. The potential transfer market value of each player was calculated based on an economic model that takes into consideration variables relative to players and their teams.[7]

The level of concentration of players per individual agent or agency across the five seasons is first analysed on the whole, then by league, and finally according to different types of players.

4.2.1 Market concentration in the big five

Before the FIFA reforms on agents were introduced in April 2015, more than 2,400 licensed agents were domiciled in England, France, Italy, Spain and Germany, organised as 1,505 individual agents or companies active at the beginning of 2015. Between them, these agents and agencies represented 1,945 players for whom we were able to collect information. This average ratio of 1.3 players to each agent suggests that the market for agents is very competitive.

However, as we know from Chapter 2, not all licensed agents represent any players. The actual market concentration can be seen in more detail in Figure 4.1.

Indeed, 104 agents or agencies represent half of the players' market share. On average, these agents manage the career of more than one football player in the big five, and one-quarter of the players are represented by 27 agencies, corresponding to 3.2 per cent, on average, of the representation market in football. In terms of market power, half of the players' market value is managed by 71 individual agents or agencies, 8.3 per cent on average over the five year period, while one-quarter of players' market value is represented by only 20 agents on average, equal to 2.4 per cent of the representation market on average.

Despite anecdotal evidence that established agents dominate the market and with clear barriers to entry, as discussed in Chapter 2, the levels of HHI were actually very low: 39 points for market share and 60 points for market power, both of which are below the limit of 100 points which is seen as a benchmark for dominance; as such the market can be thought to be operating competitively. However, considering the trend over time, it is clear that the market has been becoming less competitive, with the HHI decreasing from 41 to almost 37 points in terms of market share but increasing from 52 to 70 points in terms of market power, suggesting that even though there is a greater spread of representation, the value of work being conducted is becoming more concentrated among a small number of agents.

From this perspective, it seems that the change in regulation to remove the barrier to entry associated with a bond system and replacing it with a licence introduced by FIFA with the revised agents' regulations in 2001 has contributed to reaching the desired goal of improving competition. However, insofar as clubs

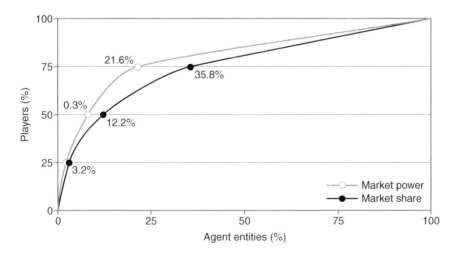

Figure 4.1 Market concentration in the big five (from season 2010/2011 to season 2014/2015).

and players rely on and trust few agents, regulations alone cannot make the market for agents more balanced. As Chapter 6 explains, the agents' market is driven by complex networks which are developed over time and therefore is not open and accessible to all intermediaries. With relatively few superstar players, who are distributed unevenly, there are inherent difficulties for new agents in joining the market.

4.2.2 *Concentration per league*

While overall across the big five leagues the picture is good, as the market seems to be operating fairly freely, when we look at domestic leagues in isolation a different pattern emerges. Figure 4.2 shows how the market is concentrated in each country. The gap between market share and market power gives an indication of the difference between how talent is distributed in terms of the number of players represented and their potential transfer values and hence the level of competitive balance. At first sight, the highest level of market concentration at league level has been found for Primera Liga in Spain, while the opposite holds true for Serie A in Italy.

The high level of concentration measured in Spain reflects the dominant position in this market held by local intermediaries who have strong links with local clubs within specific regions domestically. This situation is emphasised by the highest gap between the levels of market share and market power which reveals the high level of talent concentrated in a few clubs that dominate the transfer market. Similarly, in Germany, agencies are also central to importing players

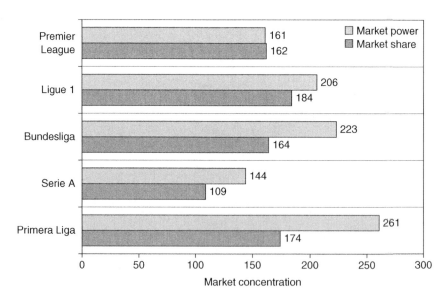

Figure 4.2 Market concentration per individual agent or agency, according to league.

from specific countries. Typically, agents develop knowledge of a specific market and the necessary contacts to facilitate the transfer of players. These transfer routes become more and more entrenched over time, particularly as agents and clubs are able to develop relations of trust. This can in turn lead to a concentration of talent in a few clubs. This is evident from the data explored above and in fact reveals a lack of competitiveness within the leagues.

At the opposite end of the table, the high proportion of expatriate players in both the English PL and the Italian Serie A means that many agents are operating. As the wealthiest league in the world, the English clubs are able to attract the best players worldwide (Deloitte, 2015). This market scenario favours the presence of foreign agents and contributes to a greater diversification in the composition of the representation market. The level of talent is less concentrated with the best players spread across different agents and the gap between market power and market share is almost zero. This reveals that clubs are competing fiercely to acquire talent in the transfer market and agents can benefit from this. Conversely, the Italian Serie A demonstrates a very competitive market for agents as it has traditionally had the highest number of active agents, but the gap between market share and market power is higher than in England, suggesting that the competition for talent between clubs has been reduced and agents tend to be working as gate-keepers with certain clubs.

4.2.3 Concentration per club

When they occur domestically, these imbalances are driven, to a large extent by practices at specific clubs. By looking at the market concentration per club we can ascertain the differences between the elite clubs, who are facing a monopsonistic market for superstar players, compared to clubs who are at the lower end of the top five leagues – competing to stay in the best leagues, but typically with much lower levels of resources with which to do that. This analysis follows the approach presented in the ECA study on the transfer system in Europe (ECA, 2014).[8] Figure 4.3, demonstrates that, as the level of club increases, so too does the concentration of agents.

This finding reflects a higher market concentration for top and high middle clubs than for low middle and bottom clubs. This trend within the five-season period is increasing and it reveals the tendency of agents and intermediaries to anticipate and forecast top and high middle clubs' transfer strategies. This evidence is strongly supported by the longer average stay of players within top clubs compared to those in middle and bottom clubs (CIES, 2015).

While the analysis above indicates that market share and market power are both important to assess competiveness within a market overall, it is also important to consider the level of concentration in the representation market by club. This is done using the Gini Index[9]: put simply, the higher its value, the higher the level of concentration. The reason for a high concentration of players per agent at a clubs is open to interpretation: on one hand, hiring many players represented by the same agent or agency can be interpreted as a club strategy to

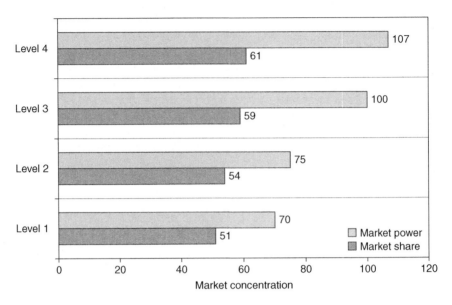

Figure 4.3 Market concentration per individual agent or agency, according to club's level.

enhance loyalty, both from agents themselves and from their protégés. On the other hand, this situation can reflect the existence of a closed circle of trust hiding conflicts of interests and financial misconduct. This is considered from a qualitative perspective in Chapter 6.

In Table 4.2, the two clubs with the highest market share, defined by the total percentage of professional players represented by an agent or an agency, are Basque: Athletic Bilbao and Real Sociedad. Since these teams mainly or exclusively employ Basque players, local intermediaries are very influential – contrary to the suggestions that FSAs are taking over the market. In fact, for some clubs,

Table 4.2 Market share concentration per individual agent or agency, according to club

Bottom 10 clubs	Gini Index	Top 10 clubs	Gini Index
Udinese	0.051	Athletic Bilbao	0.400
Arsenal	0.062	Real Sociedad	0.302
Newcastle United	0.065	Atletico Madrid	0.246
Manchester City	0.079	AS Saint-Étienne	0.245
OSC Lille	0.081	Olympique Lyon	0.245
Montpellier	0.083	Schalke	0.229
Chievo	0.088	Liverpool	0.226
Stoke City	0.101	Bayer Leverkusen	0.219
Malaga	0.101	Everton	0.216
Borussia Mönchengladbach	0.107	Real Madrid	0.215

agents with strong local knowledge and ties are more relevant. The Basque football agency Servicios Deportivos IDUB represents many players in both clubs. The other two Spanish clubs in the top ten are Real Madrid and Atletico Madrid, both of which have a strong relationship with Gestifute, while Manuel Garcia Quilón has an equivalent influence at Atletico Madrid. Conversely, only one Spanish club, Malaga, is ranked in the bottom ten clubs suggesting that in Primera Liga there is a strong likelihood that agents will be linked to specific clubs.

There are four English clubs in the bottom ten ranking, confirming the high level competitiveness for agents within the PL. Three of them, Newcastle United, Stoke City and Manchester City, are also present in the bottom ranking in terms of market power. The scouting team at Newcastle United is managed by the former player Graham Carr and has recruited players all over Europe and in particular in France and the Netherlands: as a consequence, their internal network is able to identify talent which is then signed by the club, as opposed to relying on agents to identify talent. For the French transfer market, Carr is assisted by the former player and agent Simon Stainrod who played for RC Strasbourg and Rouen in the 1980s and is well connected with several French agents (Douglas, 2015). At Stoke City, the technical director is a former player and agent Mark Cartwright. With a background working as an agent he too has a big network of people through which new players are identified (Stoke City, 2012). Udinese has the lowest concentration of players represented by the same agent. This is unsurprising given its transfer strategy, which is based on a continuous search for young talent from all over the world. However, almost all of Udinese's foreign players have former Udinese player Claudio Vagheggi, as their representative in Italy since he is the main intermediary for the club's owner, Gino Pozzo. It is not unusual for players to have two agents, particularly when they have transferred from a club overseas.

While we have looked at the market in terms of the numbers of players represented by each agency, it is now instructive to consider how this translates to value. In Table 4.3 we can see clear differences in the power that an agent is able to have at a club in the sense of the value of the players that he or she

Table 4.3 Market power concentration per individual agent or agency, according to club

Bottom 10 clubs	Gini Index	Top 10 clubs	Gini Index
Stoke City	0.345	Athletic Bilbao	0.570
Levante	0.351	Real Madrid	0.511
Manchester City	0.352	Napoli	0.510
Chelsea	0.367	Wolfsburg	0.505
Newcastle United	0.384	Schalke 04	0.505
Valencia	0.386	Toulouse	0.504
West Bromwich	0.396	Barcelona	0.499
AS Saint-Étienne	0.398	Fiorentina	0.498
Espanyol	0.398	Borussia Mönchengladbach	0.496
Malaga	0.406	Roma	0.495

represents there. Athletic Bilbao remains the club with the highest concentration of market power, followed by Real Madrid. The presence of Napoli in the top ten is simply explained by the appointment of Rafa Benitez as manager – his own agent, Manuel Garcia Quilón, also represents players including Raul Albiol, Jose Callejon and Pepe Reina, who have been brought to the Italian club.

The clubs in the top ten typically have a trusted agent who works with them on transfers. Rogon Sport Management has a strong presence at both Schalke 04 and Wolfsburg, representing the most valuable and promising players within these clubs (Psotta, 2015). At Fiorentina, Lian Sport, the agency run by Fali Ramadani, has a strong presence, having transferred players such as Stevan Jovetic, Adam Ljajic and Valon Behrami. The fact that the order of clubs differs for market power and market share demonstrates that, even though some clubs cooperate with a lot of agents, many of their best players are represented by a small number. While it is understandable that clubs form strong relationships with certain agents whom they trust, it is also possible that conflicts of interest can arise if an agent can make demands based on the players they represent having power to hold clubs to ransom.

4.3 Dominant agencies in the big five

Agents holding a dominant position in the big five leagues, both in terms of the market share and according to the average total amount of the estimated transfer value of their protégés during the five-year period, typically have influence in the clubs that they work with, giving them a route to promote new talent. This analysis offers a detailed overview of the most influential agents and intermediaries, from both a numerical and a financial perspective, allowing also an assessment of the agencies which have been able to increase their market power and influence over the time period.[10]

4.3.1 Agents with the highest market shares

The 20 individual agents or agencies with the most clients among the players in the big five leagues managed the careers of roughly 479 players, equal to 20.2 per cent of the players' market, as shown in the following table. In terms of the typology of agents presented in Chapter 2, the top agencies are all global specialists, meaning that they focus predominantly on football representation. The exception to this is WMG which is involved in other commercial elements of sport and entertainment.

As Table 4.4 shows, Groupe USM has the highest market share, representing 1.39 per cent of all of the players across the big five leagues across the full five seasons. Founded by the French agent Christophe Mongai, and with five associates, the agency operates as a full-service company on an international level on behalf of almost 100 players. Currently, its main representatives are Fabien Lemoine, Romain Danzé, and the promising Jordan Amavi and Idriss Saadi. Another important French agency is Mondial Promotion, ranked third and run by

Table 4.4 Top 20 football agencies with the highest market shares

Rank	Agency/agent/intermediary	Type[1]	Market share %	Average number of represented players	Market trend
1	Groupe USM (FRA)	GS	1.39	33	↔
2	Bahia Internacional (SPA)	GS	1.3	31	↔
3	Mondial Promotion (FRA)	GS	1.3	31	↓
4	WMG (US)	GG	1.3	31	↔
5	Stellar Group (UK)	GG	1.29	31	↔
6	Sports Total (GER)	GS	1.281	30	↔
7	Servicios Deportivos IDUB (SPA)	GS	1.116	26	↔
8	Promoesport (SPA)	GS	1.049	25	↔
9	Pro Profil (GER)	GS	1.04	25	↑
10	Gestifute (POR)	GS	1	24	↑
11	Manuel Garcia Quilón (SPA)	GS	0.998	24	↓
12	Base Soccer (UK)	GS	0.98	23	↑
13	Tecnosport Immagine (ITA)	GS	0.875	21	↑
14	Pastorello & Partners (ITA)	GS	0.86	20	↓
15	SVF Foot Consulting (FRA)	GS	0.85	20	↓
16	Rogon Sport Management (GER)	GS	0.79	19	↑
17	Branchini Associati (ITA)	GS	0.76	18	↓
18	T21 Plus Sportmanagement (GER)	GS	0.683	16	↓
19	Frédéric Guerra (FRA)	GS	0.675	16	↔
20	Jörg Neubauer (GER)	GS	0.632	15	↓
Total			20.2	479	

Note
1 As illustrated in Chapter 2, we use Poli's taxonomy to categorise the types of agencies as follows: GG=Global Generalist; GS=Global Specialist; RG=Regional Generalist RS=Regional Specialist.

Pierre Frelot, former financial and administrative director of Paris Saint-Germain. In 2004 his company, XL Sport, merged with Mondial Promotion, having acquired the shares owned by the former journalist and agent Pape Diouf, who had also been president of Olympique Marseille from October 2004 to June 2009 (Diouf and Boniface, 2009). Mondial's most well-known clients are Didier Drogba, Steve Mandanda and Mamadou Sakho. The third French agency, SVF Foot Consulting, is ranked fifteenth and run by Franck Belhassen in collaboration with former French player Fabrice Picot and Cameroonian agent Maxime Nana. The company works mostly within the French market and its client portfolio includes Alphonse Areola and Gaël Danic. Finally, ranked nineteenth is the veteran French agent Frédéric Guerra, who was informally classed as the main agent at Olympique Lyon during the glory years of the early 2000s. Having represented French internationals such as Sidnei Govou, Lasanna Diarra and the Malian international Mamadou Diarra, Guerra now works on behalf of Maxime Gonalons, Anthony Mounier and Alassane Pléa.

With five entrants, German agents feature most in the top 20 ranking. Volker Struth's Sports Total is ranked sixth with around 11 employees assisting German

Internationals such as Mario Götze, Marco Reus and Toni Kroos. Ranked ninth is the former professional player Thomas Kroth's agency Pro Profil, which represents the German players Manuel Neuer and Sebastian Rode and the Austrian international Aleksandar Dragovic. Since 2003 Kroth has held a monopoly in the representation of Japanese players transferred to Germany and his client list includes the current Bundesliga players Shinji Kagawa, Atsudo Huchida and Makoto Hasebe. Roger Wittmann and former Germany goalkeeper Wolfgang Fahrian's company, Rogon Sport Management, is listed sixteenth, representing international players such as Marko Arnautovic, Eric Choupo-Moting, Julian Draxler and Roberto Firmino, Luis Gustavo and Rafinha. In eighteenth position is T21 Plus, founded by Jürgen Milewski in collaboration with former German international Jans Jeremies. Both had previously worked for IMG Germany as agents and marketing consultants. They now represent players such as Thomas Kraft, Martin Harnik and Philipp Bargfrede. Finally, the last German agent in the top 20 ranking is Jörg Neubauer, former spokesman of the DDR football association. His portfolio includes German internationals such as Sami Khedira, Jerome Boateng, Rene Adler, Roman Weidenfeller and Sebastian Kehl.

Across the Italian market, Tecnosport Immagine, founded by the former player Tullio Tinti with his business partner Tiberio Cavalleri, lies in thirteenth position. They have a strong reputation in the representation of promising young players from the best Italian youth academies, supported by a strong network of observers especially in the northern regions of Italy. Their rich portfolio of clients includes international players such as Roberto Soriano, Giancarlo Pazzini, Andrea Pirlo, Luca Toni, Alessandro Matri and Matteo Darmian. The next Italian agency, placed one position below, is Pastorello & Partners, founded by Federico Pastorello, the son of the former Parma and Genoa technical director Giambattista Pastorello. Having an international recognition in the major transfer markets, the company now represents players such as Giuseppe Rossi, Patrice Evra and Samir Handanovic and has recently expanded its activities in Asia and North America, brokering several transfer deals with the ISL and the MLS. Giovanni Branchini, another prominent Italian agent and boxing promoter, is ranked seventeenth in the top 20 list with his company Branchini Associati. Beginning his career as an agent with his father, Umberto Branchini, working on behalf of boxers, his company now manages the careers of top players such as Riccardo Montolivo, Simone Pepe, Andrea Poli and Andrea De Sciglio. At the same time, he also works on behalf of clubs and was involved on behalf of Manchester United in the transfer of Cristiano Ronaldo from Sporting Lisbon. He also advised the manager, Pep Guardiola, when he was appointed by Bayern Munich. Branchini was among the founders of the EFAA, where he is now honorary president. He is also an executive board member and former president of the Italian agents' association, AIACS.

The Spanish agent with the most clients, Jose Antonio Martin Otin, is ranked second. Former radio commentator and writer, he manages the marketing agency Bahia International. It currently employs five licensed agents and an impressive client list which includes the Spanish national team players Fernando Torres,

Jesus Navas, Pedro Javi Martinez, Alvaro Dominguez, Dani Parejo and Cesar Azpilicueta. Ranked seventh, the Spanish company Servicios Deportivos IDUB has conquered a niche market share assisting several Basque players. The main representatives of the company, Inaki Ibanez, Peio Uralde and Vicente Biurrun, were former professional players who played for several Basque clubs during their careers (Deportivo Alaves, Real Sociedad, Athletic Bilbao, Eibar and Sestao). They have been able to take advantage of that situation to build strong relational networks and this has contributed to their achievement of dominant positions in the local transfer and representation market. Their current client list includes international players such Xabi Alonso, Mikel Arteta and Antoine Griezman as well as several Basque players. The lawyer Manuel Garcia Quilón is another influential Spanish agent ranked eleventh. Aside from top Spanish players such as Pepe Reina, Raul Albiol, Alvaro Arbeloa and Jose Callejon, he also manages the careers of four important managers: Rafa Benitez, Quique Sanchez Flores, Gregorio Manzano and Juan Carlos Mandia, which gives him a competitive advantage when it comes to attracting or placing players.

In the top 20 list, there are two global specialist English agencies, Stellar Group and Base Soccer, ranked fifth and twelfth respectively. Founded by Jonathan Barnett and David Manasseh in 1994, Stellar Group has dominated the English market for the last 20 years, representing athletes from different disciplines, such as athletics, rugby, cricket and football. Its client portfolio includes international players, including Wojciech Szczęsny, Gareth Bale, Joe Hart, Luke Shaw and Glen Johnson. Established in 1997 by Franck Trimboli and Leon Angel, Base Soccer operates through a professional network of 12 agents and 12 football consultants across the world. Its list includes international players such Aaron Ramsey and Kyle Walker.

Completing the top 20 is the American agency WMG, ranked eighth. A relative late comer to the football business, the group has been operating in this space since November 2006. Its strength has been developed through the acquisition of the leading English agency SFX. WMG also operates in several other sports, such as cycling, golf, American football, basketball and motor racing. However, the core of its football business is the English and North American markets. The WMG model is to employ 15 licensed agents and then utilise them to help each other, with bonuses awarded annually across the whole business rather than for individual deals. The agency client portfolio includes English national team players such as Ross Barkley, Chris Smalling, Stewart Downing, Mesut Ozil and Darren Bent.

It is clear that all of the agents in the top 20 can be seen to have been entrenched in the football market either through a previous career or by working closely with former players. This is a common feature of the market which has traditionally been relatively closed to outsiders. This theme is discussed further in the following chapter.

4.3.2   *Agents with the highest market power*

As alluded to previously, agents are able to gain market power according to the players that they represent. While some companies adopt a strategy of recruiting the best young players, others have been able to attract high level clients on the back of their success in representing players at a similarly high level. In this section, agents are ranked in terms of market power measured by the yearly potential total amount of transfer fees that could have been generated by players represented by them across the full five seasons. Amongst the top 20 agencies, on average, an estimated €2.73 billion could have been generated in transfer fees.

From a market power perspective, Portuguese agency Gestifute, run by Jorge Mendes, is the most valuable, representing clients with a combined projected transfer value of €390 million. Gestifute mainly represents top players such as Cristiano Ronaldo, James Rodriguez, David De Gea, Nani, Angel Di Maria, Marcos Rojo, Pepe, Ricardo Carvalho, Raul Meireles and Miguel Veloso. According to Forbes (Belzer, 2015)[11] it is ranked seventh in their list of the top 50 sports agencies, with a total portfolio worth around €850 million in players' contracts and roughly €85 million in commission fees.

Spanish agency Bahia International has the second highest market power representing players worth €215 million in transfer fees. Founded in 1997, the

Table 4.5 Top 20 football agencies with the highest market power

Rank	Agency/agent/intermediary	Type	Market power %	Represented players' total value estimation €m	Market trend
1	Gestifute (POR)	GS	3.4	390	↑
2	Bahia Internacional (SPA)	GS	1.9	215	↑
3	Stellar Group (ENG)	GS	1.8	201	↑
4	WMG (US)	GG	1.7	198	↓
5	Sports Total (GER)	GS	1.5	177	↑
6	Base Soccer (UK)	GS	1.3	145	↑
7	Maguire Tax & Legal (NDL)	GS	1.2	134	↑
8	Manuel Garcia Quilón (SPA)	GS	1.0	119	↔
9	Pastorello & Partners (ITA)	GS	1.0	115	↓
10	Mondial Promotion (FRA)	GS	1.0	109	↓
11	Servicios Depor. IDUB (SPA)	GS	1.0	109	↔
12	Rogon Sport Manag. (GER)	GS	0.9	107	↔
13	Branchini Associati (ITA)	GS	0.9	100	↓
14	Tecnosport Immagine (ITA)	GS	0.8	94	↓
15	Euro Export As. e Pr.(BRA)	GS	0.8	92	↑
16	Pro Profil (GER)	GS	0.8	92	↑
17	Twenty Two (ARG)	GS	0.8	88	↑
18	Jean Pierre Bernès (FRA)	GS	0.8	87	↓
19	Jörg Neubauer (GER)	GS	0.7	78	↔
20	Ramon Sostres (SPA)	GS	0.7	76	↓
Total			24	2726	

company is part of Atlantic Production, linked to the Spanish television network Antenna 3 and it mainly specialises in football. According to Forbes (Belzer, 2015), the company is ranked twenty-first in the top 50 sports agencies list with around €262 million in players' contracts across a portfolio of 58 players, and roughly €26 million in commission fees. The other top Spanish agencies are Manuel Garcia Quilón, ranked eighth with almost €120 million in estimated transfer fees, followed by Servicios Deportivos IDUB with almost €110 million in the eleventh position and the Catalonian lawyer Ramon Sostres, twentieth, with an estimate of €76 million. Sostres has mainly represented Barcelona players such as Carles Puyol and Andres Iniesta.

The first English agency is Stellar Group, placed third in the ranking with a potential transfer income of roughly €200 million. In the Forbes' list, the agency is ranked tenth with a portfolio of 143 athletes, worth an estimated €392 million in transfer fees and around €40 million in commissions. The other top English agency, Base Soccer, is listed sixth with players worth roughly €145 million in potential transfer fees. The agency has heavily invested in the Brazilian market, opening a branch named Base Soccer Brazil in order to exploit that market. Their clients include Brazilian internationals Felipe Anderson and Norberto Neto.

In fourth position with €198 million is the American WMG. The company is a global generalist agency representing 410 athletes in 20 sports all over the world. According to Forbes (Belzer, 2015), the entire company is ranked fourth in the top 50 sports agencies list with around €2.1 billionn in athletes' contracts and roughly €101 million in commission fees. In the last three years, the agency has gone through an expansion process which will impact on its dominant presence in the representation market. In June 2013, WMG announced the appointment of highly rated consultants, including Chiel Dekker in Netherlands, and the agents Frédéric Dobraje, Gregory Dakad, Cedric Mazet and David Martinez in France (WMG, 2013). According to Mike Watts, WMG COO, 'the appointment of these five consultants gives us a great opportunity to manage the careers of leading Ligue 1 and Eredivise players locally, which we see as a huge advantage for both the athletes and for Wasserman' (Long, 2013). In line with this expansion strategy, on 13 November 2014, WMG acquired the Dutch football agency Sport-Promotion founded and owned by Rob Jansen, one of the most respected agents in Europe, currently representing International Dutch players such as Daley Blind, Marco Van Ginkel, Daryl Janmaat and Leroy Fer. Paul Martin, EVP managing executive for global football at WMG, said of the new collaboration: 'the continued development of our European football practice is a priority for us and we firmly believe that this acquisition will enable us to go from strength to strength as we continue to grow our European presence' (WMG, 2014).

In fifth position, we find the first German agency, Sports Total, with an estimated €177 million in potential transfer fees. According to Forbes (Belzer, 2015), the agency has a portfolio of 84 football clients whose contracts are estimated to be roughly €380 million, generating €38m in commission fees. The second best

Germany agency is Rogon Sport Management, ranked twelfth, with estimated transfer fees of €107 million and listed nineteenth in the Forbes' list at €280 million with a portfolio of 75 clients. The other two remaining agencies in the top 20 list, Pro Profil and Jörg Neubauer, are respectively ranked sixteenth and nineteenth, with players' portfolios worth €92 million and €78 million respectively. Overall, these four German agencies are estimated to represent a portfolio worth €454 million.

Another prominent agent is the Dutchman Mino Raiola, ranked seventh with a client portfolio worth €134 million on average. Through his company, Maguire Tax & Legal, he works on behalf of several international players such as Zlatan Ibrahimovic, Paul Pogba, Mario Balotelli, Blaise Matuidi, Henrihk Mkhitaryan and Maxwell. Since the beginning of his career in the early 1990s, Raiola has been an active intermediary for several Dutch clubs and their players on the foreign markets, such as Italy primarily. In recent years, he has gained a relevant position in the French market, dealing extensively with Paris-Saint Germain. According to Forbes (Belzer, 2015), his company is ranked twenty-second, with a portfolio of 35 footballers worth around €260 million in players' contracts and roughly €25 million in commission fees.

Three Italian agencies are present in the top 20 list with a total portfolio worth almost €300 million. The first agency is Pastorello & Partners, ranked ninth with an estimated portfolio of €115 million. The other two Italian agencies are Branchini Associati and Tecnosport Immagine respectively ranked thirteenth and fourteenth with estimated players' portfolios of €94 million and €92 million.

In tenth position, is the first French agency, Mondial Promotion, with an estimated €109 million in potential transfer fees. The other French agent, ranked eighteenth, is the veteran and most influential Jean-Pierre Bernès, whose current portfolio is estimated at €87 million and includes players such as Nabil Fekir, Franck Ribery and Samir Nasri.

Within the top 20 agencies, there are only two South Americans, the Brazilian Euro Export and the Argentinian Twenty Two. The former is ranked fifteenth with a portfolio of €92 million and is run by former goalkeeper Giuliano Bertolucci. It works closely with Kia Joorabchian, managing players such as David Luiz, Marquinhos, Oscar, Alex, Ramires and Willian. The latter is ranked seventeenth with an estimated portfolio of €88 million. It is managed by Fernando Felicevich, whose portfolio includes Alexis Sanchez, Arturo Vidal, Gary Medel and Federico Fernandez.

4.4 The agents and intermediaries market in England

Being the most attractive and lucrative league for players and, consequently, for their agents, the English PL has adopted strict and severe regulations to govern the activities of agents, specifically calling for transparency in transfers after two major bung scandals[12] (Gardiner, 2006). The first FA inquiry into bungs in football began in 1995 in response to allegations of illegal payments made in a High Court case between Terry Venables and Alan Sugar, surrounding the transfer of

Teddy Sheringham from Nottingham Forest to Tottenham Hotspur. The FA investigation lasted three and a half years and considered several domestic and international transfers between 1992 and 1994. In September 1997, the investigation report revealed the increasing influence that agents had on financial transactions and exposed a lack of financial probity within English football. A bung culture was exposed with members of management and coaching teams regularly receiving illegal payments after transfers. The main prosecution made under FA rules was against the then Arsenal manager, George Graham, who was adjudged to have taken around £400,000 in illegal payments from Norwegian agent Rune Hauge. Graham received a one year ban before promptly returning to the world of football. However, there was no real political will from the football family to recognise the problem and discipline those involved (Gardiner, 2006). While this could have been a watershed moment for English football if those involved had been fully investigated and given more severe punishment, such as a lifetime ban from being involved in the game, that did not happen and, as a consequence, there was no deterrent that could make people change their activities since the football industry as a whole did not have the will to police transfers.

A second investigation occurred in March 2006, when Lord Stevens, former commissioner of the Metropolitan police, led an enquiry in response to allegations made by managers Mike Newell and Ian Holloway that bungs were common practice in the transfer market. Their evidence was reinforced by BBC television's *Panorama* allegations following a special investigation into corruption in English football, which showed footage of how agents, managers and high ranking football club officials accepted backhanders and were engaged in illegally tapping-up[13] players under contract to other clubs. On June 2007, Lord Stevens' inquiry issued its final report, which raised concerns over issues involving a few transfers, but stated: 'there is no evidence of any irregular payments to club officials or players, and they are identified only as a consequence of the outstanding issues the inquiry has with agents involved' (Guardian, 2007a).

Although some critics claimed a lack of hard evidence after 16 months of inquiry, Lord Stevens' investigation prompted English football to seriously confront the inadequacy of transfer regulations and practice. In the PL's own response to the findings of the Stevens investigation, it says that: 'The Premier League and the Football Association accept partial responsibility for not having effective checking and verification systems' (Guardian, 2007b). In other words, the football authorities did not try hard enough to ensure that multi-million pound transfers were complying with their rules. In response to this, 39 recommendations were provided to bring meaningful changes and improve transparency as well as giving the governing body greater regulatory control over the activity of those who are involved in the transfer market (Ellen, 2007). The main reforms included a ban on dual representation, the requirement for overseas agents to register with the FA when involved in a transfer in England, and the necessity to disclose the total amount of agents' fees paid by clubs each year.

In 2007, the FA also put in place a monitoring team which oversees and scrutinises the player transfer market and payments to football agents made through the clearing house system that gathers data on transfer operations and is set up in partnership between the PL and the FL. The FA is in charge of the monitoring and payments of commission paid to agents which are also integrated in the clearing house system. In December 2007, the FA worked closely with law enforcement authorities and came up with an extensive guide for football clubs, *Money Laundering and the Proceeds of Crime Act*, in response to requests from clubs for more guidance on the main UK legislation concerning money laundering and the proceeds of crime. This guidance set out steps a club might take in the event of a suspicious transaction, and summarised some preventative measures that clubs might take to protect themselves.

Although all these measures provide only partial solutions, the transfer market in England is now perceived as one of the most transparent and rigorous, in which agents are generally thought to be promptly and fairly remunerated in comparison to other transfer markets. This reputation was confirmed when the PL decided to ban TPO from the beginning of the 2008/09 season (KEA and CDES; 2013).

Over the last five years, three agencies have been able to dominate the English market; WMG, Stellar Group and Base Soccer. As Tables 4.6 and 4.7 illustrate, these agencies together cover 18 per cent and 16 per cent of market share and market power respectively. They are all solidly structured around a core team of agents that works cohesively in the international markets. This consolidation was also fostered by the market decline of First Artist and the closure of agencies such as Formation and SEM over the last ten years. This market gap was partially compensated by the arrival of James Grant Group, created in July 2009 by the buyout of five businesses acquired from Formation to become a leading agency in sport, music and entertainment (Barry, 2009). Present in the top 10 list, its football division managed by former MLS player, Lyle Yorks,

Table 4.6 Top 10 football agencies with the highest market shares in the English PL

Rank	Agency/agent/intermediary	Type	Market share %	Average number of represented players	Market trend
1	WMG (US)	GG	6.6	30	↔
2	Stellar Group (ENG)	GS	6.6	29–30	↑
3	Base Soccer (ENG)	GS	4.5	20	↑
4	Key Sport Management (ENG)	RS	2.7	12	↓
5	James Grant Group (ENG)	GS	1.8	8	↓
6	Impact Sport Management (ENG)	RS	1.5	7	↓
7	World in Motion (ENG)	GS	1.5	7	↓
8	New Era Sport Management (ENG)	RS	1.5	7	↔
9	Gestifute (POR)	GS	1.3	6	↔
10	Willie McKay (ENG)	RS	1.3	6	↔

Table 4.7 Top 10 football agencies with the highest market power in the English PL

Rank	Agency/agent/intermediary	Type	Market power %	Represented players' total value estimate €m	Market trend
1	WMG (US)	GG	6	192	↓
2	Stellar Group (ENG)	GS	5	165	↑
3	Base Soccer (ENG)	GS	4.1	136	↑
4	Gestifute (POR)	GS	2.8	92	↓
5	Triple S Sport Enter. (ENG)	RG	2	64	↓
6	Key Sport Management (ENG)	RS	2	64	↑
7	Euro Export As. e Pr. (BRA)	GS	1.8	59	↑
8	Bahia Internacional (SPA)	GS	1.75	57	↑
9	Interfootball Manag. (SPA)	RS	1.7	55	↑
10	SEG Sport Enter. Group (NDL)	RG	1.5	50	↓

operates in Mexico, the US and Europe, representing players such as Clint Dempsey, Jozy Altidore, Jack Rodwell and De Andre Yedlin.

Another agency of note is Key Sport Management, founded in 1999 by former players Colin Gordon and John Colquhoun. The agency was bought out on 3 September 2013 by Swiss based private investor Legion Group, who sought to expand its sport division beyond rugby. Its players are together worth €64 million and include James Vardy, Theo Walcott and Phil Jones (Legion, 2013).

The main difference between the English market and the other markets in the top ten lists is the presence of five foreign agencies in the top ten list of market power. The most likely explanation for this is the sheer number of foreign players in the English PL. As well as the most famous agencies, such as Gestifute, Bahia Internacional and Euro Export, Spanish agency Interfootball Management – founded by the former player Julio Llorente in 1991 and representing David Silva and Santi Cazorla – is also noteworthy. In addition, the multi-service agency SEG, which operates with a team of 50 employees in more than 15 European countries, looks after the interests of Dutch internationals such as Roben Van Persie, Ibrahim Afellay, Stefan de Vrij and Memphis Depay, having been founded and managed by Alex Kroes and Kees Vos.

4.5 The agents and intermediaries market in Italy

The Italian transfer market is unique in that the market occurs in real time and as such has always been followed by media, fans and professionals. The event is organised by the football association, FIGC, in partnership with the professional leagues and consists of a real football market wherein agents, players, football directors and club owners meet in a hotel to arrange transfer deals during the winter and summer transfer windows. Traditionally, Italian football had the highest numbers of licensed football agents in the world, and until the early 2000s the highest transfer fees involved Italian clubs.

However, in the last decade Italian football has been deeply affected by a number of major scandals which involved players, referees, club chairmen, managers from football associations and leagues, and football agents (Hamil *et al.*, 2010). The biggest of them has been the 2006 Calciopoli match-fixing scandal, which revealed the dominant position of the agency GEA World in the Italian transfer market with its average market share of 10.2 per cent from 2002 to 2006, and its representation of players whose transfer values equated to 18.9 per cent of the whole market – twice the amount of the second biggest agency, PDP (AGCM, 2006).

Recognising that the industry was wholly corrupt, FIGC introduced new agents' regulations in February 2007. Reform guidelines were adopted with the aim of widening access to the profession and controls were put in place to prevent the establishment and the abuse of market dominance. More specifically, the controls were implemented across the following areas: (1) the integrity of people admitted to the profession of players' agent, (2) standardisation of contractual relationships between agents and players, (3) restrictive clauses, (4) suitability of the current conflict of interest provisions to guarantee equal opportunities for players' agents operating in the market place. According to Ferrari (2007), the reform mainly focused on combating the establishment and subsequent abuse of dominant positions by agents by introducing numerous prohibitions and regulatory incompatibilities to prevent potential conflicts of interest. These included specific clauses relating to the presence of family ties as well as the number of clubs and players that were represented by the same group. Paradoxically, the restrictions on the exercise of the profession of the agent increased, made even stronger by the imposition of a new standard agents' agreement and foreclosure of recourse to state tribunals. The provisions designed to prevent conflicts of interests, in particular, ended up by actually impeding business activity, curtailing the freedom of choice of players and clubs, and creating obstacles to the competitive development of the agents' business.

Apart from the three agencies present in top 20 lists, the Italian transfer market has seen the consolidation of some agencies that filled the void left by GEA World. On this matter, the top ten lists include the marketing agency Reset Group, founded by Davide Lippi, former GEA World agent and Marcello Lippi's son, and Carlo Diana, former Juventus marketing manager. Started as a specialised football agency, the group has diversified its business activities in recent years and its current main client is Giorgio Chiellini, whose twin brother Claudio worked as an agent for the Group before becoming a Juventus scout.

Amongst the top Italian agencies, PDP was probably the first to transfer Italian players abroad, starting with the transfer of Gianluca Vialli to Chelsea. Funded and run by the veteran agent and lawyer Claudio Pasqualin, its client list includes players such as Sebastian Giovinco, Domenico Criscito, Alberto Aquilani and Salvatore Bocchetti. Lawyer Giuseppe Bozzo, former collaborator of the PDP agency for the South Italian market has also become a prominent agent in his own right, creating AGB Sport Management. He started his career assist-

Table 4.8 Top 10 football agencies with the highest market shares in Serie A

Rank	Agency/agent/intermediary	Type	Market share %	Average number of represented players	Market trend
1	Tecnosport Immagine (ITA)	GS	3.8	20–21	↑
2	Pastorello & Partners (ITA)	GS	3.3	18	↓
3	Branchini Associati (ITA)	GS	3.2	17	↓
4	PDP (ITA)	GS	2.7	14–15	↓
5	AGB Sport Management (ITA)	GS	2.3	12–13	↓
6	E3 Sports (ITA)	GS	2.2	11–12	↓
7	Reset Group (ITA)	GS	1.9	10	↓
8	Player Management	RS	1.7	9	↑
9	World Soccer Agency (ITA)	GS	1.6	8–9	↑
10	Sergio Berti (ITA)	GS	1.8	8–9	↓

ing his current client Antonio Cassano who was at Bari Calcio academy and has grown to become one of the most influential agents, gaining an international reputation. His portfolio is worth €67 million and includes players Fabio Quagliarella, Federico Peluso and Leandro Greco. He was actively involved as club agent in the transfer of Martin Caceres and Alvaro Morata to Juventus and Mateo Kovacic to Inter Milan.

Present in the top ten list is also the agency E3 Sports, founded in 2013 through a merger between the agency Law Sport, led by the renowned agent Claudio Vigorelli, and the private equity house E3 Partners. The company is quite active in the Italian and English markets and it represents the interests of players such as Mattia Destro, Emiliano Viviano, Davide Santon and Christian Abbiati. Another emerging agency in these five years has been World Soccer Agency run by the lawyer Alessandro Lucci with a team of seven collaborators that covers the national and international markets. The company has worked on

Table 4.9 Top 10 football agencies with the highest market power in Serie A

Rank	Agency/agent/intermediary	Type	Market power %	Represented players' total value estimation €m	Market trend
1	Tecnosport Immagine (ITA)	GS	4.2	94	↓
2	Pastorello & Partners (ITA)	GS	3.9	89	↑
3	Branchini Associati (ITA)	GS	3.85	87	↓
4	AGB Sport Management (ITA)	GS	3	67	↓
5	Maguire Tax & Legal (NDL)	GS	2.3	53	↑
6	PDP (ITA)	GS	2.3	53	↓
7	E3 Sports (ITA)	GS	2.25	51	↓
8	World Soccer Agency (ITA)	GS	2.2	50.5	↑
9	Sergio Berti (ITA)	GS	2.05	46	↓
10	Reset Group (ITA)	GS	1.8	41	↓

behalf of several foreign players and currently represents players such as Luis Muriel, Juan Cuadrado, Matias Vecino and Filip Djordjevic. Amongst its Italian clients are Leonardo Bonucci, Andrea Bertolacci and Alessandro Florenzi. Finally, the last agent in the top ten list is the veteran Sergio Berti, who has strongly collaborated with Fali Ramadani, the agent of Adem Ljajic and Stefan Jovetic, to import foreign talent in the Italian Serie A. Currently, he represents the interests of Daniele De Rossi, Alessio Romagnoli, Alessio Cerci and Lorenzo De Silvestri.

Ten years after the GEA World case, the market representation of agents has increasingly become more competitive and it is possible to see that the reform of the agents' regulations has had a positive impact on the level of competitiveness between football agencies. Undoubtedly, the representation market is strongly linked to the current condition of Italian football, which has lost its attraction to some extent. In this context, Italian agencies are expanding their activity in emerging markets such India, the US and China.

4.6 The agents and intermediaries market in Spain

The transfer market in Spain has traditionally centred on the transfers of the two most prestigious clubs, Barcelona and Real Madrid, who have beaten all the transfer records to sign the best talent available. This has been supported at high levels with legislation even being rewritten to facilitate it – the *Beckham Ley*, for example, was passed in 2005 and operated until 2010. The law earned its nickname after David Beckham became one of the first expatriates in Spain to take advantage of the opportunity to be subject to a flat rate of 24 per cent tax. It was seen as a way to make Spanish football attractive to foreign talent. Then, top clubs were able to maximise their income from broadcast rights to fund their spending. However, from the 2015/2016 season, rights are being collectively sold, as happens in many other leagues and therefore the difference in fees generated by the top and bottom clubs is likely to narrow, with the intended consequence of improving competitive balance (Torres, 2015). Under the previous system of individual selling of rights, Barcelona and Real Madrid each earned €140 million annually from broadcasting income, offering them a competitive advantage domestically (El Mundo, 2015). However, the Spanish government pushed for a new law that gave the Spanish league control over the collective sale of broadcasting rights in a move to improve the clubs' finances, collect outstanding taxes, and increase competitiveness. The new legislation brings Spanish football in line with the PL and Serie A.

The general economic conditions in Spain have also impacted the transfer market over the last decade, with some clubs hit hard by the post-2008 financial crisis in which several indebted clubs were forced to seek bankruptcy protection. This situation was also exacerbated by the critical condition of the banking system on which clubs relied for financial support. Prior to this, in 2003, the Spanish government had enacted a new insolvency law, the *Ley Concursal*, which allowed companies to defer their outstanding payments in order to keep their business running (Szymanski, 2015). Twenty-seven Spanish clubs embraced this law, which enabled them to renegotiate their debts between 2003 and 2014. The financial crash meant that clubs would have struggled to secure finance from banks and have had to seek alternative forms of funding. It is not a coincidence that, in December 2013, the EC began disciplinary actions against seven Spanish clubs over possible favourable tax treatment from the state, aid for the construction of new stadia and loans and bank guarantees from regional governments (EurActiv.com, 2013).

In these conditions, where finance has been at times difficult to secure, new sources of funding have come to the fore. In particular, TPE agreements supported by investment funds have proliferated enormously in Spain, operating as an entry point into the transfer markets for alternative investors using innovative forms of investment. DSI,[14] a subsidiary of Doyen Group, is a private equity fund primarily dedicated to providing an alternative, significant and growing source of funding to clubs (Russo, 2014). DSI started by operating through TPO agreements and sponsorship agreements with clubs such as Atletico Madrid, Getafe and Sporting Gijon. In the first phase of its activity, the DSI fund invested roughly €100 million, becoming the most widely recognised private investment fund in the football sector. DSI's investment strategy has increased its brand awareness, allowing it to position itself as a serious and credible player in the financial sector for the football industry, working closely with many teams including: Atletico Madrid, Benfica, Granada, Porto, Santos, Sevilla, Valencia and Twente FC.

According to the FIFA TMS (2014, 2015), 1,333 players have left Spanish clubs to go abroad since 1 January 2011 and for two consecutive years, 2013 and 2014, Spanish clubs recorded the highest transfer receipts of €520 million and €600 million. Undoubtedly, football agencies have played a relevant role in exporting Spanish talent abroad and this is partially confirmed by the presence of agencies like Bahia Internacional and Interfootball Management in the market representation of the English PL.

Amongst the agencies with the highest market share in Table 4.10, is Promoesport. Based on six regional divisions in Spain, one in France and one covering the Scandinavian countries, the company was founded by the football agent Jose Rodriguez Baster who has expanded the business activities to the African continent and, with a team of 16 agents, operates at international level, assisting clubs and players worldwide. Its portfolio is worth €51 million and includes players such as Diego Alves, Felipe Melo, Aleix Vidal, Iago Aspas and Antonio Reyes. The only global generalist agency in the list is U1St founded by Alvaro Torres. The agency mainly operates in basketball and football and provides marketing services to athletes in various disciplines such as golf, sailing and tennis. Its client list includes Diego Perotti, Guilherme Siqueira, Javi Lopez and Andres Guardado.

The other remaining football agencies in the top ten lists are regional specialists. Tackle Players 80 is managed by the former player Magico Diaz and follows the interests of Marc Bartra and Oriol Romeu. In the area of Valencia,

Table 4.10 Top 10 football agencies with the highest market shares in Primera Liga

Rank	Agency/agent/intermediary	Type	Market share %	Average number of represented players	Market trend
1	Bahia Internacional (SPA)	GS	5.4	25–26	↓
2	Servicios Deportivos IDUB (SPA)	GS	5.2	24–25	↔
3	Promoesport (SPA)	GS	4.8	22–23	↑
4	Manuel Garcia Quilón (SPA)	GS	4.5	21	↓
5	Gestifute (POR)	GS	3.2	15	↑
6	U1st (SPA)	GG	2.6	12	↑
7	Tackle Players 80 (SPA)	RS	1.8	9–8	↓
8	Toldra Football Consulting (SPA)	RS	1.7	8	↔
9	Interstar Deporte (SPA)	RS	1.7	8	↑
10	Eugenio Botas As. Depor. (SPA)	RS	1.6	8–7	↓

two main agencies operate. Toldra Football Consulting is one of the oldest football agencies in Spain, with its founder Alberto Toldra operating since the 1970s. Currently, the company represents players such as Paco Alcacer, Jaume Costa, Ruben Garcia and Juanfran Torres. The other agency is Interstar Deporte managed by Vicente Fores and Jose Tarraga whose main clients are Jordi Alba, Juan Bernat and Bruno Soriano. Finally, in the regions of Galicia, Asturia and Cartabia, the agent Eugenio Botas has always been quite active, working with Celta Vigo, Deportivo La Coruna, Sporting Gijon, Real Oviedo and Racing Santander.

Looking at the top ten agencies with the highest market power in Table 4.11, undoubtedly a wide gap exists between the leading Gestifute and the other agencies. While the top five together are worth €630 million, Gestifute's supremacy means its market power is more than double that of its closest rivals in the top

Table 4.11 Top 10 football agencies with the highest market power in Primera Liga

Rank	Agency/agent/intermediary	Type	Market power %	Represented players' total value estimation €m	Market trend
1	Gestifute (POR)	GS	9.9	257	↑
2	Bahia Internacional (SPA)	GS	4.9	127	↔
3	Servicios Depor. IDUB (SPA)	GS	3.6	94	↑
4	Manuel Garcia Quilón (SPA)	GS	3.1	81	↓
5	Ramon Sostres (SPA)	GS	2.7	71	↓
6	Jose Maria Orobitg (SPA)	RS	2.4	62	↑
7	Activos (SPA)	RS	2.1	54	↔
8	Promoesport (SPA)	GS	2	51	↑
9	Gines Carvajal (SPA)	RS	1.8	46	↔
10	Txus Medina (SPA)	RS	1.6	40	↔

five positions, revealing an imbalance within the representation market that is not present in any other league.

Activos was born out of IMG Futbol after the American sports agency made the decision to leave the business of football players' representation in 2011. The agency was formed by the merger of ACT Talent Sport & Entertainment and VOS Sportsmarketing & Entertainment with the involvement of Arturo Canales, former director of the IMG football division in Spain, and Victor Onate, former marketing director of Valencia. Its client portfolio is estimated to be worth around €54 million and includes players such as Gerard Pique, Ander Herrera, David Villa and Koke.

Finally, at the bottom of the top ten list are the agents Gines Carvajal and Txus Medina. The former is a veteran agent who dominated the representation market in the 1990s and 2000s, representing players such as Raul Blanco, Michel Salgado and Fernando Morientes. With a portfolio worth €46 million, he works on behalf of Jese, Victor Valdes and Gerard Deulofeu. The latter is a Basque agent who began his profession working mainly with players from Athletic Bilbao from 1990. He currently represents players such as Iker Munian and Ander Iturraspe.

To conclude, competitiveness within the market of representation in Spain depends on the EU Competition Commission's ruling on the challenge launched by the Spanish league, LFP (2015a), jointly with the Portuguese league, LPFP, against FIFA's ban on TPO, which states that:

> The prohibition of third-party ownership constitutes an economic agreement that restricts the economic liberty of clubs, players and third parties without any justification or proportionality. This ban damages the clubs, principally those with less economic resources, preventing them from sharing with third parties the economic rights of professional players in their squads and managing their financial obligations in the most prudent form.

This statement reveals the tensions within Spanish football due to the clear opposition to TPO of the football association, RFEF, and players' union, AFE, which favoured its complete ban.

4.7 The agents and intermediaries market in France

In France the agency business was less popular compared to the other big five leagues until French Clubs spent more on players during the 1980s. As the industry developed, the French government introduced the first national regulation for the profession of sports agents in 1992 (Berenger, 2012). While the 1992 act recognised sports agency law as distinct from general agency law and as running in tandem with the FIFA licence, the law was ineffective in controlling the actions of French sports agents regarding any improper conduct and conflicts in the conduct of their profession. Consequently, the French government passed a more detailed sports agency law in 2000; the Code du Sport. Its articles regulate sports agency and takes on board a licensing system organised by the FFF, with further strict revisions in 2010. In 2013, only 15 per cent of candidates obtained the FFF licence to act as official agents. In line with the need to increase the transparency of the representation market, the FFF has required that, every year, each agent should reveal the name of each player and coach or manager they have represented. In 2014, there were 338 official agents registered by the FFF. With the approval the new FIFA intermediary system, the FFF has decided that the current French licensing should stay in force until 2020.

This strict regulation has also led to unionisation of agents. UASF and SNAS are two competing agents' associations (Frenkiel, 2014). The former includes the agents' federal commission, CFAS, and is a member of the EFAA. It has denounced the fact that some agents have a criminal record and has supported a limit on access to the profession, stricter control of transfers via Bureau Veritas and the signing of a charter of ethics between FFF agents and clubs. SNAS, on the other hand, has opposed the recent qualification of sports attorney granted to lawyers. It participated in the States-General of football in 2010 and is open to sports agents from others disciplines. It is committed to the protection of mandates to act and the fight against the illegal exercise of the profession of sports agent.

The reputation of agents in France has been tarnished by several high profile cases of misconduct involving secret fees or bungs and dual representation and activities carried out by unlicensed agents (Frenkiel, 2014). One case involved the former Olympique Marseille manager Rolland Courbis, who was convicted in 2006 by the Correctional Court of Marseille for 'misuse of company assets, complicity in misuse of company assets, forgery and use of forged documents' (Le Figaro, 2009). Courbis was found guilty of receiving personal commissions alongside trades involving his players. In fact, he was acting as a sports agent without the right to do so. His son, Stephane, is currently one of the most influential agents, representing high profile managers such as Willy Sagnol and Alain Casanova and international players such as Laurent Koscielny and Cedric Carraso. While the Marseille case was noteworthy, it was certainly not the last – two former presidents of Paris Saint-Germain, a Nike representative and several sports agents, including Richard Bettoni, Rajko Stoijic and Milan Calasan, were convicted of 'forgery, use of forged documents and covert employment' in a judgement from the Correctional Court of Paris in 2010 (Le Monde, 2009). The matter concerned fake documents and more than 20 trade contracts that included unlawful remunerations estimated at €9 million to players and their agents, resulting from illegal tax savings. Perhaps the biggest problem of late has been dual representation. Licensed agent Jean Pierre Bernès who represents Laurent Blanc (former coach of the French national team) and Didier Deschamps (current coach of the French national team) as well as several players, was accused of influencing the selection of players in the national team (Lagoutte, 2011). This situation clearly raises conflicts of interest which need to be closely monitored. As a matter of fact, in France, football agents have been authorised to represent football coaches and managers since 9 June 2010, with the approval of law n. 2010–626 (Frenkiel, 2014).

The French clubs have traditionally been viewed as sellers in the transfer market with their best players leaving for the richest foreign clubs in England, Italy or Spain. Most French clubs relied on these fees to meet the financial conditions imposed by the French financial control, DNCG, and have tended to be well run financially, without the over-investment in players which has been a feature of other markets. In the 2014/2015 season, the French clubs recorded a net surplus in transfer fees of €121 million, spending €189 million on foreign players, but received €310 million from the sale of players to clubs abroad (LFP, 2015b). However, following the arrival of Qatar investment fund, QSI, at Paris Saint-Germain, as well as the Russian owner, Dmitry Rybolovlev at AS Monaco, the market has radically changed and Paris Saint-Germain alone spent 64 per cent of the total expenditure of the French clubs in the 2012/2013 season to recruit top international players (FIFA TMS, 2014). Aside from the aforementioned clubs, and to a lesser extent Olympique Lyon, French clubs are still not able to attract international star players as wages tend to be lower because far less is generated through broadcast revenue.

The impact of foreign ownership has been visible in the representation market, with foreign agencies becoming important in the transfer strategies of clubs that were traditionally linked to French agents. For example, Group USM and the IMG agent Bruno Satin's presence at Paris Saint-Germain have been superseded by Mino Raiola and Giuliano Bertolucci. Similarly, Jorge Mendes, with Gestifute, is at the core of AS Monaco's strategy, transferring several Portuguese and Spanish players and intermediating transfers by Yannick Ferreira-Carrasco to Atletico Madrid, Geoffrey Kondogbia to Inter Milan, Anthony Martial to Manchester United and Aymen Abdennour to Valencia on behalf of the club. These last two players are both represented by the French agent Stéphane Canard, who has become Mendes' main collaborator in France. While foreign agents helping top clubs has previously been an anomaly in this transfer market, this is

Table 4.12 Top 10 football agencies with the highest market shares in Ligue 1

Rank	Agency/agent/intermediary	Type	Market shares %	Average number of represented players	Market trend
1	Groupe USM (FRA)	GS	7	30	↔
2	Mondial Promotion (FRA)	GS	5.6	24	↓
3	SVF Foot Consulting (FRA)	GS	4.6	20	↓
4	Frédéric Guerra (FRA)	GS	3.3	14	↔
5	S.C.S.M.I. (FRA)	RS	2.7	11	↔
6	Gilino Sport (FRA)	RS	2.5	10–11	↓
7	CLK Foot (FRA)	RS	2.4	10–11	↑
8	Sport G Conseils (FRA)	RS	1.8	8	↑
9	FP Sport (FRA)	RS	1.7	7–8	↔
10	Jean Pierre Bernès (FRA)	GS	1.6	7	↓

changing and the trend looks set to continue. According to Bertrand Gardon, the president of the agents' association UNFP, 'the fact that the market is fully open favours the arrival of stronger foreign intermediaries, that gain exorbitant commissions' (Dupré, 2014). As reported by the financial annual report on French football (LFP and DNCG, 2012), the total commission paid by Ligue 1 clubs to agents increased from €40 million to €60 million in the 2011/2012 season, revealing a substantial growth in the representation market in France.

Apart from the most relevant agencies aforementioned, Karim Aklil with his agency Gilino Sport has gained a relevant position in the representation market. He has largely operated with Olympique Marseille since 2004, when he started his profession as an unlicensed agent, till 2009 when he worked on behalf of Karim Ziani, Mamadou Niang and Souleymane Diawara. Aklil currently represents several Algerian international players, such as Ryad Boudebouz, Foued Kadir, Islam Slimani and Hilel Soudani. Similarly, another influential agent in the top list, David Venditelli, has operated without a licence for his company Score Agencies. Strongly linked to AS Saint-Etienne and Olympique Lyon, he was the agent of the former French international Eric Abidal and currently represents players such as Loic Perrin, Jeremy Clement, Alexandre Lacazette and Kourt Zouma.

Finally, the last agent to mention is Jean Christophe Cano, the former football player and football director of Olympique Marseille, Cano has operated as a licensed agent since 2002 and he currently represents players such as Paul-Georges Ntep, Timothée Kolodziejczak and Benoit Trémoulinas.

In June 2013, in front of the Council of State, the two French agents' associations appealed against the fee cap of 6 per cent imposed by the Executive Committee of the FFF, under pressure from clubs' association UCPF (France Football, 2013). For the first time, the UASF and the SNAS worked together and the cap was removed. However, a similar cap of 10 per cent for any wages below €1.8 million per annum gross remains.

While agents' commissions are not typically in the public domain in France, the Court of Commerce published the information in Table 4.14 covering agents

Table 4.13 Top 10 football agencies with the highest market power in Ligue 1

Rank	Agency/agent/intermediary	Type	Market power %	Represented players' total value estimation €m	Market trend
1	Mondial Promotion (FRA)	GS	5.5	72.4	↓
2	Groupe USM (FRA)	GS	3.95	52.5	↑
3	Frédéric Guerra (FRA)	GS	3.75	50.5	↑
4	SVF Foot Consulting (FRA)	GS	3.5	47	↓
5	S.C.S.M.I. (FRA)	RS	3.1	41.7	↓
6	Jean Pierre Bernès (FRA)	GS	2.9	37	↓
7	Jean Christophe Cano (FRA)	RS	1.8	24	↓
8	Score Agencies (FRA)	GS	1.75	23	↑
9	Christophe Horlaville (FRA)	RS	1.7	22	↔
10	Gilino Sport (FRA)	RS	1.6	21	↓

Table 4.14 Average early earnings of individual agents from 2010 to 2013

Individual agent	Average yearly remuneration €m
Pierre Frelot	4.3
Jean-Pierre Bernès	3.6
Frédéric Guerra	1.7
Christophe Mongai	1.49
Thierry Gras	1.25
Bruno Satin	1.22
Franck Belhassen	1.14
Philippe Flavier	0.79
Stéphane Canard	0.75
Alexandre Bonnefond	0.74
Jonathan Maarek	0.69
Karim Djaziri	0.55
Karim Aklil	0.54
Lyes Ghilas	0.41
Patrick Glanz	0.39
Guillaume Sola	0.21

Source: Tanguy (2014).

domiciled in France who provided their accounts[15] (Tanguy, 2014). In commenting on the disclosure of this list, Franck Belhassen, the agent and vice-president of the agents' association, UASF, affirmed that agents face huge expenses and must make a long term investment in players who often do not make it as professionals. Similarly, there is a lot of risk involved, even once a player is playing professionally, as contracts signed for representation tend to be unstable.

4.8 The agents and intermediaries market in Germany

With an average crowd of 43,500 per game, the Bundesliga is the best attended football league in the world. German clubs' commitment to supporters has been at the forefront of the Bundesliga business model for a number of years, leading to match revenues increasing year on year, even though every game is broadcast live on domestic television (Peck, 2014). Ticket prices are kept low in an effort by clubs to support their football communities. The power of a German football clubs thus lies with its members, as opposed to business investors.

The league's profitability is also due to tight ownership rules which ensure that those in charge of clubs do not take excessive risks which could lead to debt. The logic behind this approach is to ensure the integrity of professional football by preventing one person having control over one, or more than one, team (Dietl and Franck, 2007). As registered non-profit associations, the so-called *verein*, clubs, are legally required to hold at least 50 per cent of the voting rights plus one voting right of the club. These *verein* are managed by representatives and elected by the members, who are usually fans. This restriction results in a special structure which is not allowed to distribute any of its assets to representatives or members or to sell individual membership rights. Instead, club representatives have strong incentives to reinvest all available funds. The German club structure discourages outside investors and foreign ownerships that have rescued clubs in the other top European leagues (Hesse, 2013). The great advantage of the German system is that the German football association, DFB, has a large network and wields a certain amount of power, for instance through the licence process. These aspects could lead German clubs to adopt more moderate transfer strategies than leagues usually do (FIFA TMS, 2014).

A further interesting element to consider about the German transfer market is that, until the season 2007/2008, there were only two professional leagues. On September 2006, the DFB announced the formation of the 3.Liga starting from 2008/2009 (Price, 2015). Since then, the league has operated at a financial loss, with a record deficit of €20,9 million. The 2013/2014 season was the first to register a profit (€4.9 million), making it the third-most economically successful professional sports league in German sports, well behind the two Bundesligas. This made the German transfer market more competitive and attractive for players and consequently for the expansion of the profession of intermediaries within the national market.

The representation market is highly transparent, with information about agents more readily available than in the other markets. German agents tend to provide reliable information on the activity of their agencies through their website social media. For the majority of top agencies, it is possible to verify their updated clients' list and how they are organised internally in terms of the work team and individual employees' functions and responsibility. Moreover, agencies tend to show which partnerships are established with different service agencies and other football agencies. Unsurprisingly therefore, the German representation industry has been relatively immune to scandals in the transfer market, suggesting that the collaboration between clubs and associations in terms of governance might minimise the impact of opportunistic behaviours from the market representation side.

While, in 2011, players' agents received €71.6 million in fees, this amount had risen to more than €100 million during the 2013/2014 season, the highest amount in Bundesliga history (Buschmann, 2015). According to Table 4.15, the top five German agencies analysed above account for around 20 per cent of the market share.

Apart from the increasing growth of the Bundesliga as an international league, the German market has become a bridge between Eastern European leagues and Western European leagues. Consequently, it is quite common to see football agencies that develop Mitteleuropean networks to facilitate players' transfers. Agencies ISMG and Soccer Talk, for example, are both linked with the Croatian market through their founder and main agent, respectively Gordon Stipic and Alen Augustincic, who have managed the careers of several players from former Yugoslavian countries moving to Bundesliga and other main European markets. Having founded his company in December 2000, four years later Augustincic was involved as TLO for the Croatian under-21 national team during the

Table 4.15 Top 10 football agencies with the highest market shares in Bundesliga

Rank	Agency/agent/intermediary	Type	Market shares %	Average number of represented players	Market trend
1	Sports Total (GER)	GS	5.8	29	↑
2	Pro Profil (GER)	GS	4.9	23	↑
3	Rogon Sport Management (GER)	GS	3.4	16–17	↑
4	T21 Plus Sportmanag. (GER)	GS	3.4	16–17	↓
5	Jörg Neubauer (GER)	GS	2.8	14	↓
6	Marketing Sports (GER)	GS	2.4	12	↑
7	Stars & Friends (GER)	GS	2.3	11	↓
8	Soccer Talk Sportmanag. (GER)	RS	2.3	10–11	↓
9	Avantgarde (GER)	GS	2	10	↑
10	IFM (SUI)	GS	1.9	9	↔

European U21 Championship in Germany. His company currently comprises four agents and eight employees who represent players such as Lukas Rupp, Sebastian Jung and Stefan Aigner. Stipic started his career as an agent in 2001 with his company Marketing-Sports, later renamed ISMG, and has been the main agent in Germany of Ivica Olic. Currently, he represents Denis Aogo, Matthias Ginter and Sead Kolasinac. Stars & Friends was founded in early 2005 by the fusion of the Austrian Star Factory and the German Strunz & Friends. The company operates throughout Mitteleuropean markets with offices in Austria, Germany, Slovakia, Norway and Hungary. The company is part of a holding group composed of 40 employees which acquired a stake in Sport Investment International Group, the leading sports agency in the Czech Republic. Its current client portfolio includes some international players such as Ron-Robert Zieler, Sebastian Prödl, Bas Dost and Zlatko Junuzovic. Finally, there is a deserved mention for the Swiss agency IFM. Founded by the former German player Wolfgang Vöge in the late 1980s, the agency has always been active in transfers between Swiss and German clubs. Currently, the agency works on behalf of international players such as Jacob Blaszczykowski, Yann Sommer and Pirmin Schwegler.

A big market player is undoubtedly the agency Avantgarde. Founded in 1985, the company is a leading marketing agency that operates in 11 countries with 400 employees. Its football division is managed by the lawyer Robert Schneider, who joined the company in 2000. Since then, the company has become a prime actor in the international transfer market, promoting several international German players. The company has consulted several players for their advertising contracts and offers complete PR assistance to its clients. This modus operandi is quite unique within the German market and offers a strong competitive advantage. Its current portfolio includes players such as Bastian Schweinsteiger, Fabian Johnson, Daniel Ginczek and Manuel Schmiedebach.

Since 2002 the DFB has built a wide network of youth centres, training camps, district clinics, coaches and scouts to systematically develop and integrate young

Table 4.16 Top 10 football agencies with the highest market power in Bundesliga

Rank	Agency/agent/intermediary	Type	Market power %	Represented players' total value estimation €m	Market trend
1	Sports Total (GER)	GS	8.5	165	↑
2	Rogon Sport Manag. (GER)	GS	4.3	83.5	↑
3	Pro Profil (GER)	GS	4.15	83.4	↑
4	Avantgarde (GER)	GS	3.85	71.5	↔
5	Jörg Neubauer (GER)	GS	2.8	53	↔
6	IFM (SUI)	GS	2.8	53	↑
7	Fair-Sport Marketing (GER)	RS	2.3	43	↓
8	Jean Pierre Bernès (FRA)	GS	2.15	40.5	↓
9	Kögl & Partners (GER)	RS	2.15	40.5	↑
10	T21 Plus Sportmanag. (GER)	GS	1.95	36	↓

players into the world of football (Price, 2015). This vast network of 36 Bundes-liga organisations flows into more than 25,000 clubs with over 100,000 registered youth teams where young players receive basic training and development. As part of the revival of systematic youth support, all 36 football clubs from 1.Fußball-Bundesliga and 2.Fußball-Bundesliga have been mandated to have a youth development centre as part of their licensing process in order to develop home grown talent. In general, the ten-year plan has succeeded: in the 2002/2003 season, just 50 per cent of all Bundesliga players were Germans. Ten years later, this figure climbed to 57 per cent, achieving 71 per cent in the second division. The average age of all players deployed also fell by 1.32 from 27.09 to 25.77 (Price, 2015). Since the launch of the plan, clubs and the DFB have invested more than €700 million. In the 2013/14 season alone, clubs from the top two divisions invested €120 million in the youth academies.

4.9 Conclusions

While other reports have suggested that a small number of agents dominate the entire market place, we do not find that to be true, based on the available data. Across a single season it is fair to say that some agents make significant sums while others do not, but the nature of the market is such that this dominance does not seem to last across a five year period. In fact, the market appears to be very competitive. While in a one-off season it is evident that some agents do dominate, it is unlikely to be the same agent season after season. The job of an agent means that it is difficult to represent a large number of players in different markets at the same time and, therefore, the market seems to operate in cycles based on when the biggest players move.

Nevertheless, when we look at the situation on a market by market level, there are clearer patterns emerging and a small number of agents tend to represent a disproportionately large number of players relative to the number of agents operating. This is particularly noticeable in terms of the market power of agents, which seems to support the conjecture that for agents, success breeds success.

There are clear differences between the agents' landscapes within each market. While England has faced problems relating to agents, the authorities have been forced to put measures in place to actively oversee their activities. This has meant that the level of concentration is fairly low, with many agents active in representing players. As one might expect, given the large number of foreign players in the English PL, it is notable how many foreign agents have a strong presence. However, that is not to say that there are no issues of clubs favouring specific agents.

In Italy too, scandals have forced a restructure of the market, which now operates on a more equitable basis. Restrictive measures have been introduced by the authorities in an effort to stop conflicts of interest from occurring. The popularity of Italian football post-Calciopoli has made it less attractive to foreign stars who can earn much higher wages in other leagues. As such, the majority of agents active in the market are based in Italy. These factors together make Serie A at present the most balanced league in terms of agent dominance.

Market conditions have proved important in Spain too, where the credit crunch has had a profound impact on the ability of all but the top clubs to sign players. As such, we have seen various funding models emerge and it is not surprising that some of the most active agents are known to have been involved with TPE to players. There is a split market in Spain where Real Madrid and Barcelona have typically dominated the transfer market, employing the world's best players and working with their associated agents. However, aside from these clubs, many teams still recruit from their locality. As such, market share on a club by club basis is often high. This has also translated to the league level where one agency, Gestifute, controls almost 10 per cent of the market power.

As in the UK and Italy, French football has also faced various scandals relating to agents and, as a consequence, strict controls have been put in place. While in recent years Ligue 1 has been less attractive to the world's best players than the English and Spanish Leagues, the recent takeovers of Monaco and Paris Saint-Germain by foreign owners has signalled a change in the market place. Both clubs are closely linked with specific agents and their dominance has increased as a result. However, the most powerful agents across the league are all France based at present. This is expected to change in the years ahead.

The German Bundesliga is increasingly viewed as the best model for football to follow, with a division of responsibilities between operational and commercial imperatives. Through this governance structure it has largely been able to avoid the issues which have occurred in other markets. Similarly, its strong youth structure, enforced across all clubs, has limited the reliance of clubs on agents. However, the success of German clubs in international competition has had an impact on the value of their best players and as such the related market power of some agents is significant.

The question then arises of whether we should be concerned by the levels registered in this analysis. It is difficult to say that there is any problem when we consider a European single market and look at the Leagues overall. However, in reality the leagues themselves operate very separately and there are clear opportunities for conflicts of interest to arise when a small number of agents represent a disproportionately large number of players – which has been demonstrated across all leagues. However, as football is a relatively volatile market in which promotion and relegation create a constant churn of clubs, it is difficult for agents to retain a dominant position for too long outside of the elite clubs. It has been shown that at the very top level of clubs the concentration of agents is in fact low and comparable to the structure of supply and demand relationships across many other industries.

The agents who have been able to achieve a high level of power have done so by virtue of the players that they represent. From an agent's perspective, given that a player's career tends to be short and the risk of injury is high, it is essential for agents to insure against their careers relying on just a small number of players.

The analysis suggests that governing bodies need to be alert to the possibility for potential conflicts of interest to occur and monitor accordingly. The next chapter now sets out the legal framework in place to do this.

Notes

1 This figure takes into consideration the fees paid by English clubs from the beginning of the summer transfer window of the 2008/2009 season to the end of the summer transfer window of the 2015/2016 season.

2 The study adopts the definition of club agents seen as intermediaries who manage the transfers on behalf of the engaging or releasing clubs, in contrast to player agents who act in the interest of the player in transfer.

3 When a player is transferred, the sum used is the actual transfer fee paid by the buying club.

4 The HHI index is calculated by squaring the market share of each firm competing in a market of a given industry and then summing the resulting numbers. The HHI index takes into account the relative size distribution of the firms in a market. It approaches zero when the market is occupied by a large number of firms of relatively equal size and reaches its maximum of 10,000 points when a market is controlled by a single firm. The HHI index increases both as the number of firms in the market decreases and as the disparity in size between those firms increases. Markets in which the HHI index is between 1,500 and 2,500 points are considered to be moderately concentrated, while those in which the HHI index is in excess of 2,500 points are considered to be highly concentrated. Highly competitive markets register an HHI index below 100 points.

5 The Gini index is a measure of inequality of distribution. It is defined as a ratio with a value between 0 and 1, where 0 corresponds to perfect equality and 1 represents a situation of perfect inequality. Thus, a low Gini coefficient indicates more equal distribution, while a high Gini coefficient represents an unequal distribution.

6 By cross checking a plurality of sources, we managed to ascertain the intermediary for almost 91 per cent of the players: 82 per cent in France, 84.9 per cent in England, 94.8 per cent in Spain, 96.5 per cent in Italy and 96.8 per cent in Germany.

7 Transfer values were estimated on the basis of 1,500 fee-paying transfers involving big five European league clubs. It is important to remember that the official transfer fees in any European football leagues are not always disclosed, therefore those that were unavailable have been estimated based on an extrapolation and cross-referenced with various media sources.

8 The level of each club has been assigned by looking at the final ranking in their respective leagues during the five sporting seasons from 2010/2011 to 2014/2015. Subsequently, clubs are divided into four cluster levels. For all the big five leagues, with the exception of the German Bundesliga, each cluster is made of five clubs: Cluster 1 includes clubs ranked from first to fifth; Cluster 2 includes clubs ranked from sixth to tenth; Cluster 3 includes clubs ranked from eleventh to fifteenth; Cluster 4 includes those ranked from sixteenth to twentieth. For the German Bundesliga, because there are 18 clubs playing in the league, the first two clusters each comprise four clubs, whereas Clusters 3 and 4 comprise five clubs per season.

9 We considered only the clubs that were present in the leagues during the five-year period in question – a total of 58 clubs out of 141.

10 As the transfer market is highly volatile, our use of a five-season period can better determine which agencies have a stable and constant position within the market.

11 The American business magazine Forbes publishes the list of the 50 most influential sports agencies in the world. The data reported are updated to September 2015. The valuations of the rankings were compiled through extensive research into the client lists and contracts negotiated by each agency. The total contract value under management was then multiplied by the maximum agent commission as allowed by the regulations. Thus, agencies are ranked in order of the maximum commissions obtainable from the negotiated contracts, instead of the total value of the contracts. While agencies also earn income from negotiating marketing and endorsement contracts for their clients, the overall value derived from any such deals is negligible for the average player. While no concrete data exists, Forbes estimates that average professional players may make an additional one or two per cent maximum of their overall contract in endorsement earnings, and their agents earn just 20 per cent to 25 per cent maximum of that.

12 In football, a bung is essentially a payment undeclared for tax purposes made to a club official by a player agent or intermediary to facilitate completion of a transfer deal.

13 Tapping up is an attempt in professional sports to persuade a player contracted to a club to transfer to another club, without informing the player's current club. This approach is usually made with the help of the player's agent. In several leagues, this practice is expressly forbidden.

14 DSI is the only investment fund which has a website, makes its business public, declares it to national and international regulators, and is registered in the various leagues in which it operates. DSI operates in two different ways: the first is providing traditional loans to football clubs in the same way that banks operate, so they can meet their financial obligations and treasury needs; and the second, known as Third Party Investment, provides loans for clubs to acquire the talent they need to build a successful team that can compete. In DSI contracts, control over whether a player is transferred lies entirely with the club, and the ultimate decision lies with the player himself. As stated, DSI short term objectives are to continue to boost marketing and image rights and to further enhance a presence in the Netherlands, Belgium, Italy and Germany, increasingly working as an important available service for clubs.

15 Some agents, such as Stéphane Courbis and Jeannot Werth, are domiciled abroad and other agents such as Yvan Le Mee and Fabrice Picot did not provide their personal accounts.

Bibliography

AGCM (2006). *Indagine Conoscitiva sul Settore del Calcio Professionistico*. Roma: Autoritá Garante della Concorrenza e del Mercato.

Barry, C. (2009) Formation sells showbiz and sports division in £20m deal. *Business Desk* [online]. Available from: www.thebusinessdesk.com/northwest/news/14862-formation-sells-showbiz-and-sports-divisions-in-20m-deal.html [accessed 13 February 2012].

Belzer, J. (2015) The world's most valuable sport agencies 2015. *Forbes* [online]. Available from: www.forbes.com/sites/jasonbelzer/2015/09/23/the-worlds-most-valuable-sports-agencies-2015/ [accessed 10 December 2015].

Berenger, J. (2012) Acces a l'activite d'agent sportif. In: Karaquillo, J. P. and Lagarde, F. (eds) *Agent Sportif.* CDES: Limoges: 19–29.

Buschmann, R. (2015) Bundesliga: Spielerberater kassieren mehr als 100 Millionen Euro. *Spiegel* [online]. Available from: www.spiegel.de/sport/fussball/bundesliga-spielerberater-kassieren-mehr-als-100-millionen-euro-a-1011123.html [accessed 20 November 2015].

CIES (2015) Big-5 data. *CIES football observatory* [online]. Available from: www.football-observatory.com/Indicators [accessed 20 December 2015]

Deloitte (2015) *Deloitte annual review of football finance, 24th Edition*. Manchester: Deloitte.

Dietl, H. M. and Franck, E. (2007) Governance failure and financial crisis in German football. *Journal of Sports Economics*. 8(6), pp. 662–669.

Diouf, P. and Boniface, P. (2009) *De but en blanc*. Paris: Hachette Litteratures.

Douglas, M. (2014) Has the va-va gone from Newcastle United's relationship with French players? *Chronicle Live* [online]. Available from: www.chroniclelive.co.uk/sport/football/football-news/va-va-voom-gone-newcastle-uniteds-7977887 [accessed 1 December 2015].

Dupré, R. (2014) Football: Jorge Mendes, un infiltré à la conquête de la Ligue 1. *Le Monde* [online]. Available from: www.lemonde.fr/sport/article/2013/08/08/l-infiltre_3459198_3242.html [accessed 25 November 2015].

ECA (2014) Study on transfer system in Europe. *ECA* [online]. Available from: www.ecaeurope.com/Research/Study%20on%20the%20Transfer%20System%20in%20Europe/ECA%20Study%20on%20Transfer%20System%20in%20Europe_WEB%20version.pdf [accessed 15 January 2015].

El Mundo (2015) Objetivo: 1500 milliones para el fútbol. *El Mundo* [online]. Available from: www.elmundo.es/deportes/2015/04/30/554262b3ca4741a87a8b4572.html [accessed 29 November 2015].

Ellen, L. (2007) Football agents: A critique of the Football Association's new regulations. *Sport and the Law Journal*. 15(3), pp. 18–25.

EuroActiv.com (2013) Brussels will investigate Barça, Real Madrid over illegal stat aid. *EuroActiv* [online]. Available from: www.euractiv.com/video/brussels-will-investigate-barca-real-madrid-over-illegal-state-aid-307380 [accessed 20 January 2014].

FA (2008) *Money laundering and the proceeds of crime act: Guidance for football clubs*. London: FA.

Ferrari, L. (2007) Italy. In: Siekman, R. C. R., Parrish, R., Martins, R. B. and Soek, J. (eds) *Players' agents worldwide: Legal aspects*. The Hague: T. M. C. Asser Press, pp. 309–335.

FIFA TMS (2014) *Global transfer market report 2014*. Zurich: FIFA.

FIFA TMS (2015) *Global transfer market report 2015*. Zurich: FIFA.

France Football (2013) Transferts. La guerre des agents est déclarée, France Football, 29 October.

Frenkiel, S. (2014) *Une histoire des agents sportifs en France: Les imprésarios du football (1979–2014)*. Neuchâtel: Editions CIES.

Gardiner, S. (2006) Football bungs and brown paper bungs revisited. *Sport and the Law Journal*. 14(3), pp. 6–10.

Guardian (2007a) Key findings from the Stevens report. *Guardian* [online]. Available from: www.theguardian.com/football/2007/jun/15/newsstory.sport2 [accessed 20 February 2014].

Guardian (2007b) Stevens names and shames 17 transfers in bungs inquiry. *Guardian* [online]. Available from: www.theguardian.com/football/2007/jun/15/newsstory.bolton wanderers [accessed 20 February 2014].

Hamil, S., Morrow, S., Idle, C., Rossi, G. and Faccendini, S. (2010) The governance and regulation of Italian football. *Soccer & Society*. 11(4), pp. 373–413.

Hesse, U. (2013) Learning to press: The tactical revolution that led to the transformation of the German game. *The Blizzard – The Football Quarterly*. 11.

KEA and CDES (2013) The economics and legal aspects of transfer of players. Brussels: Sport EC.

KEA, CDES and EOSE (2009) *Study on sport agents in the European Union*. Brussels: Sport EC.

Lagoutte, A. (2011) Bernès, l'agent double. *Football* [online]. Available from: www.football.fr/mag/articles/bernes-l-agent-double-60098/ [accessed 23 March 2013].

Le Figaro (2009) Retour a la case prison pour Rolland Courbis. *Le Figaro* [online]. Available at: www.lefigaro.fr/actualite-france/2009/09/20/01016-20090920ARTFIG00024-rolland-courbis-va-retourner-en-prison-.php [accessed 15 March 2012].

Le Monde (2009) Le PSG et Nike renvoyés en correctionnelle dans l'affaires des transferts fraudoleux. *Le Monde* [online]. Available from: www.lemonde.fr/sport/article/2009/11/02/le-psg-et-nike-renvoyes-en-proces-dans-l-affaire-des-transferts-frauduleux_1261434_3242.html [accessed 23 March 2013].

Legion (2013) Legion announce the launch of Legion Football Advisory. *Legion* [online]. Available from: www.legionworldwide.com/news/legion-announce-the-launch-of-legion-football-advisory/+&cd=1&hl=it&ct=clnk&gl=uk [accessed 23 January 2014].

LFP (2015a) Las ligas española y portuguesa denuncian ante la Comisión Europea la prohibición de los TPO de la FIFA. *LFP* [online]. Available from: www.laliga.es/noticias/las-ligas-espanola-y-portuguesa-denuncian-ante-la-comision-europea-la-prohibicion-de-los-tpo-de-la-fifa [accessed 15 November 2015].

LFP (2015b) Le bilan du mercato estival. *LFP* [online]. Available from: www.lfp.fr/corporate/article/le-bilan-du-mercato-estival-2015-2016.htm [accessed 15 November 2015].

LFP and DNCG (2012) Situation du football professional: Saison 2011/12. *LFP* [online]. Available from: www.lfp.fr/dncg/rapport_annuel_2011_2012/1112_rapport_dncg_all.pdf [accessed 10 March 2010].

Long, M. (2013) Wasserman expands European soccer practices. *SportsPro* [online]. Available from: www.sportspromedia.com/movers_and_shakers/wasserman_expands_european_soccer_practice [accessed 25 May 2015].

Peck, T. (2014) English tickets prices in Germany would led to 'a s***storm', claims Bundesliga CEO Seifert. *Independent* [online]. Available from: www.independent.co.

uk/sport/football/news-and-comment/english-ticket-prices-in-germany-would-lead-to-a-sstorm-claims-bundesliga-ceo-christian-seifert-9667352.html [accessed 15 November 2015].

Price, L. (2015) *Bundesliga blueprint: How Germany became the home of football.* Oakmoor: Bennion Kearny Editions.

Psotta, K. (2015) *Der paten der Liga: Spielerberater und ihre Geschäfte.* Munich: Piper.

Russo, P. (2014) *Gol di rapina: il lato oscuro del calcio globale.* Firenze: Edizioni Clichy.

Stoke City (2012) City appoint technical director. *Stoke City* [online]. Available from: www.stokecityfc.com/news/article/technical-director-536547.aspx [accessed 20 March 2013].

Szymanski, S. (2015) *Money and soccer: A soccernomics guide.* New York: Nation Books.

Tanguy, G. (2014) Le palmarès des plus gros agents du foot. *Capital* [online]. Available from: www.capital.fr/a-la-une/actualites/le-palmares-des-plus-gros-agents-du-foot-994584 [accessed 25 January 2015].

Torres, L. (2015) The Spanish TV rights distribution system after the Royal decree: An introduction. *Asser International Sports Law Blog* [online]. Available from: www.asser.nl/SportsLaw/Blog/post/the-spanish-tv-rights-distribution-system-after-the-royal-decree-an-introduction-by-luis-torres [accessed 25 October 2015].

WMG (2013) Wasserman expands football division. *WMG* [online]. Available from: www.wmgllc.com/wasserman-expands-football-division/ [accessed 25 May 2015].

WMG (2014) Wasserman acquires Dutch football agency Sport-Promotion. *WMG* [online]. Available from: www.wmgllc.com/wasserman-acquires-football-agency-sport-promotion/ [accessed 25 May 2015].

5 The historical evolution of player agents' regulations by FIFA

Overview

The question of player agent regulation is relatively new and, for a long time, the profession operated without specific supervision as, prior to the 1980s, for most players the services of an agent were not required and where they were employed, a form of self-regulation took over. However, as agents became more popular and the sums of money at stake for players and clubs in transfer negotiations increased, so did the role for agents and, in tandem, the potential to operate in self-interest. As agents' fees increased, the level of distrust increased and rules were introduced in response to calls from agents themselves who sought to professionalise their industry and from governing bodies who sought to curb their activities. In football, regulation of players' agents has been rather challenging for FIFA, whose rules, as a result, were only adopted in 1994 and have undergone various amendments over the last two decades before being withdrawn completely in 2015 in favour of regulating the activities of players and clubs in relation to transfers instead.

This chapter aims to identify and review the regulatory changes which have occurred in recent decades and consider specifically how these changes affected the profession of football agents. To do so, the principles of agency theory are first outlined to demonstrate the need for some regulation. In line with this, the legal framework of sports agent regulations within the EU is presented and analysed to highlight the different levels of regulation. Then, the original regulations of FIFA are illustrated within the wider structure of football governance that underpinned the development of the licence-based regulatory framework by FIFA. Hence, we analyse the impact of the EU's single market approach to regulations in the context of EU sport policy. Finally, we conclude by presenting problems in the activities of players' agents, raising questions as to the effectiveness of the regulations, and the new regulatory framework based on the concept of FIFA intermediaries is briefly introduced.

5.1 The principal-agency theory for the market of sports agents

Agency theory is central to the necessity of regulating and monitoring the profession of football agents and intermediaries (Mason and Slack, 2001a, 2001b). At a very basic level, it applies to situations where a principal hires an agent to do a job the principal is unable or unwilling to do; i.e. the agent acts on behalf of the principal. The theory helps to determine the optimum incentive relationship between the principal and the agent so that both parties are satisfied. In the context of football, a number of principal-agent relationships exist within the matrix of contracting relationships that comprise the industry, as players acquire the services of an agent to perform various duties. Typically, we can think of a player as being the principal who hires an agent or intermediary to secure him the best job offer or possible transfer (Holt *et al.*, 2006).

Agency theory is concerned with self-interest within the context of principal-agent relationships and relies on two basic assumptions: bounded rationality and opportunism (Barney and Hesterly, 1996). While bounded rationality assumes that individuals are unable to have complete information about all situations and circumstances, opportunism identifies the possibility of actors acting in self-interest. Because of the presence of bounded rationality, the principal cannot completely monitor the behaviour, abilities and effort of the agent, which therefore provides the opportunity for the agent to act against the principal's interests without detection (Nilakant and Rao, 1994). As such, agents' opportunism in this setting is always present. The focus of agency theory is concerned with the means through which principals can lessen the opportunity that agents have to act in ways detrimental to the interests of the principal (Eisenhardt, 1989).

In football, when a player hires an agent to represent him, both want to maximise their own objective function, i.e. their profit or utility. When the goals of players and agents are not perfectly aligned, the agent may pursue his own goals at the expense of the player. This misalignment, supported by the assumptions of bounded rationality and opportunism, can respectively lead to two improper market behaviours: adverse selection and moral hazard. Both behaviours generate inefficiencies and failures in the labour and transfer market for athletes.

Adverse selection occurs where the agent misleads the principal by overestimating his or her level of competence or training; the principal thus contracts with an agent who might not be capable of performing the services needed (Greenwald, 1986). This implies asymmetric information between the principal and the agent must exist. In a classic football scenario, the player has imperfect information about the activities of the agent and the wages paid to other players of comparable skills and experience. Additionally, the agent has more knowledge about the bargaining process and the market conditions, because of his experience in other negotiations, and he is also more aware of his own efforts and behaviour. It is this knowledge that potentially allows the agent to act in self-interest, at the player's expense, while working on the player's behalf. Moral hazard implies that the agent behaves not fully in the interest of the principal since the principal cannot perfectly observe the effort of the agent (Holmstrom, 1979). This means that the player cannot completely monitor and/or evaluate the agent's efforts. For example, a sports agent can make a quick deal with a club, which is more beneficial for him than for the player.

When these market behaviours occur, agency problems arise, and the agency costs and solutions they incur become the focus of agency theory (White, 1992). These costs are the resources spent and are usually associated with designing, implementing and evaluating contracts and/or governance mechanisms (McGuire, 1988). Thus, agency theory has practical value in identifying courses of action that ideally reduce market inefficiencies by suggesting more cost-effective means of controlling agents' behaviour. In sport, to overcome these problems, the player has to give the right incentives to the agent. When an athlete has a sports agent, it is important to keep in mind that the sports agent has to do what the athlete wants. An agent has to prioritise the business affairs of his principal, not his own. However, an agent also needs to build a working relationship with the club he is negotiating with since there is the potential for him to deal with them in future for other players. According to Smienk (2009), there is a three-way relationship in this case as clubs also need agents, both to contract a particular player when the agent acts as a gate-keeper and potentially to attract other players on their behalf in the future. Agents are therefore able to extract fees from clubs as a result of the strategic competition between clubs to sign players and the fact that agents can play a gate-keeping role. This role induces clubs to pay fees because they recognise that other clubs have an incentive to pay fees to agents in order to sign players (Holt *et al.*, 2006). The three parties in the beginning of the process have different interests but, by using the right incentives, the conflict between the sports agent and the athlete can be mitigated (Smienk, 2009). Clubs can also try to realign the interests of an agent and an athlete in order to get a lower salary in future contract negotiations in the clubs' interests. Clubs could reward sports agents, when they act in their interest and not in the interest of their principal. As Smienk (2009) argues, the three-way relationship between the clubs, the sports agents and the athletes is very complex and it cannot be said who has a more powerful position in the relationship.

To minimise agency problems and costs, two types of controls are available (Eisenhard, 1989): monitoring mechanisms and performance-contingent contracts. Monitoring mechanisms provide information regarding the qualifications and conduct of agents. In doing so, they decrease the information asymmetry that favours the agent by allowing the player to know more about the agent's abilities efforts and performance. In this context, the principal is less likely to contract with an unqualified agent if he performs background checks or seeks recommendations from other players, for example; and the agent, who deliberately attempts to act opportunistically, has less incentive to do so for fear of being detected or punished (Mason and Slack, 2001a). Various sports industry stakeholders from players' associations to international sporting federations have been involved in creating monitoring mechanisms to more closely regulate and control agent behaviour. Where it is difficult to assess agents' behaviour or knowledge, the use of a performance-contingent compensation system is most appropriate, as the agent's compensation is contingent on his or her performance (Eisenhardt, 1989). Quite simply, it typically provides an effective deterrent by increasing the agent's reward on the basis of increasing the principal's reward. In this respect, player agents have traditionally charged the player a percentage of the player's contract in order to negotiate both playing and endorsement deals (Greenberg, 1993). This tends to align the interests of player and agent. These two solutions to agency problems are highly interrelated and the different combinations of their application can have different results in solving the agency theory problems (Mason and Slack, 2001a).

A number of safeguards that pertain to the contract between players and their agents and possible solutions for market failure are already in place in most sports. These include mechanisms of reputation, supervision by the players' unions, national and international governing bodies, and legal remedies that are all included in a regulatory framework. As White (2007) argues, the appropriate level of agents' regulation is a vexed issue. However, despite the prevalence of these solutions in the professional industry, there have still been widespread examples of abuse. Player agents' malpractice has always been highly reported in both academic and trade journals. Clearly, a major concern is to ensure that sport is seen to be as 'clean' as possible and, in this regard, the more safeguards that can be put in place the better. Furthermore, acting as a player agent brings employment regulations into play with specific duties, which agents must observe and which governing bodies must consider in their own regulations.

International and national governing bodies have implemented mechanisms and systems that improve the transparency of financial dealings and transactions within the transfer markets against abusive, elusive, and fraudulent practices that threaten the fairness and competitive balance of competition. By spending on players without controls or limits, clubs' financial instability has become the biggest threat to the stability of players' contracts. Consequently, financial malpractice and excessive transfer fees and wages in particular are causing alarm amongst supporters, the general public and public authorities. Monitoring systems track transfer market operations and control their validity as does the enforcement of transfer rules, notably registration periods and the protection of minors, as well as the payment of financial compensation. In 2010, FIFA introduced the transfer matching system, TMS, which is designed to regulate the international transfers of professional players.

Case study: FIFA TMS

A decision to replace the old procedure for registering transfers based on agreements signed on paper with an online system was taken at the FIFA Congress in 2007 (FIFA, 2010). The tool TMS was developed and tested over the next three and a half years, with training given to FIFA member associations and to clubs. It came into effect on Friday 1 October 2010 with the aim of making international transfers more transparent and protecting minors, based on the fact that fraud is very difficult to carry out online and this guarantees transparency. Initially, the system was designed to regulate the international transfers of male professional footballers and later it was extended to cover so-called 'domestic' transfers, i.e. those between clubs of the same association.

The TMS has a dedicated compliance and monitoring team plus a number of additional tools that oversee each transfer. The system is composed of four independent and interconnected systems: the International Transfer Matching System, ITMS; the Domestic Transfer Matching System, DTMS; the Global Player Exchange, GPX; and the Intermediary Regulations Tool, IRT.

The ITMS is the first original and mandatory online application, used by over 6,500 professional football clubs and 209 member associations worldwide to transfer professional players internationally (FIFA TMS, 2015a). In order for a transfer to be validated the two clubs involved must enter the relevant information on the deal. Member associations must keep all information relating to the league season in question up to date, as well as information on player registrations, clubs and agents.

The following information must be given (FIFA, 2010): the names of the clubs, the member associations, player details (date of birth, nationality, first last and middle names), type of transfer (permanent, loan, exchange), possible commission payments, the total transfer fee, details of any training compensation or solidarity contributions, payment deadlines (of which there may be one or more), the payment schedule (including dates, amounts paid and recipients) and details of payments already made (including information on the paying bank, the payee bank, the amount paid, the date of payment and the recipient).

As well as the information above, clubs and associations are required to upload a series of documents to the system as follows (FIFA, 2010): documents providing proof of nationality and the correct spelling of the name and age of the player; a copy of the player's new contract of employment, a copy of the transfer agreement and proof of payments. Prior to forwarding information, clubs are required to tick a box confirming that no third parties are involved in the transaction. Each club and association has its own system account and this allows the TMS teams to view the information they provide immediately, enabling them to identify each party involved along with any irregularities.

Based on this information, member associations use the system to request and deliver international transfer certificates, ITCs, electronically. The ITC allows the association to which the player is transferring to register him, so that he can participate in official matches for his new club.

The DTMS is an online platform modelled on and fully integrated with the ITMS (FIFA TMS, 2015b). It works with one single sign-on and was developed following feedback from numerous national football associations and clubs expressing the need for a domestic transfer system based on ITMS. The Dutch association, KNVB, was the first member association to start using DTMS. The KNVB and its clubs manage and monitor their domestic transfer activity, generate statistics and reports, communicate more efficiently to speed up the transfer process and store required documents online, safely and securely. Moreover, as an extension of ITMS, the system allows the KNVB to access international and domestic transfers in one place.

The GPX was launched in 2015. It provides a direct and discreet channel for secure and intimate stakeholder communication across the entire global professional football network (FIFA TMS, 2015c). The platform offers the most comprehensive player profile database on the market, giving clubs market access as well as pre-transfer functionalities to improve their reach, competitiveness and decision-making. In these terms, GPX widens the scope of player employment opportunities at the national and international level as well as allowing clubs and stakeholders to build their professional identity.

Finally, the IRT is designed to assist member associations to meet their regulatory obligations, as set out in the intermediaries' regulations known as FIFA RWI (FIFA TMS, 2015d). The IRT is integrated with the ITMS and the DTMS so that professional player transfers and related intermediary involvement can be managed in one system. The information to be submitted includes: all agreed remunerations or payments that have been made or are to be made to an intermediary, the intermediary declaration, the representation contract, and the necessary consents and declarations about conflict of interest for all involved intermediaries as defined by the FIFA RWI.

National federations and confederations are also taking steps to develop monitoring of national transfers (KEA and CDES, 2013). Before the implementation of the FIFA TMS at international level, some national associations had already established monitoring schemes for national transfers. Table 5.1 maps the different initiatives and their scope.

The scope and the extent of monitoring differ between the analysed countries. France and Germany were the first to implement their domestic licensing model, considered as the most sophisticated mechanisms to control clubs' finances. However, it is possible to see heterogeneity amongst the monitoring mechanisms which differ in their scopes and purposes country by country.

In relation to the activities of agents in particular, the clearing house system in place in England, which has been set up between the PL and the FL, guarantees the transparency of payments related to players' transfers between clubs by controlling financial flows. Specifically, it gathers data on every aspect of transfers, such as the fees payable to each party including agents' commissions. With information entered by both the buying and selling clubs, a transfer certificate is only issued when all of the information input by both clubs matches. Thus, the monitoring concerns the destination of funds and verifies the consistency of the amounts reported with the information contained in the transfer contract.

In practice, in a player's transfer, the transfer fee is paid through the intermediary of the leagues in question. The buying club pays the amount into a bank account identified by the league that is then responsible for re-allocating this to the selling club. In the case of a default payment, the league can execute compensation either on other payments or on an outgoing domestic transfer made by this club. If it is not possible to execute either of these solutions the league has the ability to impose various sanctions, including a transfer embargo, fines and payment of default interest.

Table 5.1 National specificities on monitoring domestic transfers of football players

	England	France	Germany	Italy	Spain
Countries that monitor transfer	Yes	Yes	Yes	Yes	Yes
Scope of the monitoring (if it exists) — *Transfer fees*	Yes	Yes	No	N/A	No
Contracts	Yes	Yes	Yes	Yes	Yes
Payments related to contracts	Yes	No	Yes	N/A	No
Commissions paid to agents	Yes	Yes	Yes	N/A	No
Names of clubs and players	Yes	Yes	Yes	Yes	Yes
Purpose of the monitoring (if it exists)	Registration of Players Clearing house system.	Registration of Players Financial Control of Clubs.	Registration of Players Financial Control of Clubs.	Registration of Players Financial Control of Clubs.	Transfers are always stamped, monitored and, where appropriate, approved by the Department of Licenses and the Register of RFEF.

Source: adapted from KEA and CIDES (2013).

A 5 per cent tax on the amount of each transfer is collected to cover administrative expenses. A player's registration is completed only after the buying club pays the first installment of the transfer fee. In case of any dispute, an independent arbitration tribunal is set up. The FA is in charge of monitoring incoming international transfers whose transfer fees are paid by the English clubs and has two objectives: supervision of the consistency of the periodic payments, as agreed in the transfer contract, and control of the destination of the paid amounts. Moreover, the FA monitors and transfers the commissions paid to agents through the clearing house, after having verified the consistency of the amount paid with the remuneration contained in the contract and also the information provided on the recipient.

In France, in June 2013 a committee of 20 members from the world of football and politics was formed to produce a report on building a sustainable model for French football (Sports.gouv.fr, 2014). Six months later, on January 2014, the Glavany report was submitted to the Ministry of Sport with nine proposals to reform football in France. In particular, proposal N.4 recommends the strengthening of the regulation of the transfer market and the supervision of the activity of agents. Hence, to regulate financial flows related to player transfers, the commission issued two actions: the set-up of a clearing house following the model provided by English football and the reform of the models of agents' remuneration.

5.2 The legal framework of agents' regulation: the European case

The regulation of sports agents has a dual nature, falling under the jurisdiction of both state and sporting governing bodies (KEA *et al.*, 2009). As a consequence, both governments and (international and/or national) sport federations have become embroiled in the regulatory process. While state authorities seek to legalise the activities of sports agents, sports federations have typically controlled any activity which can have a direct impact on their members and hence on the proper functioning of competitions and their public image. It is therefore unsurprising that there are a large number of requirements applying to sports agents which derive from the *lex sportiva* of national and international federations. As Pinna (2006) argues, the legal obligations generated by both orders do not always coincide and at times in fact collide. In this way, there are, in effect, three tiers of agent regulation: international law, national law and the law of sport bodies. From an international perspective, therefore, the hierarchy of laws always has to be taken into consideration: International Treaties and EU law prevail over national law; national law prevails over rules made by sports associations Martins (2007).

In legal terms, the profession of sports agent can be defined as a private job placement activity whereby agencies are involved in employment intermediation services (Hendrickx, 2007). Until 1997, according to ILO Convention N.96 of July 1949, job placement was considered a duty of public authorities and private employment intermediation was prohibited. It was only in June 1997 that the ILO recognised – by means of Convention C181 – that profit-driven private employment agencies could legitimately operate in the labour market. Whilst labour market liberalisation has been a theme in many states, particularly within the EU, where the principles of the single market are influential, some countries are still reluctant to cede control in this field. In most EU member states, sports agents essentially provide services as intermediaries between sportspersons and clubs through an employment contract and they are affected by the regulations concerning private job placement. In these countries, the activities of sports agents are regarded, essentially, as exceptions to the public monopoly on employment services, but they are subject to the more or less stringent rules applicable to private employment agencies. It is apparent, however, that these general regulations on private employment agencies are, in practice, difficult to apply to sports agents, particularly because, often, sports agents are completely unaware that such regulations apply to them or because of the difficulty of pre-cisely defining activities – such as the procurement and negotiation of endorse-ment deals for a player or assistance with day to day administrative matters – that are not regulated by the sports authorities (White, 2007). One of the central concepts of the Convention is laid down in Article 7, where it is provided that private employment agencies shall not charge directly or indirectly, in whole or in part, any fees or costs to workers, although exceptions are formu-lated (Hendrickx, 2007).

In this legal context, Shropshire (1992) and Martins (2007) distinguish between interventionist systems and non-interventionist systems. The interven-tionist legal system applies to member states which have introduced one or more public sport laws to regulate their sport sector (Martins, 2007). Sports governing bodies are autonomous, but their autonomy is based on the sports laws enacted as semi-public laws due to a 'trickle-down' mandate issued by the public legis-lative authority. It is possible that a specific sports law is in force and serves as a legal basis for the official regulation of the profession of sports/players' agents. Such a formal sports law is only present in the EU member states that embrace an interventionist system. Many states, through general statutory interventions or common laws such as contract law, regulate agency work while others have established a sport specific statutory basis for agent regulation. Consequently, there is a wide pattern of regulation through national laws which govern both the exercise of agent activities and also access to the profession. France has been the one of the leaders in this respect, having adopted legislation governing the profession of sports agent in 1992 which runs parallel to the regulations of gov-erning bodies (Verheyden, 2007). Across the EU, there are vast differences in how the industry is regulated. Some states require agents to pass a state licence to undertake their duties whilst others do not. In circumstances in which the state requires a licence, this raises the prospect of agents requiring two licences, one issued by the state, and the other by the sports association (Parrish, 2007). A non-interventionist system, in contrast, is characterised by a high degree of self-regulation by sport governing bodies and a lack of legislation in the field of sport from the state. Within this system the regulations of associations are considered as 'association law' and national legislation prevails over their rules if there is ever a conflict; so if public law regulates a certain situation in sport which is also regulated by association law, then the association regulations are formally not binding for those to whom they are addressed.

The pattern of transposition has been varied and conflicts and inconsistencies remain applicable to players' agents, causing incoherence and uncertainty in the application of the regulations that directly affect the effectiveness of the system (Martins, 2009a). As White (2007) argues, any football association must ensure that football is clear about and fully in compliance with applicable employment agency regulations. This is crucial as clubs should not be overly constrained in terms of their ability to do deals and to trade in players. Due to the influence of player agents in the transfer market, if an agent finds it harder to operate in a particular territory, he is likely to focus on other markets where it is easier for him to do deals and secure the commission he seeks. The regulators must therefore be wary of creating a regulatory regime which impacts on teams' ability to attract the best players. Moreover, of course, football governing bodies want to ensure that their regulations are legal and resist challenges from parties affected by them, particularly on the grounds of restraint of trade. So while, generally, the courts are reluctant to interfere in the sporting regulatory process, they are not immune from legal challenge. Whilst 'cleaning up' the game is often the publicly stated ambition of regulators, ensuring the market works effectively for the stakeholders in it is often the real aim. Rules therefore often do not reflect industry norms and thus have a tendency to be breached and/or not enforced. As Parrish (2007) illustrates, in the UK this tension was clear when considering the approach to the agents' regulation adopted by the two professional leagues; the FL covering the Championship, League One and League Two actively embraced agent regulation whilst the PL, perhaps fearful of damaging its chances of attracting top quality overseas players, resisted greater controls.

5.3 The original FIFA regulations: establishing the regulatory framework based on licensing

The first FIFA regulations on players' agents adopted a licensing-based framework and they need to be contextualised within the wider football governance structure, which establishes a single governing body for each national territory, a single confederation in each continent and a single worldwide federation (Holt, 2007). With a hierarchical competency to regulate football, FIFA makes the rules at international level and ensures their applicability at all levels through a membership mechanism that also creates contractual chains for jurisdictional competency to sanction any regulatory breach. The national associations and the continental federations are FIFA members and they agree to comply with its internationally applicable rules and regulations as well as enforcing them within their territory. On the other hand, clubs and players are not formally FIFA members, albeit that clubs generally agree to abide by rules and regulations, whilst playing contracts incorporate provisions compelling players to comply with them. The integration of all participants as stakeholders through one framework based on a vertical hierarchy ensures that FIFA, continental federations and the national associations monopolise the regulation and organisation of football. This breakdown of responsibility also applies to the regulation of players' agents (Holt, 2007). As the global governing body, FIFA is the organisation that sets the guideline regulations on agents. The national associations then use the FIFA regulations to inform their own individual set of rules, and they are obliged to draw up their own regulations based on the FIFA regulations and requirements. Despite the existence of continental confederations, there is no regulation at a continental level. The transposition of the FIFA regulations into the rules of the national associations aims to achieve a coherent application worldwide. National associations then have jurisdiction over transfers between their member clubs while FIFA have jurisdiction in respect of transfers of players between associations.

Within this framework, on 20 May 1994, the FIFA Executive Committee adopted the first regulatory licensing system to govern the profession of player agents in order to bring them under the realm of the governance structure. The integration of agents into the FIFA framework meant that agents were considered 'participants' in the game, and as such must in theory adhere to the rules and regulations of football's governing bodies (Holt *et al.*, 2006). Effectively, player agents had to enter into contractual agreements with governing bodies through the grant of a licence allowing the imposition of regulatory obligations. FIFA adopted the regulations setting out principles determining how a licensed player agent should operate and required the national associations to adopt their own regulations incorporating those principles. The candidates who did not satisfy certain criteria or who were not prepared to comply with FIFA's and the national associations' regulations on player agents were not allowed to obtain a licence and the validity of any licence was subject to continuous compliance with the regulations in place.

Under this system, which was amended on 11 December 1995 and came in to force on 1 January 1996, the exercise of this profession was subject to obtaining a licence, and clubs and players were obliged only to use licensed players' agents during transfers and contract negotiations. While the licence was to be issued either by FIFA for all types of transfers or by the national associations for domestic transfers, agents were named as FIFA licensed agents. The profession was reserved for natural persons only and legal persons, such as companies and organisations, were not admissible. Players' relatives and qualified lawyers, legally authorised in compliance with the rules in force in their country of domicile, were defined as exempt individuals with a right to exercise the profession without licence (FIFA, 1994: Article 1). To obtain the licence, the candidates had to attend an interview to ascertain their level of knowledge relating to football regulations and civil law and they also had to meet certain criteria, including not having any criminal record or bad reputation (FIFA, 1994: Articles 2 and 3). The competent national associations then decided the admissibility of the candidate into the profession. If there were no objections to the grant of the licence, as a next step, the candidate had to deposit a bank guarantee of 200,000 Swiss francs (FIFA, 1994: Article 9). Upon receipt of the bank guarantee FIFA issued a licence that was personal and non-transferable (FIFA, 1994: Article 11).

The first regulations also provided provisions governing the relationship of licensed players' agents with their principles, i.e. players or clubs, and laid out sanctions for regulatory breaches. A licensed player agent had the right to contract with any player not contracted to clubs or to represent the interest of any player or club requesting him to negotiate or/and conclude contracts on his/its behalf. Player agents were required to enter into a written representation contract to exercise these rights which could not run for more than a maximum period of two years before it needed to be renewed (FIFA, 1994: Article 13). In the case of infringement of the regulations, licensed agents could be subject to a number of sanctions, including a fine and the withdrawal of the licence (FIFA, 1994: Article 15). Clubs and players were prohibited from using the services of unlicensed agents and could also be liable to sanctions such as; disciplinary suspensions for players and a ban on all national and international footballing activity for the clubs (FIFA, 1994: Article 16, 17, 18 and 19). The Players' Status Committee was the designated body within FIFA for the supervision of the regulations.

5.4 The transformation of the governance structure and the amendments of the original FIFA regulations

The decision by FIFA to regulate the activities of players' agents also coincided with some important developments that were to eventually become catalysts for the transformation of the governance structure in football. Since the early 1990s, the changing media landscape had brought the traditional hierarchical nature of the governance structure under pressure. Increased media involvement had also significantly contributed to the increased commodification of football and, as a result, clubs and leagues sought greater autonomy to exploit their market power and emerged as powerful stakeholders, contesting their lack of participation in the governance structure (Boyes, 2000; Holt, 2007).

In the discourse of transformation of football governance, the EU became a key terrain in which the stakeholders challenged the decisions of governing bodies. The commercialisation and commodification of football ran parallel to the completion of the EU's Single European Market project and the EU sought to oversee all commercial entities respecting the economic basis of the Union. The EU was particularly concerned with the rules and regulations of governing bodies interfering with competition and free movement rules. On the basis of their remit as the single market regulator of sport, the EC and the ECJ dealt with a significant number of cases resulting from the EU's internal market competences (Parrish, 2003). In particular, the Directorate-General for Competition took the view that the organisation and operation of sport might have fallen within the scope of EU competition law and there were significant numbers of complaints to the Commission in the form of private rights actions (as this was a cheaper and easier option) against governing bodies for acting in an anti-competitive manner (Foster, 2000). In this respect, the Directorate-General examined various aspects of football, including the applicability of revised transfer rules following the Bosman ruling, ticketing arrangements for major international football events and broadcast rights (Parrish, 2000). The result of this on-going battle was that the EU established a supervisory role, offering governing bodies a degree of supervised authority in exchange for greater stakeholder representation within the governance structure (Garcia, 2009).

It was in this context that the authority of FIFA to regulate players' agents and the compatibility of its original regulations with the EU law came under scrutiny, first before the Commission and then before the CFI. On 20 February 1996, Multiplayers International Denmark lodged a complaint to the Commission alleging that the regulations were contrary to Articles 101 and 102 of the TFEU, formerly Articles 81 and 82 of the EC Treaty. French national, Laurent Piau,[1] submitted another complaint on 23 March 1998. In his complaint, Mr. Piau alleged that the original regulations by FIFA were contrary to the provisions of the EU's free movement rules related to services, in particular Article 59 TFEU, formerly Article 49 of EC Treaty. The challenge was based first on the fact that opaque examination procedures, the requirement for a bank guarantee, and controls and sanctions imposed under the regulations constituted restrictions on access to the profession and second, on the fact that no legal remedy was available against the decisions of governing bodies or against the sanctions imposed under the regulations (Martins, 2007). Finally, he also questioned the discriminatory nature of the regulations between citizens of different member states.

As a result of these complaints, the EC examined the FIFA regulations and sent a statement of objections to the governing body on 19 October 1999 (Martins, 2007). The EC concluded that the FIFA regulations constituted a decision by an association of undertakings as per Article 101 TFEU. Furthermore, the EC questioned restrictions under regulations related to the licensing requirement, making it available only to natural persons, the prohibition on using unlicensed agents, and the compulsory bank guarantee requirement. In response to the objections, on 10 December 2000, FIFA adopted new regulations governing the activity of players' agents which entered into force on 1 March 2001 and were amended again on 3 April 2002. The objective of the new regulations was to remove alleged infringements of EU provisions under the original regulations. This new regulation maintained the licence obligation, as well as the exclusivity of its assurance for the benefit of natural persons and the official wording became 'Agent licensed by the respective football national association' (FIFA, 2001: Articles 1 and 2). The procedure to obtain a licence required applicants to undertake a written examination, consisting of multiple-choice questions, to assess their knowledge of law and sport and they needed to satisfy the requirement to have an impeccable reputation (FIFA 2001: Articles 2, 4 and 5). The candidates needed either to take out a professional liability insurance policy or to deposit a bank guarantee for the amount of 100,000 Swiss francs prior to the issue of the licence (FIFA 2001: Articles 6 and 7). The player agents were also required to sign a new code of conduct annexed to the regulations (FIFA 2001: Article 8). Using the services of unlicensed players' agents was still forbidden whilst player agents were prohibited to approach any player under contract with any club with a view to arranging a transfer without the consent or the knowledge of the player's current club. The written representation contract was still required in order to enter into a relationship with either club or player, and could only last two years though it could be renewed, and there was a standard contract annexed to the regulations which players' agents were required to use in their activities. The contract was to be signed by both parties in quadruple and lodged with the national association and FIFA whilst both parties also kept a copy. Under the representation contract, player agents' remuneration was to be stipulated. If the contract did not specifically state a level of remuneration it was fixed at 5 per cent of the player's basic gross salary and payable either in a lump sum or in periodic instalments (FIFA, 2001: Article 12). The previous sanctions for player agents, clubs and players remained in place (FIFA, 2001: Article 15, 17 and 19). The Players' Status Committee and the competent national association were given authority to deal with disputes (FIFA, 2001: Article 22).

Despite the changes that FIFA had made to its regulations, the legal dispute continued between the parties. The final decision was reached when the CFI initially assessed the nature of FIFA and its regulations from a competition law perspective to determine whether FIFA constituted an association of undertakings and its players' regulations a decision by an association of undertakings, in order to establish the applicability of Articles 101 and 102 TFEU to the case. On this point, the CFI recalled that, in principle, only public authorities are legitimated to regulate a profession through appropriate regulations (Martins, 2007). Although an association has the freedom to draw up rules and regulations for its internal organisation, an exemption exists only when an organisation receives a formal mandate, based upon public laws. In the case of sport, The European authorities can only grant an exemption to the regulations of a profession if such regulations could fall under the specificity of sport principle. The CFI made it clear that FIFA could not rely on the specific nature of sport to derogate from the rules of competition law (Martins, 2007). In the case of player agents' regulations, FIFA is not a public authority and had drafted its rules unilaterally. Because FIFA is an association of associations, with the national football associations as its members, its player agents' regulations covered the entire world. In other words, no international organisation composed of national public authorities, through their official and formal channel, awarded FIFA a formal mandate to regulate the profession of player agents. Hence, FIFA lacked a legal basis to issue a set of rules that controlled access to the profession of players' agent in the EU. In several cases, national formal legislation regulates the profession of sports agent and guarantees professionalism and high moral standards. The FIFA regulations created an artificial barrier for parties wishing to enter the services market as players' agents and were in breach of international law. On a global level, a specific ILO Convention exists and it offers a framework of rules for private employment agencies. The FIFA PAR were in conflict with this Convention on a crucial point: the payment of a fee to the agent by the worker is strongly prohibited in the ILO Convention; in the FIFA regulations the payment of a fee to the agent by the player is obligatory, whenever the player engages the services of an agent (Martins, 2007). The CFI concluded that FIFA held a collective, dominant position on the player agents' market but that position was not abused by FIFA. For this reason, the FIFA PAR stated that, when drawing up their regulations, the national associations had to take the statutes and regulations into account as well as their own national legislation and international treaties.

Despite FIFA lacking the public authority to regulate the profession of players' agent, the CFI argued that the rule-making action of FIFA was justified due to the fact that (Parrish, 2007; Martins, 2007):

- the type of player agent regulation adopted by FIFA was necessary in order to introduce professionalism and morality to the occupation of players' agent in order to protect players whose careers are short;
- the profession of players' agent did not have an internal organisation and certain activities of players' agents could have harmed players and clubs financially and professionally;
- there is a general lack of legislation in the Union, apart from France, governing the activities of players' agents.

As Pinna (2006) argues, whilst the pattern of agent regulation, both current and potential, varies somewhat, FIFA regulations are by no means the only form of regulation applicable to agents. This varied pattern of regulations created tensions between national law and FIFA rules, particularly over issues concerning restricting access to the profession and questions of remuneration. FIFA regulations can be thought of as international norms that take into consideration national idiosyncrasies in a federative purpose. The scope of FIFA regulations was essentially limited to the agent's role in the transfer of players from one club to another, or in the negotiation or renegotiation of a player's contract with a club, with no jurisdiction to govern any other commercial agreements.

5.5 The effectiveness of FIFA's regulatory framework: the problems and a call for alternatives

As Martins (2007) illustrates, ensuring the participation of all the relevant football authorities, apart from FIFA, was a reason for maintaining the system of licensing agents, or creating a form of regulation that is binding upon agents. In line with this view, on 29 September 2006 UEFA's CEO, Martin Olsson, expressed UEFA's views at a meeting of the Council of Europe during the Fair Play with Sport Conference, stating: 'The issue of players' agents is one of the key problems that we have to address today. We are not afraid to act against agents. What we are asking for is firm legislation on agents and their activities'

(UEFA, 2006). This statement highlighted a need for better control of agents and their activities, because of the financial sums they are handling or as a result of agents' conduct. As a result, UEFA's Professional Committee established a working group on the role of agents in Europe. On 28 and 29 November 2005 the working group produced draft recommendations for its member associations. These were divided into three categories: the first related to access to the profession, the second related to the activity of an agent and the third category was about enforcement of these rules. The extension of the use of compulsory licences is an elaboration of these categories. It was clear that UEFA sought firm regulation of the profession.

The problems associated with the activities of player agents which raised questions about the effectiveness of the FIFA players' agents regulations also led to increased calls for the EU to regulate players' agents by taking EU-level action (Martins, 2009b). For the EU, the problems generated by player agents were detrimental to the overall image of sport and its socio-cultural role within European policy and this position was highlighted in a number of policy documents. In 2006, the Independent European Sport Review, also known as the Arnaut Report (a semi-official document) originated from the UK Presidency of the European Council as a member state initiative, emphasising the necessity for a more rigorous form of regulatory enforcement in relation to problems with the activities of agents (Arnaut, 2006). The problems were pressing concerns for the efficient administration and financial well-being of football and for the image of the game. UEFA fully endorsed these findings. The European Parliament was particularly concerned with the economic reality surrounding the activities of agents. In March 2007, its report on the future of professional football in Europe, known as the Belet report and prepared by the Committee on Culture and Education of the European Parliament, underlined the necessity of improving the rules governing players' agents (Belet, 2007). The emphasis was on the immense impact a lack of clear standards for the profession was having on European football. The Parliament urged football governing bodies at all levels, in conjunction with the EC, to work towards an improved regulatory framework with strict standards and criteria. It recommended that UEFA should regulate and amend the present framework whilst, if necessary, the EC would present a proposal for a directive concerning agents in order to support the efforts of UEFA in the field. In July 2007, the EC published the White Paper on Sport that highlighted bad practices in the activities of some players' agents, such as corruption, money laundering and exploitation of minor players (EC, 2002). For the EC, these problems were undermining the image of sport in general and raising serious concern for governance. The EC also confirmed that, for all of these reasons, there had been repeated calls on the EU to regulate agents by adopting an EU legal instrument. Therefore, the EC made a commitment to undertake an impact assessment to establish a clear overview of the activities of agents in the EU, to evaluate whether EU-level action was required, and if so, to analyse different options.

In 2007, EFAA was funded to improve the image of licensed agents and to create a common ground for them in Europe (Martins, 2009b). At the end of

2008, EFAA drafted a list of ten urgent issues to be tackled by stakeholders in European football. In particular, three of them were said to deserve particular attention: the creation of a solid legal framework for the regulation of the activities of licensed agents, monitoring and banning the activities of unlicensed agents, and provision of better protection for youth players and minors. The remaining elements of the list focused on money laundering and criminal activities such as corruption and the protection of players' careers. The EC recognised the work carried out by EFAA and pushed to further strengthen the representation of agents. For this reason, EFAA was formally recognised as an official stakeholder by the EC.

Meanwhile, the new FIFA PAR came into force on 1 January 2008 following further amendments to provide more control over the activities of players' agents (FIFA, 2008). Various requirements established by the FIFA PAR 2001 still remained under the provisions of the new regulations. However, there were some significant changes. The validity of licences was limited to five years instead of running for an indefinite period and the agent had to take an exam in order to renew it. If he or she failed the exam, their licence was suspended until the examination was passed (FIFA, 2008: Article 17). The other important change was in relation to the level of remuneration. If the player and players' agent had not agreed on the level of remuneration, it was stipulated that the agent would be entitled to 3 per cent of the gross annual income of the player, whereas under the previous regulation it was 5 per cent (FIFA, 2008: Article 20). Several shortfalls were identified in the new licensing-based regulatory framework, creating regulatory deficiencies that undermined the effectiveness of whole system. Enforcement was a particular problem for FIFA and the national associations due to their restricted jurisdictional reach. Players' agents were not direct members of FIFA and the national associations and FIFA aimed to overcome the lack of a contractual link for effective enforcement by establishing the licence-based system. By using its direct contractual relationship with clubs and players, FIFA obliged them to work with licensed players' agents and aimed to create a regulatory hook for players' agents through the grant of a licence. Nevertheless, it meant that FIFA had no power regarding players' agents operating without a licence. As a result, unlicensed agents were able to operate freely in the transfer market and it was literally impossible for FIFA and the national associations to impose any disciplinary sanctions on them.

On 3 June 2009, FIFA decided to conduct in-depth reform of the licensing system through a new approach based on the concept of intermediaries in order to overcome the deficiencies of the existing regulatory system (FIFA, 2015e). The member associations of FIFA acknowledged that almost three-quarters of international transfers were organised through unlicensed agents and they sought to deregulate the profession of agents through this new approach. The reform resulted from an extensive consultation process that involving all stakeholders in football, except agents. A sub-committee was established by FIFA's Committee for Club Football with a mandate to develop the new system. The sub-committee undertook a lengthy and extensive consultation process with representatives of member associations, confederations, clubs, FIFPro and professional football leagues. The draft regulations on the concept of intermediaries were analysed by various working groups, including the Players' Status Committee and the Legal Committee. As a result, the EC commissioned an impact assessment study into the activities of sports agents to evaluate whether Community action was necessary. Despite the fragmented legal framework applicable to the activities of sports agents, the study determined that there were no major obstacles to the free provision of the services of agents across the EU. Moreover, it identified ethical issues, such as financial crimes and exploitation of young players, which do threaten the fairness of sporting competitions and the integrity of sports people. Concerns also focused on the lack of transparency of the financial flows involved and several issues related to the governance of agents in team sports and, in particular, football, should have been discussed to improve the existing system. In order to create a discussion with stakeholders about these issues and to allow FIFA to present its draft regulations the EC appointed an EC expert Group on Good Governance, consisting of representatives of FIFPro, EFAA, FIFA, UEFA, ECA and EPFL to assist the organisation of a conference in Brussels in November 2011 (FIFA, 2015e). In October 2013, after a year of assessment and interviews with stakeholders, the group recommended that the existing legal framework was appropriate and that sports stakeholders were best fitted to regulate their own activities, but that the EU could assist. Methods of supervision of sports agents should be aimed at transparency in transactions, protection of young players and creating higher standards for agents, with clear and universal rules and appropriate sanctioning systems attached. The expert group suggested that a system of training for agents should be created with national and international control on the quality of activities and it also promoted the creation of universal minimum standards that could be further adapted to the needs of every individual country or confederation.

The FIFA RWI were approved by the FIFA Executive Committee on 21 March 2014 and the sixty-fourth FIFA Congress on 11 June 2014 approved the amendments to FIFA Statutes and to the RGA of FIFA Statutes that were necessary for the implementation of new regulations (FIFA, 2015e). The new regulations came into force on 1 April 2015 in order to allow their member associations enough time to adapt to the new system. FIFA established an overarching regulatory framework for efficient control of the activity, rather than regulating access to the profession. The new framework superseded the existing regulatory framework and the licence requirement was abandoned. The framework laid down minimum standards and requirements as well as a registration system for intermediaries who represent players or clubs in the conclusion of employment contracts or transfer agreements. FIFA considers the new system to be more transparent and simple to administer and implement which they propose will result in better enforcement at national level. In essence however, there is no licence, no insurance, no agent regulation and no activity control. However, control at the end of the transfer process, through the actions of clubs and players, has been implemented and guaranteed.

5.6 Conclusions

In line with the strong support of agency theory, regulations on sports agents have never been implemented in any sport. A permanent tension between civil law and sport law has constrained the implementation of a coherent legal framework at national and international levels. This limitation has directly affected the adoption of valid and robust mechanisms of monitoring and control on sports agents' activities, no matter which sport, country and league we refer to. In football, the issue of agents' regulations has never been so popular due to the power that agents are able to have in the transfer and labour markets and the ethical issues related to player exploitation, match-fixing, financial crime and the trafficking of youth players which has put the agents' activities and their regulations high on the agenda of football governing bodies and of political and legislative institutions alike. In this context, the evolution of FIFA's regulations on players' agents has been shaped by different factors. The EU has been an important catalyst for the development of its evolutionary regulatory discourse. It became an avenue for unsatisfied stakeholders to challenge the decisions of the governing bodies and in this regard, the regulations of FIFA came under the scrutiny of EU law. Also a single market approach to sport by the EU resulted in the development of sport related case law that had a profound impact on sport. The Bosman judgment caused the transformation of labour relationships in football and revolutionised the player market within which players' agents blossomed while the problems in their activities led to FIFA questioning the efficacy of the licence-based framework.

FIFA has now opened up the market for the regulation of the activities of agents. The reasons for the regulations that have been applicable for almost 20 years are still, or maybe even more, pressing than at the time of previous regulation applicable to the sector. There is no evidence that the need for the protection of (young/minor) players, for transparency in transactions and for a certain level of quality in relation to the services of the agent, has changed. The new FIFA regulations place responsibility for the activities of agents on the shoulders of the clubs and the players. Especially for the players, this is now a double burden. Where they initially needed more protection they now lose the protection offered by the FIFA PAR and, paradoxically, will now be responsible for the activities of the agent/intermediary. The move back from the FIFA PAR will mean that in the case of a dispute, the agents are no longer in any way under the jurisdiction of FIFA. Taking the international aspects of the activities of agents into consideration, problems might occur with dispute resolution and enforcement of decisions if disputes are addressed solely through civil courts. If the national associations fail to create a harmonised system, there could be serious dissonance in the freedom to provide services in the EU. The stakeholders now need to find the best framework for implementing enforceable rules that are in line with their wishes and in accordance with EU law.

The search for a solution by means of a negotiated settlement is under pressure, as is proven by the activities of the English agents' association, the AFA, which has lodged a complaint with the EC alleging that the new system leads to widespread corruption and is potentially in breach of European law. The concept of intermediaries has been introduced and is already subject to scrutiny by the EU. The AFA has requested an investigation by the EC into the new system. Although FIFA has adopted the new system, whether or not the forthcoming decision by the EC will force another twist in the regulatory evolution of FIFA regulations remains to be seen.

Note

1. Piau objected to the fact that he could only carry out the profession of player agent on the condition that he possessed a compulsory licence. He particularly objected to the necessity of passing a written exam before being able to receive such a licence. His complaint also concerned the necessary financial deposit that a player agent needed to make as a type of insurance, FIFA's power to sanction and the fact that FIFA PAR did not foresee the possibility of appealing against a FIFA sanction or decision in court.

Bibliography

Arnaut, J. (2006) *Independent European sport review*. Brussels: EC.

Barney, J. B. and Hesterly, W. (1996) Organizational economics: Understanding the relationship between organizations and economic analysis. In: Clegg, S. R., Hardy, C. and Nord, W. R. (eds) *Handbook of organization studies*. London: Sage, pp. 111–146.

Belet, I. (2007) *Report on the professional future of football in Europe*. Strasbourg: European Parliament.

Boyes, S. (2000) Salary caps in sport: Objectives, problems and the law. *Sports Law Bulletin*. 3(1), pp. 120–130.

EC (2002) *White paper on sport*. Brussels: EC.

Eisenhardt, K. M. (1989) Agency theory: An assessment and review. *Academy of Management*. 14(1), pp. 57–74.

FIFA (1994) *Players' agents regulations*. Zurich: FIFA.

FIFA (2001) *Players' agents regulations*. Zurich: FIFA.

FIFA (2008) *Players' agents regulations*. Zurich: FIFA.

FIFA (2010) The TMS explained. *FIFA* [online]. Available from: www.fifa.com/governance/news/y=2010/m=9/news=the-tms-explained-1310345.html [accessed 29 November 2015].

FIFA TMS (2015a) Domestic Transfer Matching System – DTMS. *FIFA TMS* [online]. Available from: www.fifatms.com/en/Products/DTMS/ [accessed 29 November 2015].

FIFA TMS (2015b) International Transfer Matching System – ITMS. *FIFA TMS* [online]. Available from: www.fifatms.com/en/Products/ITMS/ [accessed 29 November 2015].

FIFA TMS (2015c) The Global Player Exchange – GPX. *FIFA TMS*. FIFA TMS: Zurich.

FIFA TMS (2015d) The Global Player Exchange – GPX. *FIFA TMS*. FIFA TMS: Zurich.

FIFA (2015e) Working with intermediaries – reform of the players' agents system. *FIFA* *[online]*. Available from: www.fifa.com/governance/news/y=2015/m=4/news=working-with-intermediaries-reform-of-fifa-s-players-agents-system-2583543.html [accessed 19 November 2015].

Foster, K. (2000) Can sport be regulated by Europe? In: Caiger, A. and Gardiner, S. (eds) *Professional sport in the European Union: Regulation and re-regulation*. Den Haag: T. M. C. Asser Press, pp. 43–63.

Garcia, B. (2009) Sport governance after the white paper: The demise of the European model? *International Journal of Sport Policy*. (1)3, pp. 267–284.

Glavany, J., Bret, C., Geneteaud, M. and Mauvilain, S. (2014) Pour un modèle durable du football français. *Ministère de la ville, de la jeunesse et des sports* [online]. Available from: www.sports.gouv.fr/IMG/pdf/footdurable_rapport_m3.pdf [accessed 13 May 2015].

Greenberg, M. J. (1993) Drafting of players contracts and clauses. *Marquette Sports Law*. 4(5), pp. 51–70.

Greenwald, B. C. (1986) Adverse selection in the labour market. *Review of Economic Studies*. 53(3), pp. 325–347.

Hendrickx, F. (2007) Belgium. In: Siekman, R. C. R., Parrish, R., Martins, R. B. and Soek, J. (eds) *Players' agents worldwide: Legal aspects*. The Hague: T. M. C. Asser Press, pp. 105–115.

Holmstrom, B. (1979) Moral hazard and observability. *Bell Journal of Economics*. 10(1), pp. 74–91.

Holt, M. (2007) The ownership and control of elite club competition in European football. *Soccer and Society*. 1(8), pp. 50–67.

Holt, M., Michie, J. and Oughton, C. (2006) *The role and regulations of agents in football*. London: The Sport Nexus.

Karcher, R. T. (2007) United States. In: Siekman, R. C. R., Parrish, R., Martins, R. B. and Soek, J. (eds) *Players' agents worldwide: Legal aspects*. The Hague: T. M. C. Asser Press, pp. 693–727.

KEA and CDES (2013) *The economics and legal aspects of transfer of players*. Brussels: Sport EC.

KEA, CDES and EOSE (2009) *Study on sport agents in the European Union*. Brussels: Sport EC.

Martins, R. B. (2007) The Laurent Piau case of the ECJ on the status of players' agents. In: Siekman, R. C. R., Parrish, R., Martins, R. B. and Soek, J. (eds) *Players' agents worldwide: Legal aspects*. Den Haag: T. M. C. Asser Press, pp. 37–57.

Martins, R. B. (2009a) The Laurent Piau case of the ECJ on the status of players' agents. In Gardiner, S., Parrish, R. and Siekman, R. C. R. (eds) *EU, sport, law: Regulation, re-regulation, and representation*. Den Haag: T. M. C. Asser Press, pp. 247–257.

Martins, R. B. (2009b) Players' agents: Past, present ... future? *EPFL Sports Law Bulletin*. 5, pp. 33–42.

Mason, D. S. and Slack, T. (2001a) Industry factors and the changing dynamics of the player-agent relationships in professional ice hockey. *Sport Management Review*. 4(2), pp. 165–191.

Mason, D. S. and Slack, T. (2001b) Evaluating monitoring mechanisms as a solution to opportunism by professional hockey players. *Journal of Sport Management*. 15(1), pp. 37–61.

McGuire, J. B. (1988) Agency theory and organizational analysis. *Managerial Finance*. 14(4), pp. 6–9.

Nilakant, V. and Rao, H. (1994) Agency theory and uncertainty in organizations: An evaluation. *Organization Studies*. 15(5), pp. 649–672.

Parrish, R. (2000) Reconciling conflicting approaches to sport in the European Union. In: Caiger, A. and Gardiner, S. (eds) *Professional sport in the European Union: Regulation and re-regulation*. Den Haag: T. M. C. Asser Press, pp. 21–41.

Parrish, R. (2003) The politics of sports regulations in the European Union. *Journal of European Public Policy*. 10(2), pp. 246–262.

Parrish, R. (2007) Regulating players' agents: A global perspective. In: Siekman, R. C. R., Parrish, R., Martins, R. B. and Soek, J. (eds) *Players' agents worldwide: Legal aspects.* The Hague: T. M. C. Asser Press, pp. 1–13.

Pinna, A. (2006) The International supply of sport agent services. *International Sports Law Journal.* 1–2, pp. 20–27.

Shropshire, K. L. (1992) *Agents of opportunity: Sports agents and corruption in collegiate sports.* Philadelphia: University of Pennsylvania Press.

Smienk, M. (2009) Regulations in the market of sports agents. *International Sports Law Journal.* 3–4, pp. 70–92.

Sports.gouv.fr (2014) Pour un modéle durable du football Français. *Sports Gouv* [online]. Available from: www.sports.gouv.fr/IMG/pdf/footdurable_rapport_m3.pdf [accessed 28 February 2015].

UEFA (2006) Agents in the UEFA spotlight. *UEFA* [online]. Available from: www.uefa. org/stakeholders/newsid=462974.html [accessed 23 March 2012].

Verheyden, D. (2007) France. In: Siekman, R. C. R., Parrish, R., Martins, R. B. and Soek, J. (eds) *Players' agents worldwide: Legal aspects.* The Hague: T. M. C. Asser Press, pp. 207–225.

White, N. (2007) United Kingdom. In: Siekman, R. C. R., Parrish, R., Martins, R. B. and Soek, J. (eds) *Players' agents worldwide: Legal aspects.* The Hague: T. M. C. Asser Press, pp. 611–635.

White, W. D. (1992) Information and the control of agents. *Journal of Economic Behaviour and Organization.* 18(1), pp. 111–117.

6 Football agents and transfer networks

Overview

The principal-agent theory discussed in Chapter 5 raises important questions about both the structure of the player labour market and the role of agents. The economic justification for the presence of intermediaries is that asymmetric information exists between players and clubs. Thus, economic theory assigns middlemen a cognitive role, mobilising the necessary information to conduct transactions (Bessy, 1997). For clubs, agents specialise in revealing information about players which is difficult to find, such as their ability to adapt to new surroundings, languages spoken, health, lifestyle, capacity to progress, etc. (Autor, 2001). For players, who are not usually in a position to access information about potentially interested clubs, or to negotiate with employers, agents help by using their networks to access information about which clubs are offering work (with a view to a transfer but also with a view to salary enhancement) and prioritising the most interesting clubs according to the selected criteria (wealth, stability, location...).

This chapter considers the supply chain for footballing talent in more detail and looks at how networks have become important for the flow of information between stakeholders and in gaining access to decision makers. Using data from the author's involvement in a study on football agents conducted for the EC, we are able to tease out how agents' backgrounds can help them to enter the marketplace. Applying network theory to the football labour market, we consider why agents have become even more important following liberalisation of the labour market. Acknowledging the global nature of the game today, we look at migratory flows of players and consider how the roles of intermediaries have developed in this context, before switching attention to how the nature of networks can lead to more negative outcomes whereby well connected agents may be able to abuse their power.

6.1 Building a network

Networks can be thought of as evolving social structures with interdependencies between individuals or groups in society (Fulse, 2008; Poli, 2008). They are differentiated by their size and quality and are constantly developing as opportunities arise for individuals within the network to change their function or make new connections. While a combination of different elements determines the strength of networks, including time invested and emotional intensity, reciprocal exchanges in particular are thought to create a sense of trust which increases the probability of future cooperation whilst also helping an individual to develop a good reputation (Granovetter, 1985). However, even with a good reputation, people usually base their choices on who they know personally; so, if an individual is not in some way connected to another individual, the two are unlikely to cooperate – even if they have heard of each other. In football, networks are particularly important for the passing of information between buyers (clubs) and sellers (players). Recognising that information does not necessarily flow directly between these parties, the agent has become an entrepreneur who notices and takes advantage of these gaps in networks, known as 'structural holes' (Burt, 1992).

Given this necessity for agents to be well connected, the main obstacle to entering the profession is the capacity to develop relations with relevant people in order to have access to reliable and, ideally, exclusive information. Indeed, the outcome of competition amongst agents depends on intricate knowledge of the football landscape, developing know-how not only with players but also with their employers, pin-pointing the needs of clubs, gaining access to the decision makers and entering into a productive relationship with them (Demazière and Jouvenet, 2013). As knowledge circulates more quickly within groups, people become aware of information at different rates according to how well connected they are. Having access to information therefore creates social capital.[1] This is clear when we look at the profile of current active agents; there is a bias towards people who have previously worked in the football industry as shown in Figure 6.1. Drawing on our work in Chapter 2, we know that 56.7 per cent of agents in

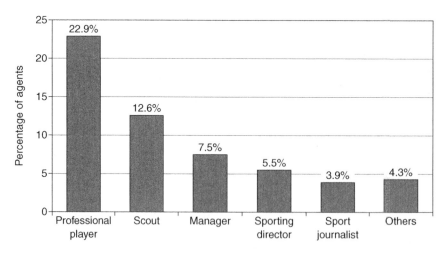

Figure 6.1 Percentage of agents with previous work experience in football, per type of job.

the five top European leagues had significant experience in the world of football prior to becoming agents.

Competition in the marketplace with a large ratio of agents to players means that former players have an advantage since they are able to rely on the relationships forged with the footballing fraternity in their playing careers to start their business, capitalising on existing mutual respect and trust, and it is not unusual for a player, on retirement, to join the agency that he was previously represented by. Interestingly, having experience of scouting players also appears to be a good pathway into the profession as these individuals are more likely to be able to evaluate players' skills, thus being able, at an early stage, to pick out players who are likely to be valuable assets in future, as well as having the ability to recognise clubs' needs in order to provide a matching service. Pierre Garonnaire, for example, ex scout and sporting director of AS Saint-Etienne from 1950 to 1988, started his agent career when he retired (Frenkiel, 2014). His business began with him representing players he met while he was a scout, including Fabien Barthez, Christophe Pignol, and Mohamed Chaouch. Observing that the players he met during his scout period trusted him, he decided to develop his own activity as a career manager. Scouts have not only established trust with players, but also with clubs and agents that they worked with in the past, thus putting them in an enviable position in terms of having contacts.

Other roles in professional football are less likely to be a route into becoming an agent. However, some managers do switch sides: the former Danish international Søren Lerby managed Bayern Munich during the 1991/92 season before becoming a licensed agent in 1993, when he founded his company Essel Sport Management, looking after the career of international players such as Wesley Sneijder, Thomas Vermaelen and Toby Alderweireld. Likewise, in 2013 Yvon Poliquen became a football agent after a long career as a football player and later a football coach in France (Frenkiel, 2014). An estimated 7.5 per cent of agents have previously been football managers, while even fewer have been sporting directors – 5.5 per cent. In this respect, after several years as Peterborough United football director, in 2006 John Kay launched Emerging Sport Talents and began to operate as an FA licensed agent, setting up a network of scouts covering all the leagues in England.

Sports journalists often find themselves becoming agents as their profession also permits contact with many key actors in the transfer market and representation business. The well-known agent Pini Zahavi, for example, concluded his first deal in 1979 while he was still a journalist (Jackson, 2006). In France, Pape Diouf switched from being a journalist to an influential football agent assisting, among other players, Roger Boli, Joseph-Antoine Bell, Marcel Desailly, Bernard Lama, William Gallas and Didier Drogba. He finally left the agency business to become Olympique Marseille's general manager and then president (Diouf and Boniface, 2009).

Finally, a minority of agents also had a professional career in football as a referee, club board member, chairman, team manager, etc. It is not rare to find professionals who have covered different positions within clubs and associations;

Federico Bonetto, for example, worked for Torino between 1973 and 1980 as club secretary, team manager, PR manager and technical director before moving to other Italian clubs, again as technical director, before becoming a licensed agent at the prestigious IFA Bonetto agency which had been founded by his uncle, Giuseppe Bonetto, himself former general director of Torino and Napoli during the 70s and 80s. A similar career path was taken by Jean Pierre Bernés who spent most of his early career in football as administrative secretary, general secretary and club general secretary at Olympique Marseille before moving into the representation industry. These relationships and the tacit knowledge developed between key football stakeholders appear to make it relatively easy for these actors to switch roles within the industry; however, it is not essential to have previous football experience to be successful as an agent.

While the benefit of being well networked is understandable in that it creates a greater likelihood of having knowledge of how the game operates, the necessity of having connections in the industry in order to make a living creates a barrier to entry. It also creates a de facto segmentation among agents between the 'insiders', who have the necessary network and the 'outsiders' who may have the technical skills but have an empty address book.[2] In the representation market, the 'outsiders' in the big five leagues are the remaining 46 per cent of agents who do not have previous experience in the football industry. For them, building a network requires an investment of both time and financial resources. As Pirel (2013) states, a new agent only has two options to enable him to quickly make a living if he is not already involved in the football industry: having a close friend whose professional career is on the up, or being affiliated to one of the few agencies already active in the market. Even if agents seem to be very reluctant to share their personal networks, collaborations are possible when an 'insider' faces excess demand and offers another agent (possibly an 'outsider') the opportunity to deal with some of his minor clients.

According to our study, the individuals who have managed to become successful agents without a football background all made an early decision to develop closer ties with people already connected in the industry. Philippe Flavier, for example was a former physiotherapist who launched his representation career in 1989 by collaborating with retired footballers in order to use their network. The necessity of having these contacts to open doors in the football world is clear. The thickness and quality of an agent's address book bears witness to his integration in the network of professionals: it is a status symbol. The telephone numbers of decision-makers in professional clubs are an all-important resource and source of information. Being able to call them means having an essential tool to work with and is a show of trust on the part of an insider (Demazière and Jouvenet, 2013).

6.2 The networking structure and the strength of connections

Normally agents conduct two key roles – working on behalf of a player to find them a club, or working on behalf of a club to secure the right talent for them. Both of these roles need agents to use their network in different ways. As Granovetter (1983) argues, networks have two types of ties, strong or weak, according to how well people are connected in a relationship. In a close network of people with strong ties, it is likely that most members of the group know each other very well. However, in a group with weak ties the members of the group are more likely to be acquaintances. These acquaintances are likely to have other close relationships of their own and therefore be enmeshed in a closely knit clump of social structure, but one that is different to the rest of their acquaint-ances. The weak tie between two acquaintances, therefore, becomes a crucial bridge between the two densely knit close networks. It follows, then, that indi-viduals with few weak ties will be deprived of information from distant parts of the social system and will be limited to information from people close to them. This will limit their access to new knowledge but also put them at a disadvantage in knowing about job openings at the right time (Granovetter, 1973).

In the context of football, it is therefore important for agents to have both strong and weak ties according to the role that they are playing. For an agent who represents only players, it is very important to have a lot of weak ties in order to both hear about new opportunities and also hear about other good players who need representation. Without these weak ties, the opportunities for their players to move clubs will be very limited. According to Poli and Ravenel (2005), international transfers only occur for the very best players or those with a very good network. Similarly, if a player wants to go to a particular club it will be necessary for someone in his network – usually his agent – to be connected to that club (Poli, 2009). This is even more relevant for players who have not yet gained a footballing reputation so that few clubs are actively scouting them. Clubs are inundated with requests for trials and videos of young players; however, they are unlikely to be watched without a recommendation. Normally, this will come from an agent or an ex player who will talk directly to a club. For agents working for clubs, it will have been essential for them to have strong ties with people at the club in order to gain a position of trust.

Agents normally need at least three types of network connections to be suc-cessful; players, clubs, and other agents. Players are not only represented by their agents, but also help them to both broaden their networks and be seen as trustworthy. According to Bulliard (2010), players are a source of information for agents both in recruiting new players and also in providing information about other players. Typically, by being seen to operate professionally for the players an agent represents, he will also attract attention from other players and clubs. However, conflicts of interest can arise if an agent represents numerous players in the same position, or who play for the same club, as it would become more difficult to lobby on their behalf to play for the national team, for example. Some agents therefore limit the number of players of the same type that they are willing to represent (Semens, 2012b). By working closely with their stable of players, agents can therefore also develop closer ties with clubs. It is not unknown for an individual at a club to talk to an agent to find out about players he does not directly represent, but whom he has knowledge of by virtue of his ties to other players in the same team. This helps to also develop the relationships which are needed with clubs to be able to transfer players. With regards to building relationships with clubs, the most straightforward way would be to place a good player with them. This can be tricky without having already developed a relationship with that specific club and therefore other agents might be needed to help smooth the process, particularly when placing an unknown player. For this reason, networking events such as Wyscout forum, a well-known world leading event, are specially organised and dedicated to global networking and international transfers (Wyscout, 2015). Twice a year, in different locations, this networking forum is reserved for transfer decision makers, football club executives, scouts, player agents and intermediaries, bringing together the international football community for two days.

It is known that some clubs have preferred agents that they use consistently to sign new players (Anon., 2014). This is usually an agent who has delivered good players to them in the past and who has built their relationship with the club over time. In representing a good player at a club, an agent will be seen at matches and around the club with the player, and he will naturally come into contact with decision makers, becoming aware of the club's needs and requests. In the context of discussions about the player he represents, he is also likely to develop a greater understanding of what the club wants and the type of player that would fit in, as well as of their internal structures on discipline and finance. Therefore, an agent with this knowledge could be useful in bringing another player to the same club and, having developed a relationship, a club is more likely to offer the agent a mandate in future to work on their behalf either to help buy or to sell players.

Given the importance of trust, it is not surprising that many agents are family members of managers and other football decision makers. However, there are many concerns that these relations also lead to conflicts of interests. The case study below of GEA World, an agency that was intimately entwined with the *Calciopoli* scandal in Italian football, looks at this in more detail and clearly illustrates the importance of monitoring mechanisms on agents' activities and their network development.

Case study: GEA World

Imagine a scenario where a club football director has to negotiate with his own son to determine the transfers of players signed up with his son's agency; dealings that would naturally entail transfer commissions. Such a scenario could manipulate the transfer market, inflate transfer fees and players' wages as the two parties saw fit, and offer the opportunity for 'under-the-table' tax-free payments. This was indeed the case regarding the football management agency GEA World. In 2006, the agency was managed by the sons and daughters of four prominent Italian business-men directly involved in football: Juventus general manager Luciano Moggi, the leading player in the Calciopoli scandal, Calisto Tanzi, the former head of the Par-malat dairy conglomerate and Parma Calcio, Sergio Cragnotti, the former head of the Cirio food business conglomerate and Lazio and Cesare Geronzi, one of the most influential bankers in Italy.

Founded in September 2001 following the merger of the activities of three smaller agencies (General Athletic, Football Management, and Riccardo Calleri), GEA World described itself as a flexibly structured organisation whose aim was to define, improve and consolidate the image of companies. It also sought to optimise the career prospects for athletes, who they suggested may be too busy to manage their finances properly. The agency structure and its complex network are illustrated in Figure 6.2. Significant shareholders in General Athletic included Andrea Cragnotti, son of Sergio Cragnotti; Francesca Tanzi, daughter of Calisto Tanzi; and Chiara Geronzi, daughter of Cesare Geronzi. Another significant shareholder was Romafides, a company owned by Capitalia bank, which subse-quently merged with Unicredit bank. Capitalia was the major investment bank in football, financing clubs including Lazio, Parma Calcio, Perugia and Roma. All of these clubs faced several financial crises and this investment bank had influ-ence, directly or indirectly, with the respective club boards. Capitalia's role in the collapse of both Cirio and Parmalat was prominent as it was a leading advisor to both companies. Capitalia owned shares in MMC, an investment bank, whose chairman was Franco Carraro, the FIGC President who resigned in 2006 as a direct result of the Calciopoli scandal. The Football Management company was controlled by prominent Italian football agents; Alessandro Moggi, son of the former Juventus General Director Luciano Moggi – a key figure in the Calciopoli scandal, and Franco Zavaglia. Other leading figures connected to the company through collaborative business links were Giuseppe De Mita, son of Ciriaco De Mita, former Italian Prime Minister, and Davide Lippi, son of Marcello Lippi, former Juventus and Italy manager (Monti, 2005). GEA World managed around 200 contracts for managers, club directors and players (AGCM, 2006). The majority of these were players, around 154 in total, of whom 99 played in Serie A and Serie B. Considering the volume of players' contracts dealt with from 2002 to 2006, it is estimated that GEA World's share of the player transfer market was approximately 10.2 per cent, with 4.30 per cent and 3.74 per cent accruing to Moggi and Zavaglia respectively, more than any other football agents operating in Italy. Moreover, GEA World controlled 18.9 per cent of the total turnover of all agencies in Italy, double the share of PDP, the second largest. Over the shorter period from 2004 to 2006, GEA World's share was approxi-mately 17.9 per cent, with Moggi responsible for 12.3 per cent and Zavaglia 4.8 per cent (AGCM, 2006).

On 1 August 2006, GEA World was dissolved; in theory the cartel had been destroyed (Foot, 2007). Following the Calciopoli scandal and several allegations and investigations, most of its leading executives were put on trial, having been accused of manipulating the transfer market by using threats or violence. Clearly, the dissolution of GEA World had a profound influence on the review of the rules and code of conduct which was undertaken by the FIGC. Jones (2007: 273–274) summarises the problem of GEA as follows:

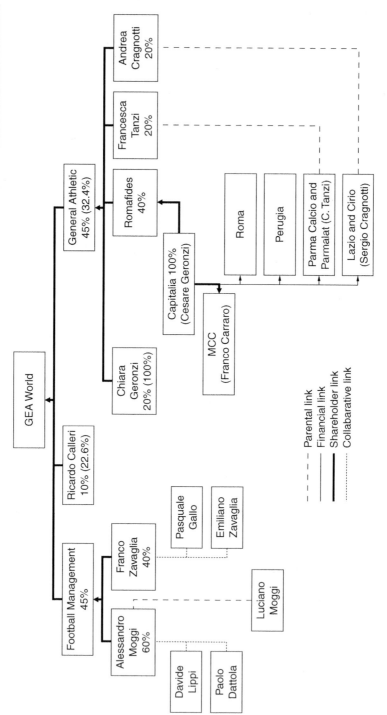

Figure 6.2 GEA World structure and network (source: Hamil *et al.* (2010)).

The overlap of interests whereby Moggi senior could buy a player represented by his son, or Lippi could sell a player represented by his son, meant that, as always, nothing was ever 'disinterested'. There was always a hidden agenda to most deals which had absolutely nothing to do with football tactics and talent.

The GEA World case demonstrates how even a highly regulated transfer and labour market could become inefficient and highly influenced by the network developed by a sports agency. It raises the question of whether weak monitoring mechanisms themselves had a negative impact on the efficiency and transparency of the transfer market, leading a high concentration of agents dominating the market, potentially through improper conduct. Despite the scandal, in January 2013 GEA World return to fully operate in the sports industry, having expanded its service to offer advice on sports systems, event organisation, image management, marketing and corporate social responsibility as well as providing a mentoring support service for athletes, with the goal of helping them to transition in both their personal and professional lives as their careers come to a close (Laudisa, 2013). On 15 January 2014, the Italian High Court of Justice annulled the sentences against Luciano Moggi and his son Alessandro after the Italian Court of Appeal had earlier thrown out the conspiracy to commit crime charge, but sentenced them to one year and five months and five months respectively for intensively putting pressure on players to be represented by agents from GEA World.

Inevitably, an agent representing the club's best players will have power in negotiations with a club. The more players at a club the agent represents the more power the agent is likely to have. If the agent is close to all of his players he can easily ask them to behave in a certain way in order to ensure that the club meets his demands for both the player and himself in negotiations. For example, in the negotiation of Seydou Doumbia's contract at Young Boys in Switzerland it is believed that the agent managed to negotiate a large third party entitlement for himself when the player is sold in future (Bulliard, 2010).

Agents usually limit the number of clubs that they have strong relationships with so that they can deliver the players that the club wants. If an agent had mandates from a lot of clubs it would be difficult to fulfil their needs – particularly if the clubs were all interested in the same type of player. It is not unusual for clubs to conduct all of their transfers through an agent, even when a player is known to them. This makes it very important for agents to also have at least weak ties to other agents too. These will naturally develop for agents representing players in the same teams or from similar markets as well as through football events when the industry comes together. If a player wants to move to a particular club the only route for this to happen if the club only conducts business through an agent will be for the player's agent to work with the club's agent to complete the move. The club's agent in this case can act as a gate-keeper and the player's agent may share his own fee with that agent in order to secure the move. In cross border transfers in particular this would be normal since, without an agent trusted by the club, it is unlikely that the player in question would be seen.

With an established reputation, agents can therefore be offered opportunities to collaborate in order to bring together complementary networks. This is the case for Kirin Soccer, the football agency funded by Joseph Lee that has become the main intermediary agency between the Chinese and Brazilian football markets, building a strong partnership with the Brazilian agency Traffic (Marques, 2014). Interagency cooperation is increasingly common and many agents indicate that they represent players on behalf of other colleagues, mainly to introduce players to a specific national market or to a specific club. Strategic partnerships concluded by agents at transnational level are a key globalising factor.

For agents who are not established, the network is even more important. However, as football is a relatively closed industry for new agents who are not able to collaborate with people who have more connections, the remaining option is to search for young prospects. In this case, it would take many years for newcomers in the industry to develop a portfolio of clients and benefit from relations of trust they build up with clubs and players. Even then it is less likely that these agents will make a living in the industry as they have a lower probability of discovering a 'star'. Even if they do, there is no guarantee that the player will not decide to be represented by a 'bigger' agent with more connections once he is recognised as a good player. According to our study in Chapter 2, on average, licensed agents had seven years of work experience in the transfer market. The majority of licensed agents were not active in the market, and never had been. In reality, even though a large number of people held a licence, this did not mean that they were insiders. In fact, becoming an insider does not depend on a licence. Kia Joorabchian, Tévez's representative, has always operated as an unlicensed agent, defining his activity as intermediation. For this reason, he has involved licensed agent and business partner, Nojan Bedroud, during transfer negotiations to avoid any irregularities in his deals. Similarly, Pini Zahavi worked for several years as an unlicensed agent before becoming licensed by the FA.

From a theoretical perspective, relational frameworks are thus very important in helping us to understand the football labour market where human interactions generate global dynamics that make migration go beyond the simple supply and demand logic (Meyer, 2001). As changes in legislation have presented opportunities for players to move more freely, the networks operating in football have become even more important.

6.3 Labour migration and football agents

Although labour migration has occurred throughout history, the labour market for footballers has usually been one in which clubs have held power over the players who are registered with them. While the labour market liberalisation of the 1990s had a profound impact on the composition of teams by making it easier for players to move, it was clearly not the only reason why players chose to migrate to different leagues. Some migratory routes had been established decades previously.

International transfers had existed since the advent of professional football, largely built around colonial ties: English clubs had recruited from 23 countries before 1985 and from 41 countries by 1995, with 22 nationalities represented in the English PL alone (Williams, 2007). However, the numbers of foreign players increased exponentially after the Bosman ruling. Whereas, in the 1992/1993 season there were 11 foreign players in the English PL; this rose to 66 in the 1995/1996 season and reached 166 by 1998/1999. In 2000, the first year that the new rules were fully embedded, 1,478 international transfer requests were processed by FIFA (Lanfranchi *et al.*, 2004). Post-colonial connections were still evident, with 69 per cent of the African footballers in Portugal coming from former colonies, 59 per cent in France from former French territories and, even though Belgium has become the de facto route for African footballers to enter Europe, its equivalent figure was still 31 per cent (Darby, 2000; Lanfranchi and Taylor, 2001; Taylor, 2006). In the big five European leagues 43 per cent of players were migrants by 2008/2009 (Poli, 2009).

Standard neoclassical economics explain that individuals choose to move when they can exploit differences in supply and demand to be able to make themselves better off. In the case of footballers, if a player at one club is more valuable to another club then he is likely to be transferred – this remains the case irrespective of where that club is. Allowing for transaction costs, if a player's marginal revenue product is higher at a club elsewhere, then an optimal solution would be for the player to transfer. Traditionally, this was often manifested as players moving from Africa and South America to the richer leagues in Europe. Following Krugman (1991), Magee and Sugden (2002) contextualise player migration as a movement from the economic periphery to the economic core, with Europe at the core acting as a magnet for football migrants on a global scale. While this provides a useful starting point, it does little to explain the complexity of the migration process, or to explain why some countries are peripheral and others core. In contrast to general economic and commercial conditions outside of football, developed northern European countries have been exporters of talent to the poorer south. As Stead and Maguire (2000) point out, prior to the 1980s the southern leagues attracted talented Scandinavian players whose domestic leagues were amateur and are even now mainly semi-professional.

Poli (2010a) agrees that migration is explained by more than purely economic reasons. While the patterns of movement post Bosman have reinforced older channels with historical links, geographical proximity is also important, with German leagues normally having players from Eastern Europe, whereas the English leagues have traditionally been more popular for players from Scandinavian countries and the rest of the UK and Ireland. In recent years, while these migratory routes are still evident, the rates at which these players move are not uniform, suggesting that various other dynamics are also at play.

Migratory flows are present whereby some players' moves are influenced, to a greater or lesser extent, by interpersonal networks where strategies are developed to create and to take advantage of opportunities (Poli, 2010b; Semens, 2012a). Various stakeholders (often chairmen, managers, scouts, players, agents, investors, families and other intermediaries) are involved in the football labour market, and together engineer situations which can lead to player moves. Irrespective of which party to the deal has induced the transfer, the move itself will generate economic rents for either the buying or selling club or the player and their representatives, depending on who has power in the negotiations. As well as being able to introduce otherwise unconnected individuals, the agent can control what information is shared, when, and who it is shared with in order to retain power. How much the other actors in the network know of each other often depends on whether the transfer is domestic or international. Even when the various parties do know of each other, it is likely that they operate in different networks and therefore will use intermediaries who can link the two groups.

Looking at the interactions which occur in the build up to a transfer deal in more detail can help us to understand how agents are able to gain power. Using the English PL as an example, Lonsdale (2004) demonstrates that where the surplus value accrues depends on the relative power of buyers and sellers. As revenue generation for clubs tends to be related to their on-field performance, clubs must have a successful team in order to progress, making the recruitment of the best players possible essential (Szymanski and Kuypers, 1999). However, as we saw in Chapter 2, the scarcity of superstar players means they can command a higher price in terms of wages and transfer fees. Indeed, the best English PL clubs are competing with the best clubs globally to secure talent. As the quality of player reduces, so too does their scarcity, while their utility to a club also decreases and their power in negotiation also weakens. It is the ability for players to extract surplus value in supply chains that can prompt their movement from one club or country to another. While the decision process is different in each transfer, agents mediate the market in order to help players navigate their moves.

To demonstrate this movement, we can look at the example of African players moving to the English PL. As Poli (2009) points out, African players tend to change clubs more often than the average player from other countries. They are often recruited through a complex network and looking at specific examples can help to explain these linkages. We first consider the career of Michael Essien who was playing for the Liberty Professionals FC team in Accra when he was picked to play for Ghana's youth team. In 1999 he won the U20 African Cup of nations and also took part in the U20 World Cup. He was spotted by Manchester United scouts and invited to a trial in England. He was offered a contract at feeder club Royal Antwerp in Belgium in order to adjust to a European life and style of play and also to fulfil the necessary conditions to gain a work permit in England. However, Essien already had an agent – former goalkeeper Fabien Piveteau, an associate of Sly Tetteh – president of Liberty Professionals FC. He refused the offer from Royal Antwerp and went to his agent's house in Monaco. His agent then organised a trial at Bastia – a club Piveteau had previously played for and Essien too signed for the club in 2000. After three years, he secured a move to Olympic Lyon for €11.75 million and then, two years later, moved to

Chelsea for €38 million. According to Poli (2010a), this demonstrates that the role of the agent is more important than that of clubs or managers as it is their contacts which enable migratory channels to be set up.

Another example is the career trajectory of Senegalese player Henri Camara. Camara was playing for local club ASC Jaraat Dakar when he was recruited by RC Strasbourg. Central to the arrangement of this were two intermediaries – Claude Leroy who, having spent many years as a coach in Africa, including in Senegal, had become sporting director of RC Strasbourg, and Swiss agent Nicolas Geiger, who was active in Africa and had scouts in Senegal and Cameroon. Camara transferred to RC Strasbourg in a deal which saw Team Consult, a Swiss based company belonging to Geiger, paid a commission of €1.7 million for their part in the move. Just two months after arriving in Strasbourg, Camara was loaned to Neuchâtel Xamax, whose coach was Nicolas Geiger's brother, Alain. After transferring to Grasshoppers of Zurich in 2001, Camara was freed from his contractual commitments following court proceedings in which RC Strasbourg claimed that the player's registration was still with them and a preference agreement had been signed affording them a fee in compensation if the player signed for another club. The French National League dismissed the case after Camara denied signing this agreement and the player was allowed to move without a fee. His next move was to CS Sedan, arranged by his new agent – Pape Diouf, later president of Olympic Marseille. Camara transferred after two years to Wolverhampton Wanderers for around €3 million, through Pape Diouf's associate for the UK – Willy McKay. After moving around six other clubs he finally retired.

Without the networks of their agents, the players in these two examples could have followed very different routes. Privileged relations between club officials, managers, agents, intermediaries and investors have developed in which players are often akin to a commodity moving from club to club in order to acquire more wealth – who this wealth accrues to is not always clear. As Meyer (2001: 102) points out, the emergence of people acting as intermediaries professionally 'confirms that the globalisation of the highly skilled labour market does not occur without massive network investment'. The same logic can be applied to the migration of footballers. While the examples above looked at players in isolation, the agents involved often work with a stable of players who they help to move around the world. Again, an instructive example is the career development of Jorge Mendes.

Mendes' company, Gestifute, has conducted 68 per cent of the transfers of players from Portugal's top three clubs, Porto, Sporting Lisbon and Benfica, over the last decade, with many of the players moving to the English, Spanish, Russian, Turkish and French leagues (Conn, 2014). His first major international transfer was in 2002 when he brokered an £8.5 million deal for 19 year old Hugo Viana to move from Sporting Lisbon to Newcastle United – the player started just 16 matches for them. At this time Mendes had a partnership with English agency Formation – as seen in Chapter 4, it is not unusual for two groups with specialist knowledge of a particular market to work together in international transfers. However, in Mendes' next major deal – the transfer of Cristiano Ronaldo from Sporting Lisbon to Manchester United, this partnership collapsed with Formation claiming that Mendes had breached their agreement. Formation later sued but the matter was settled out of court. At that time Peter Kenyon was CEO at Manchester United. When Kenyon moved to Chelsea, he worked with Mendes again to secure the services of Jose Mourinho as manager, as well as the signings of Ricardo Carvalho and Paulo Ferreira from Porto and Tiago Mendes from Benfica.

Mendes continued to broker deals with Manchester United too and in 2007 negotiated their £27 million transfer of Anderson, from Porto, and, Nani's £25.5 million transfer from Sporting Lisbon.[3] In the same transfer window, Mendes helped Real Madrid to sign Pepe for £24 million from Porto. His connections and relationships were demonstrated further in 2010 when he facilitated Cristiano Ronaldo's transfer from Manchester United to Real Madrid for £80 million and then Mourinho's arrival as coach. It is clear that the networks involved helped to smooth the way for these moves to take place and undoubtedly the relationships Mendes has with all of the clubs involved through previous transactions afforded him a level of trust in that network.

His record in transferring players to Real continued with the immediate arrival of Di María from Benfica for £21 million and Carvalho from Chelsea for £6.7 million, while Fábio Coentrão arrived from Benfica in a £25 million deal the following year. This has continued and, with Mendes also supporting the new Monaco revival when its owner Rybolovlev decided to restrain his spending in summer 2015, he brokered the sale of James Rodriguez to Real Madrid for £71 million and the loan of Radamel Falcao to Manchester United.

A relational approach in the football migratory process, where networks are developed over time, can therefore help us to understand the motivations of actors who take into account the opportunities and constraints linked to economic, cultural and power differentials that exist between territories. Mendes has been able to capitalise on his knowledge of football in Portugal, where he was first involved in meeting players through his nightclub business, before becoming friends with them, before going on to represent them in a professional capacity (Russo, 2014). By channelling the information that he has built up he has been able to have an influence in moulding the process of international migration.

Mendes, like other agents and intermediaries, has been able to obtain a privileged position via his connections to diverse groups (clubs, players, funding sources, scouts etc.), enabling him to collect more information than those outside of the network and therefore also exercise some influence over how that information is used and whose interests are served (Russo, 2014). At the same time as arranging the transfers above (and various others), Mendes has continued his relationship with Manchester United, arranging the transfer of Bebé from Vitória Guimarães, for £7.4 million in 2010. While most of the players transferring from Portugal to English clubs had a track record of being developed in academies then playing for the top Portuguese clubs, Bebé was discovered playing in the

Homeless World Cup before playing one season in the Portuguese third division, and then playing pre-season friendly matches with Guimarães. Mendes bought 30 per cent of Bebé's economic rights just before he moved to Manchester United and, with a 10 per cent agent's fee, was paid £2.9 million of the £7.4 million from Manchester United. Gonçalo Reis, Bebé's agent, complained to the Portuguese federation, FPF, and FIFA that Mendes had poached the player; later Portuguese police announced an investigation into the transfer, but its results are unknown and Mendes has faced no disciplinary charges.

Bebé failed to impress at Manchester United and was loaned to Besiktas, where several Mendes-represented players have gone, and then to the Portuguese clubs Rio Ave and Paços Ferreira, before Benfica bought him this summer, spending £2.4 million.

Agents acquiring a proportion of the economic rights of players they represent are not unusual in many football markets. While the example above of Mendes acquiring a proportion of Bebé's rights was a transaction conducted by an individual with some level of transparency, the situation becomes even more likely to lead to conflicts of interest when the parties involved are more opaque (Conn, 2014; Russo, 2014). In recent years it has become more popular for players to transfer to a club and be immediately loaned back to the seller club or loaned on to a different club. Concerns arise under these circumstances that the transfers are being conducted for non-sporting reasons. In this sense the networks involved are usually mediated by powerful stakeholders. The case study of bridge transfers below explains this in more detail.

Case study: bridge transfers

In March 2014, for the first time, four Argentinian clubs, Rosario Central, Racing, Indipendiente and Instituto, and one Uruguayan club, Sud América, were sanctioned by FIFA for having participated in bridge transfers (FIFA, 2014). Although there is no legal definition, FIFA (2014) define bridge transfers as follows: 'In general, bridge transfers involve clubs collaborating through a "bridge" club to a destination club where the player was never fielded by the bridge club' They occur when a club is used as an intermediary bridge for a player's transfer from one club to another to gain or retain economic benefits from a player while maintaining the legal rights of a FIFA registered club. In other words, the transfer is not conducted directly from the club of origin to the club of destination, but indirectly through a third club (the bridge), where the player is transferred first, for no apparent sporting reason. Therefore, formally, there are two transfers or registrations: one from the player's original status to the bridge club and a second from that club to the final destination. As the player never plays for the bridge club, this 'transfer' is fictitious. Duval and Torres (2015) set out three main characteristics of a bridge transfer: there is no sporting purpose underlying the transfer and three clubs are involved in a triangular structure – the club of origin where the player was first registered, the so-called bridge club, and the final destination club which the player was always intended to play for; and the player is registered for the bridge club for only a short period of time.

While extreme cases are easy to identify, in other situations the non-sporting purpose of the transfer can only be discovered after years of a continuous pattern of successive loan deals.

According to Reck (2014), bridge transfers can be used for different reasons. They originally started as a way for free agents to extract some extra money from clubs by virtue of an artificially created transfer fee that was further split between the player and the bridge club. Imagine a free agent player who wants a net salary of $1 million and is targeted by a club. If all this is deemed to be salary, taxes can be really high. So the free agent signs a contract on a lower salary, say $350,000, with a bridge club and only afterwards with the final club, while the player and the bridge club sign a transfer agreement of $650,000 which is subject to lower taxation.

Likewise, third party investors use clubs to control players' economic rights but, in the event of breach of contract, only civil remedies are offered under CAS jurisdiction. In a TPE dispute, any attempt to revert to FIFA is immediately rejected by the governing body. The bridge transfer offers TPEs a federative relationship, regulated by FIFA, with stronger protection, sporting sanctions, joint liability of the new club and an efficient execution stance, including threats of points deductions and relegation. Hence, through bridge clubs, TPE funds can enjoy this protection as they can loan the player to a third club and manage his return, or sign multi-year contracts with the player, anchoring him to the bridge club, and if the contract is breached, this would constitute a violation of Article 17 of the FIFA RSTP which could lead to sporting sanctions and to the joint liability of the new club.

Bridge clubs also protect the anonymity of the final beneficiary of the amounts received by the clubs through the transfer price. This helps real recipients of the transfer amounts to evade taxes or to circumvent the FIFA rule that prohibits third parties from TPEs. Moreover, it also explains why bridge clubs are usually located in countries that do not impose strong barriers or controls on the money flowing in and out in transfers. The transfer amounts are distributed depending on where the transfer would be subject to high taxation. To transfer the tax burden, instead of conducting a direct transfer between club A and club B, both clubs interpose a bridge club C and the real transfer price of $1m is divided between two different transfers from A to C for $200,000 and, subsequently, from C to B for $800,000, as illustrated in Figure 6.3.

In September 2012, the Argentinian tax authority, AFIP, suspended 151 football agents registered with the AFA[4] on suspicion of avoiding tax payments through bridge transfers (Levinsky, 2013). The investigation focused on 444 transfers that involved 33 Argentinian players. Argentinian clubs found it more convenient to use transfer bridges with Chilean and Uruguayan clubs where the taxes paid for each transfer were 19 per cent and 17 per cent respectively, instead of 24.5 per cent in Argentina. This system allowed the clubs and players involved to reduce their overall tax burden. To avoid these transfers in future, the AFIP passed new regulations designed to disclose the real owner of the economic rights, imposing high withholding rates for payments to economic rights owners of up to 35 per cent. The same rates and advance payments were enforced against a list of bridge clubs usually used to perform these operations as sporting tax havens. In addition, the AFIP signed an agreement with FIFA to gain access to the data contained in the FIFA TMS.

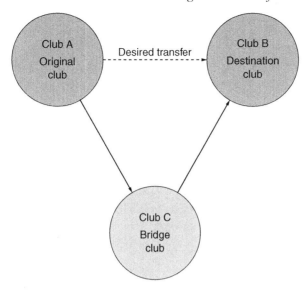

Figure 6.3 Bridge transfer in football.

A bridge club can also be used to locate an otherwise national dispute at international level for the purposes of how the dispute is regulated. For example, club of origin and destination clubs are located in the same country, while the bridge club is a foreign one. This opens the doors to FIFA jurisdiction over the dispute, which is reserved for cases with an international dimension. Finally, bridge transfers are also used to reduce training compensation paid under FIFA's solidarity mechanism.

6.4 Conclusions

Clearly, building networks can be beneficial for all parties in a transfer, potentially reducing transaction costs. Typically, agents develop expertise in a given area – possibly in their domestic market or in identifying and transferring players from another region. Normally, having built up this specialism, the routes to transferring players from these regions become easier to navigate. However, there are also potential conflicts of interest which can arise when individuals within a network decide to use their positions of trust and influence to manipulate the market. The FIFA PAR have traditionally tried to protect players from conflicts of interest where a manager could also hold shares in an agency business. However, it is well known that many agencies are owned by people with family ties to managers in particular and there is concern that managers are being offered illegal payments to hire certain players.

In a principal-agent relationship, the agent acts on behalf of the principal. However, when there are incentives for an agent to act against the best interests of the principal, problems can occur. A football agent can benefit from his intermediary position which grants him full disclosure of private information from both clubs and players. He has an incentive to use his superior knowledge to capture an 'information rent'. In this context, some agents manage to become 'indispensable go-betweens' when concluding transfers for the top clubs, thus monopolising access to resources. In this case, the way agents 'work the market' obscures the information propagated in most central places (Demazière and Jouvenet, 2013). These agents allegedly have the power to distort the allocation of talent which would grant them market power. This would be the case if they placed players in clubs according to their personal interests or connections, with no reference to the economic rationale, and could lead to situations in which agents get paid more than they actually deserve. According to former agent Peter Harrison, agents are able to use their networks to take advantage of the naivety of some club chairmen. Specifically, he stated in an interview with the Daily Mail newspaper (Ashton, 2011):

> The commission with the club is whatever you can negotiate. When I took Lucas Neill to West Ham instead of Liverpool I earned £900,000 and they put the player on £72,000 a week.... He was going to Liverpool but West Ham wouldn't take no for an answer. It was incredible. At the time I thought it was just business – I had bills to pay, office, telephone, travel – but when I look back on it now I'm embarrassed.'

In this trusted role the agent was able to earn a better contract for the player because the chairman was less powerful in the negotiation process. Trusted by both the player and the club, Harrison himself was able to make a huge commission by acting as a gate keeper. However other questions must also be asked – was the agent acting in the best interests of the player in agreeing a contract with West Ham, or would the player have been better off by moving to Liverpool where the agent's commission might have been lower?

The network again is brought to the fore when assessing why an agent is trusted by a club when he is working for a player. While this form of dual representation is banned by FIFA, there are often ways around it. Again to quote Harrison (Ashton, 2011):

> The best way is to get a 'friendly agent' to act on behalf of the club – that way you can split the commission with someone you trust.... If, for example, the agent is based in Monaco, the club will pay his commission into an offshore account and he will pay the player's agent. It's all untraceable.' As this quote explains, agents work together to complete deals in their interest – a clear principal agent problem. Even though a deal may be the best possible outcome for both the club and player, the agent is making sure that by using his network he will be better off.

Transfer networks often span various countries and usually are set up to exploit economic advantages in other leagues. As we have seen, personal networks, as well as historic trends in migratory routes, support the movement of players, who are often driven to move having been promised higher salaries in other leagues. This movement of players is lucrative not only for the players them-selves, but also for the selling club and the player's agent who seek to profit from the move. Human agency and social embeddedness are central to the opera-tion of transfer markets. Specifically, networks have developed in order to help transfer information to decision makers. Since markets are composed of people with different information, opportunities arise when resources could be more efficiently deployed in other roles – in this case players would be more effective in different clubs and therefore there is surplus value from them moving. A reac-tion from an agent can help bring this system back into equilibrium. As informa-tion diffuses over time, individuals who are informed earlier have an advantage (Burt, 2003).

The elite players and their agents have been shown to have power over clubs since they are thought of as a scarce commodity and as such are irreplaceable. Through agents, strategies can be devised to effectively 'hold clubs to ransom' and the market is such that the top clubs who compete to sign such players appear to be willing to give in to the demands of the player and agent. By acting as a gate-keeper – denying access to the player apart from through him/herself – the agent is able to hold power over the club. While it is not unusual for a number of clubs to be interested in signing the best players, it is often the relationships of the players' representatives which facilitate the final choice of transfer. Thus the most powerful agents have the ability to influence the allocation of talent, distort the placement of players in clubs and take a fin-ancial advantage from it. This is even more concerning given that business is often conducted and set up as a result of interpersonal relations that fit into a complex system of debts and credits, mutual back-scratching and reciprocal exchanges of services (Shropshire and Davis, 2008). As we have seen, agents work closely with other professionals in football. Sporting directors are felt by agents to be the most important business partners when placing players, fol-lowed by football managers. This leads to situations in which managers and sporting directors who are very close to agents organise transfer deals jointly (Ashton, 2011).

The independence of agents and club managers is then questioned and we can observe cases in which sporting directors explicitly recommend some agents to their club players. Bower (2007) gives evidence on the mechanisms of bringing in trusted 'friends' on the intermediation side to allow for deals being concluded. This was notably the case in some Italian clubs in the 2000s where players already orally engaged had no choice but to change their agents on the day of signing their contract in order to secure the transfer. In fact, some clubs will only conclude deals with one or two specific agents, even if this agent is not the one who worked the deal.

On the other hand, cases also exist where clubs have to pay an agent when no agent had any part whatsoever in the deal. This stresses the gate-keeping role of the agent and indicates the market power of agents and the current distortion between their revenues and their actual efforts. When Wayne Rooney signed with Manchester United in 2004, it appears that the player had made his choice and that the clubs had negotiated an agreement. However, Manchester United decided to bring the agent Paul Stretford in to secure the deal. He was the official agent of the player but was not active in the process. This kind of situation gives another example of the lack of parity between the amount of service provided by the agent and the level of his remuneration.

The networks can often become opaque and information available to some parties may be held back according to who an agent is working with. This can lead to conflicts of interest. Similarly, a role in the network affording agents access to more information regarding new talent has led to them being involved with third party investment in players where they have a share of a player's economic rights. This too can potentially lead to conflicts of interest and that is considered further in the following chapter.

Notes

1 Social capital is defined as the collective value of all 'social networks' [who people know] and the inclinations that arise from these networks to do things for each other ['norms of reciprocity'].
2 The insiders-outsiders theory was originally created to describe economic behaviours in the labour market. It stresses the privileged position of incumbent workers in comparison to job-seekers, allowing the former to resist competition or even harass outsiders.
3 Nani's previous agent, Ana Almeida claimed that she had been sidelined from the deal.
4 AFA: Asociación del Fútbol Argentino.

Bibliography

AGCM (2006). *Indagine Conoscitiva sul Settore del Calcio Professionistico*. Roma: Autoritá Garante della Concorrenza e del Mercato.

Anon. (2014) *The secret football agent: Inside of the world of the football agent*. Edinburgh: Arena Sport.

Ashton, N. (2011) Top agent lifts the bid on football's murky secrets. *Daily Mail* [online]. Available from: www.dailymail.co.uk/sport/football/article-2040773/Andy-Carrolls-agent-reveals-footballs-dirty-secrets.html [accessed 12 January 2012].

Autor, D. H. (2001) Wiring the labor market. *Journal of Economic Perspectives*. 15(1), pp. 25–40.

Bessy, C. (1997) Cabinets de recrutement et formes d'intermédiation sur le marché du travail. In: Bessy, C. and Eymard-Duvernay, F. (eds) *Les intermediaires du marché du travail*. Paris: Presses Universitaires de France, pp. 103–141.

Bower, T. (2007) *Broken dreams: The definitive exposé of British football corruption (updated version)*. London: Pocket Books.

Bulliard, M. (2010) *Les intermédiaires dans les migrations professionnelles: La mise en relation de l'offre et de la demande dans le football*. MSc. Université de Neuchâtel.

Burt, R. S. (1992) *Structural holes. The social structure of competition*. Cambridge: Harvard University Press.

Burt, R. S. (2003) The social capital of structural holes. In: Guillen, R., Collins, R., England P. and Meyer, M. (eds) *The new economic sociology: Developments in an emerging field.* New York: Russell Sage Foundation, pp. 148–189.

Conn, D. (2014) Jorge Mendes: The most powerful man in football? *Guardian* [online]. Available from: www.theguardian.com/football/2014/sep/22/-sp-jorge-mendes-agent-third-party-ownership-players [accessed 30 November 2015].

Darby, P. (2000) The new scramble for Africa: African football labour migration to Europe. *European Sports History Review.* 3(1), pp. 217–244.

Demazière, D. and Jouvenet, M. (2013) The market work of football agents and the manifold valorizations of professional football players. *Economic Sociology European Electronic Newsletter* [online]. 15(1), pp. 29–40. Available from: http://econsoc.mpifg.de/archive/econ_soc_15-1_docm.pdf [accessed 10 April 2014].

Diouf, P. and Boniface, P. (2009) *De but en blanc.* Paris: Hachette Littératures.

Duval, A. and Torres, L. (2015) A bridge too far? Bridge transfers at the Court of Arbitration for Sport. *Asser International Sports Law* [online]. Available from: www.asser.nl/SportsLaw/Blog/post/a-bridge-too-far-bridge-transfers-at-the-court-of-arbitration-for-sport-by-antoine-duval-and-luis-torres [accessed 25 October 2015].

FIFA (2014) Argentinean and Uruguayan clubs sanctioned for bridge transfers. FIFA [online]. Available from: www.fifa.com/governance/news/y=2014/m=3/news=argentinian-and-uruguayan-clubs-sanctioned-for-bridge-transfers-2292724.html [accessed 21 March 2015].

Foot, J. (2007) *Calcio: A history of Italian football.* Harper Perennial: London.

Frenkiel, S. (2014) Une histoire des agents sportifs en France: Les imprésarios du football (1979-2014). Neuchâtel: Editions CIES.

Fulse, J. A. (2008) *Ethnizitat, akkulturation und personliche netwerke von italieschen migraten.* Opland: Barbara Budrich.

Granovetter, M. (1973) The strength of weak ties. *American Journal of Sociology.* 78(6), pp. 1360–1380.

Granovetter, M. (1983) The strength of weak ties: A network theory revisited. *Sociological Theory.* 1, pp. 201–233.

Granovetter, M. (1985) Economic action and social structure: The problem of embeddedness. *American Journal of Sociology.* 91(3), pp. 481–510.

Hamil, S., Morrow, S., Idle, C., Rossi, G. and Faccendini, S. (2010) The governance and regulation of Italian football. *Soccer & Society.* 11(4), pp. 373–413.

Jackson, J. (2006) Profile: Pini Zahavi, football's first and only super-agent. *Guardian* [online]. Available from: www.theguardian.com/sport/2006/nov/26/football.features [accessed 12 May 2011].

Jones, T. (2007) *The dark heart of Italy.* London: Faber & Faber.

Krugman, P. (1991) Increasing returns and economic geography. *Journal of Political Economy.* 99(1), pp. 484–99.

Lanfranchi, P. and Taylor, M. (2001) *Moving with the ball: The migration of professional footballers.* Oxford: Berg.

Lanfranchi, P., Eisenberg, C., Mason, T. and Wahl, A. (2004) *100 years of football: The FIFA centenary book.* London: Weidenfeld & Nicholson.

Laudisa, C. (2013) Gea, nuova era: Moggi riparte a 7 anni dall'inchiesta. *Gazzetta* [online]. Available from: www.gazzetta.it/Calcio/03-04-2013/gea-nuova-era-moggi-riparte-7-anni-inchiesta-92809724637.shtml [accessed 10 April 2014].

Levinsky, S. (2013) The third party: A tax avoidance scandal in Argentina could have ramifications across the globe. *The Blizzard – The Football Quarterly.* 7, pp. 151–153.

Lonsdale, C. (2004) Player power: Capturing value in the English football supply network. *Supply Chain Management: An International Journal.* 9(5), pp. 383–391.

Magee, J. and Sugden, J (2002), The world at their feet. Professional football and international labour migration. *Journal of Sport and Social Issues.* 26(4), pp. 421–437.

Marques, D. (2014) Amigo de Juvenal, indonésio conduz explosão de R$130 mi no futbol chinês. Terra [online]: Available from: http://esportes.terra.com.br/atletico-pr/amigo-de-juvenal-indonesio-conduz-explosao-de-r-130-mi-no-futebolchines,b4864afc024e34 10VgnVCM20000099cceb0aRCRD.html [accessed 28 November 2015].

Meyer, J. B. (2001) Network approach versus brain drain: Lessons from the Diaspora. *International Migration.* 39(5), pp. 91–110.

Monti, F. (2005) La GEA dei figli di papa' sempre al centro dei sospetti. *Corriere della Sera* [online]. Available from: http://archiviostorico.corriere.it/2005/aprile/01/Gea_dei_figli_papa_sempre_co_9_050401716.shtml [accessed 13 March 2012].

Pirel, B. (2013) *The secret footballer. Dans le peau d'un joueur de Premier League.* Paris: Hugo Sport.

Poli, R. (2008) *Production des footballeurs, reseaux marchands et mobilite profession-nelles dans l'économie globale. Le cas de joueurs africains en Europe.* PhD. Université de Neuchâtel.

Poli, R. (2009) Labour market migration to the five major leagues in European football: The impact of national team selection. In: *Labour market migration in European football: Key issues and challenges, proceedings from the Feet-Drain Conference,* May 2008. London: Birkbeck Sport Business Centre.

Poli, R. (2010a) Agents and intermediaries. In: Hamil, S. and Chadwick, S. (eds) *Managing football: An international perspective.* Oxford: Elsevier Butterworth-Heinemann, pp. 201–216.

Poli, R. (2010b) Understanding globalisation through football: The new international division of labour, migratory channels and transnational trade circuits. *International Review for the Sociology of Sport.* 45(4), pp. 491–506.

Poli, R. and Ravenel, L. (2005) Borders of 'free' movement in European football. Towards the globalization of players 'flows'. *Espace-Populations-Societies.* 2, pp. 293–303.

Reck, A. (2014) Bridge transfers under FIFA regulation. *Football Legal.* 1, pp. 36–40.

Russo, P. (2014) *Gol di rapina: il lato oscuro del calcio globale.* Firenze: Edizioni Clichy.

Semens, A. (2012a) Bridge, gate keeper, negotiator: The sports agent as entrepreneur. In: Ciletti, D. and Chadwick, S. (eds) *Sports entrepreneurship: Theory and practice.* Morgantown: Fitness Information Technology, pp. 81–95.

Semens, A. (2012b) Agents and intermediaries in the football industry. In: Chadwick, S. and Beech, J. (eds) *The business of sport management.* London: Financial Times Prentice Hall, pp. 1–34.

Shropshire, K. L. and Davis, T. (2008) *The business of sports agents.* 2nd edn. Philadelphia: University of Pennsylvania Press.

Stead, D. and Maguire, J. (2000) Rite de passage or passage to riches? The motivation and objectives of Nordic/Scandinavian on players in English League soccer. *Journal of Sport and Social Issues.* 24(1), pp. 36–60.

Szymanski, S. and Kuypers, T. (1999) *Winners and losers: The business strategy of football.* London: Viking.

Taylor, M. (2006) Global players? Football migration and globalization, *c.*1930–2000. *Historical Social Research.* 31(6), pp. 7–30.

Williams, J. (2007) Rethinking sports fandom: The case of European soccer. *Leisure Studies.* 26(2), pp. 127–146.

Wyscout (2015) About Wyscout forum. Wyscout [online]. Available from: https://forum.wyscout.com/about/ [accessed 28 November 2015].

7 Football agents and third party entitlements

Overview

As we have seen in the previous chapter, player transfers can be mediated by third parties who may or may not have their own interests at the forefront in moving players. In the economic context of the transfer market, football players are not just workers under contract with a club, they are also commodities. Theoretically, the resource based view, RBV, suggests that they can be conceived of as strategic resources which help clubs to obtain a competitive advantage in their industry and generate value, thereby contributing to both the strategic and the financial viability of the club. It follows that different actors in football, including players' agents, create value-added chains in order to gain profit from the career trajectory of football players through their transfers between clubs (Poli, 2010).

The concept of third party entitlement, TPE, has been briefly introduced in Chapter 5 in the context of the influence of networks. This chapter seeks to understand the practice more, by considering its historic development and role in the transfer market. While TPE has grown organically and therefore can take many forms, we begin by providing a general definition before looking at the nuances of other forms of financing players. We explain TPE primarily in the context of agents and intermediaries, identifying their centrality in the process. Case studies are presented to give an exhaustive analysis of this phenomenon, which has become widespread in some markets. We finish by touching on the current position of governing bodies that are opposed to TPE.

7.1 An introduction to TPE

The TPE concept in relation to football players is a relatively new phenomenon, though it has existed elsewhere in various guises for a long time. TPE is defined as

> The entitlement to future transfer compensation of any party other than the two clubs transferring the registration of players from one to the other, with the exception of the players' training clubs as per the solidarity mechanism provided in the FIFA RSTP.

> (CDES and CIES, 2014: 2)

Forms of TPE can include club-to-club co-ownership, club-to-agent co-ownership, economic rights pledged to secure credit and player participation in transfer rights (KPMG, 2013). Behind this practice, specific forms of TPE offer alternative means of financing for football clubs.

Specifically, third party ownership, TPO, is

> usually and commonly defined as the Agreement between a Club and a Third Party, such as investment funds, companies, sports agencies, agents and/or private investors, in accordance to which, a Third Party, whether or not in relation with an actual payment in favour of a club, acquires an economic participation or a future credit related to the eventual transfer of a certain player.
>
> (KPMG, 2013: 5)

This differs from third party investment, TPI, in that there is no contractual relation with the players as the third party provides loans, like banks do, to football clubs specifically to invest in players. In this case, players' economic rights are not owned by the third parties that assist clubs' transfer market strategies by financing them.

While the TPO market share in European leagues has been estimated at between 5.1 per cent and 7.8 per cent (KPMG, 2013), TPO was valued at $359.52 million annually and represented 9.68 per cent of the global value of transfer compensation on international transfers in 2013, according to a study commissioned by FIFA (CDES and CIES, 2014).

TPE is therefore relevant in value-added chains by helping to facilitate the movement (or not) of players, without which clubs would be subject solely to the market forces which favour the bigger clubs. Agents and intermediaries have become key to the organisation of TPE deals by uniting their contacts. Before looking in detail at the empirical evidence of TPE, it is useful to understand why the concept has emerged from a theoretical perspective.

7.2 Football players as strategic and competitive resources

In recent years, academics have explained differences in the success of firms with reference to their 'competitive advantage', i.e. those resources owned and controlled by firms, which are unavailable to competitors (Penrose, 1959; Miller and Shamsie, 1996). According to the RBV, resources can be defined as those assets that are tied semi-permanently to the firm and, together with capabilities, are the foundation of the firm's long term strategy since they are the primary source of profit (Amit and Schoemaker, 1993). These strategic resources are defined as valuable, rare, inimitable and non-substitutable and any firm has then to identify how to generate, manage and control them in order to establish and enhance its sustainable competitive advantage and, in turn, its profits (Barney, 1991). The RBV therefore helps us to understand the relationships between resources, capabilities, competitive advantage and profitability and, as a consequence, can help with strategic planning. Additionally, the firm's returns from its resources depend not only on sustaining its competitive position over time, but also on its ability to appropriate these returns. The issue of appropriability concerns the allocation of rents where property rights are not fully defined.

In the football context, since players are valuable, rare, inimitable and non-substitutable for their clubs, clubs' actions in the transfer market, based on their scouting and recruitment process, can be thought of as representing the most important strategics decision that have to be made. Indeed, contrary to other professional sports (e.g. rugby, basketball), football clubs buy out the contracts of players whose registration rights are owned by other clubs in an exchange for a negotiated amount of compensation. In operational terms, this financial element to labour market moves, which must be agreed in a relatively open market, has created opportunities for third parties to compete with clubs in the market to acquire these resources and extract economic rents for themselves.

Indeed for an agent, when it comes to assessing resources[1] owned and controlled by third parties, their main asset is the network of personal relationships that they operate in. Built informally over time, and not governed by contracts which could expire over time, agents use their networks to obtain information that can help them in making deals. In the context of the transfer market, third parties have helped to turn players into resources, either explicitly or implicitly[2] and, in this respect, TPE investors buy a stake in the player's contract which entitles them to a share of the financial benefit from a player's transfer. While agents are often involved in this, there are many other potential stakeholders for TPEs, including holding companies, investment funds, club shareholders and employees, football academies and even football players and their relatives.

Given the competitive nature of the representation market, some agents and intermediaries have found ways to differentiate themselves from the competition and to make their activity profitable, despite not controlling many resources, by their access to those resources. However, as we have seen under the principal-agent framework in Chapter 5, while players are advised by agents, they are not controlled by them, or at least, agents do not have the legal means to control the moves of players and since many player agent relationships do not involve a formal contract, an agent's relationship with profitable clients is vulnerable. However, agents' revenues are tightly linked to the players they represent. By investing in TPEs, agents have found a way to convert players into property-based resources which can be protected and become a source of profit. In theoretical terms, agents have taken advantage of the transfer system that was implemented by clubs under the same resource-based rationale since TPE is derived directly from this strategy. Investing formally in players thus gives agents a competitive advantage in the market and the potential to profit from holding a share of a player's economic rights.

7.3 TPE history

The speculative nature of the transfer market suggests that the concept of TPE is likely to have been present in one form or another since its inception. However, TPE in its current sense is a more recent phenomenon. Early examples emerged in the 1960s, when Raimondo Lanza di Trabia, chairman of Palermo Calcio, used to personally invest in the economic rights of the players he signed from South America,[3] without involving the club directly in the transfer market (Ordine, 2002). Similarly, in Spain, agent Luis Guijarro is known to have invested in the economic rights of promising players in the late 1960s (Vasco, 2012). In Uruguay, TPE has been documented since the late 1970s and on 18 March 1980 'any transfer of a player's rights linked to his sport activity or his future transfer in favour of a physical or legal body that is not a sport association' was expressly prohibited (section 2, decree n.14996). This legal provision was motivated by the development of practices, initiated by intermediaries, which were believed to limit the integrity of the transfer market.

As the football transfer market has expanded globally, TPE, as a way for clubs to finance the recruitment of talent, has become more widespread (Bourg and Gouget, 2010). Through the 1990s and 2000s in particular, highly indebted clubs faced harsh credit conditions with limited access to finance and high interest rates, meaning that new financing solutions were necessary in order to stay in business. In France, FC Brest Armorique was the first club known to use TPE in 1986, when the club recruited the Argentinian Jose Luis Brown and the Brazilian Julio Cesar, with the support of a pool of local investors united under the auspices of a company named SODIBA (Allain, 1999). The LFP sought to stop this practice in order to maintain the independence of its clubs and included a provision on TPE in its administrative regulations in the 1988/89 season. Under Article 221 concerning the assignment or purchase of players' property rights, a new rule stated that

> A club may not conclude a contract, with a legal person other than another club or with a natural person, resulting in the direct or indirect assignment to, or purchase from, such persons of all or a portion of the property rights deriving from the amounts which the club may claim in connection with the transfer of one or several of its players.

In South America too TPE has become embedded owing to the imbalanced nature of the leagues. Small and medium-sized clubs face a vicious circle wherein they struggle to generate significant commercial revenues because they are not performing particularly well on the pitch. As a consequence, they cannot invest in players that would help them to compete on a bigger stage and thus increase revenues (Cravo and Castro Moreira Sordi, 2014). Despite enormous potential for the football industry, many South American football clubs have faced insolvency through bad management, bribery and financial embezzlement by directors as well as through a championship structure which favours only the major clubs (Bourg and Gouget, 2010). In Brazil, the profitable export of talent and the lucrative sponsorship of the national team have coexisted with economic and institutional instability in the championships, with clubs in debt, overstaffed professional teams, and low attendance in stadia. Moreover, instead of companies, most clubs are organised as civil associations, meaning that private investors could not inject cash into the clubs through buying shares. In this context, TPE has become the main form of investment in football in Brazil. Without legal regulation, these atypical contracts have been based on Article 286 of the Brazilian Civil Code relating to the transfer of credit. Consequently, an investment market has emerged where third parties, unaffiliated with football clubs, provide finance to clubs in exchange for a share in transfer fees. Since the mid-1990s, a system of external economic partnerships, named *parceria*, has become an alternative to private funding, allowing any company to invest in a club over a minimum period of ten years, with the right to take a share of clubs' commercial revenues and transfer fees offered in return (Bourg and Gouget, 2010). This has fundamentally changed the nature of clubs, with those playing in the Brazilian top division now generating competition between investment companies such as HMTF, MSI, and Exxel who see the potential to make huge profits when Brazilian talent transfers to European leagues and therefore want to be involved.

The widening gap between the main markets in Europe demanding talent and those countries in South America and Africa supplying it has created new opportunities for intermediaries. While agents are often spoken about with disdain in European markets and their role in TPE is vilified, the opposite is true in South American football, where agents and intermediaries are named as empresario do futbol, i.e. football entrepreneurs who go beyond the simple role of players' representatives. Similarly, as clubs have progressively implemented more sophisticated talent management methods, several South American clubs have created their own investment funds in order to sell the economic rights of their players. In 1997, Boca Juniors is thought to have become the first club in the world to create a fund to sell the economic rights of its players when it established La Xeneize Sociedad De Fondos Comunes de Inversión (Leblebidjian, 2003). The fund, that was open to any types of investor, was fully recognised by the Argentinian financial authorities and attracted significant numbers of investors, collecting $13 million at the time of its launch. In total, the fund acquired the economic rights of 12 players from Boca Juniors. Through this system, clubs had the opportunity to cash in the partial or entire sale of the economic rights of some players in advance, while their federative and labour rights remained under the control of the club.

In England, the first TPE case emerged in 2000 when the transfer of Columbian player Juan Pablo Angel from River Plate to Aston Villa was being discussed. At that time Angel's agent, Gustavo Mascardi, owned half of the player's economic rights (Bower, 2007). The English FA was informed by FIFA that it was strictly forbidden for an agent to own any part of the player's rights and the transfer looked to be in jeopardy. However, an agreement was reached and Angel arrived in January 2001. A very different form of TPE appeared in summer 2002, when the supporter run AFC Bournemouth agreed several deals with Playershare, a limited company set up by the supporters to fund player purchases and salaries in exchange for a percentage of future transfer income. The company, run by a chairman and an operating committee, even advanced funds for non-profitable loan deals in return for a financial interest in other players or a percentage of future transfer income from the entire squad. At the time, Trevor Watkins, a sport lawyer, who led the rescue of AFC Bournemouth as chairman during the supporters' buyout and advised 15 FL clubs on ways of raising finance, stated:

> The idea of buying a share of a player is something new, but it is growing in stature and growing in regularity. There will be people who want it to make money out of football out of the football club and will be prepared to lend money if they get a decent return.

(Hart, 2004)

However, it was not until two Argentinian players, Carlos Tevez and Javier Mascherano, signed for West Ham United from Brazilian club Corinthians in 2006 that TPE really became prominent. The players' economic rights were both held by third party owners, MSI and Just Sports, who contractually had exclusive power to decide on their transfer movements. West Ham United did not have a veto over this right and such a stipulation breached Rule V.20 as it meant that outside parties had material influence over the decision-making of West Ham United.[4] As, prior to this case, there was no express clause prohibiting TPE in English football, the English football authorities have since created a stringent regulatory mechanism which has had a significant impact on the regulation of player transfers, ultimately leading to an outright ban on TPE from the beginning of the 2008/09 season.

Any historical analysis of the development of TPE would not be complete without mentioning the case of Portugal, the first European country to expressly adopt TPE as a regular development system for clubs in 2000. With the country's favourable immigration legislation, Portuguese clubs have traditionally recruited players from Brazil whose citizens can easily obtain an EU passport in Portugal. This immigration system has enabled some Portuguese clubs to gain a competitive advantage over their European competitors in attracting players. Off the back of this, TPE practices have been developed to directly support clubs through the acquisition of a player's economic rights. The FPFPF was the first investment fund dedicated to football which involved Portuguese clubs. The fund was set up by First Portuguese SGPSS S.A. in 2002. In April 2004, Grupo Orey became the major shareholder via Football Players Funds Management Limited. The fund invested in three main Portuguese clubs with the following results:[5]

- Porto: the fund invested €8.5 million in 16 Porto players who were all transferred in the following years. The fund earned almost €12 million with a net profit of €3 million.

- Sporting Lisbon: almost €8.5 million was invested in 22 players acquired by Sporting Lisbon. After successful transfers the Fund reported a net profit of €2 million.
- Boavista: the investment in Boavista players was not disclosed.

In 2003 the Fund's yield peaked at 80 per cent with the sale of Cristiano Ronaldo by Sporting Lisbon to Manchester United. After the sale of Ricardo Carvalho, Paulo Ferreira, Deco and Pedro Mendes (sold by Porto for a total €74 million), the Porto fund's value increased by 37 per cent in 2004. In the same year, Sporting Lisbon and Boavista fund performance registered a loss of 8 per cent and 3 per cent respectively. Since then, the value of the portfolio has decreased due to lack of high value transfers and many investors have left the fund, having realised significant capital gains. The fund terminated its activity in January 2008, prompting several other funds to emerge.

An innovative and controversial form of TPE, specifically named ISA, has recently emerged in North America. Similar to the TPE agreements in football, ISAs enable funds to be generated now with view to receiving a return in future. The difference between these funds and the traditional TPEs is that ISAs are conducted between individual athletes who need to raise funds and third parties. In other words, as illustrated in the following case study, the athletes pledge a percentage of their future earnings to the investors over a defined period (Oei and Ring, 2015).

Case study: Fantex

Launched in 2012, Fantex is a platform that offers investors the opportunity to invest in stock linked to the cash flows generated by contracts with professional athletes in terms of playing contracts, endorsements, speaking fees, etc, known as ABIs (Fantex, 2015). In detail, this platform gives an athlete an upfront lump sum payment in return for a percentage of his ABIs. When the athlete earns money from his ABIs, Fantex receives cash from the athlete. A typical contract with Fantex, specifies that 95 per cent of the athlete's income from ABIs is attributable to the respective tracking stock. Based on the available cash for each tracking stock, Fantex intends to return a percentage of this cash to the stockholders via periodic dividend distributions. The stock price does not reflect the current perceived success of the athletes, as the investors buy shares in the company as whole and not individual players (Roberts, 2015). From October 2013 to September 2015, Fantex signed contracts with 11 athletes and has completed six IPOs worth a total of $25.8 million.

Athletes are turned into stock as follows:

1   An athlete agrees to sell Fantex a portion of his future brand-related earnings;
2   Fantex writes up the paperwork to sell a certain amount of shares to the public at a given price via an IPO;
3   The athlete goes through a pre-IPO period just like a corporation following a traditional IPO protocol and issues a prospectus;

4   While salaries go public, the athlete is paid upfront and Fantex keeps around 5 per cent. For example, in Vernon Davies IPO for $4.21 million, Davies was paid $4 million upfront and Fantex took the remaining $210,000;

5   Shares are traded on Fantex's Brokerage Service.

Based on this procedure, Fantex engages in a detailed statistical process to estimate the fair value of each contract signed by its athletes, adjusted for the risk taken (Fantex, 2015). First, a statistical model is used to estimate the athlete's future playing contracts by determining the closest set of comparable players, based on factors such as draft position, production, durability and injury history. Second, the same future playing contracts are also estimated based on historical and estimated future growth of salaries in that sport overall.

There are a number of factors that can impact the value of an investment in a Fantex stock (Fantex, 2015). First, an athlete's performance on the field – both positive and negative – has the potential to impact the value of his future playing contracts. Second, the ability or inability of the athlete to secure revenue generating opportunities away from the playing field will impact on the total income paid by the athlete to Fantex. Finally, Fantex is actively engaged in audience development with all of the athletes it has under contract. If successful, these activities may help an athlete to increase his income. These programmes, if unsuccessful, will not provide any benefit to the athlete and his ability to generate additional income.

7.4 Types of TPE and its business models

The interpretation of what constitutes TPE varies considerably, depending on individuals' knowledge of the subject and their degree of involvement in the practice, as well as their personal opinion. Since TPE has developed largely in response to the market and without formal rules, it is often subject to negotiation and varies according to the specifics of a contract. Factors like the age of the player, his past performance and the remaining duration of his contract all contribute to what a third party will expect as a return. The general understanding of what constitutes a TPE is also debatable; one could contemplate exclusion of the practices of certain actors, i.e. clubs and players from the definition of TPE, and reduce it to the activities of others, typically investment funds and companies, or only, for example, consider practices which are potentially in breach of Articles 18bis and 18tris of the FIFA RSTP as TPE.

From a legal perspective, TPE is regarded as the implementation of business law instruments, such as the assignment of future receivables in football. In this context, there is a distinction between economic rights and registration rights of football players (Burgess, 2008). The latter is understood to be the right of a club to register a player with the national association so that the player can be fielded for the club, in different competitions organised by the national association. In this regard, CAS jurisprudence (CAS 2004/A/662 *RCD Mallorca v. Club Atletico Lanus*) establishes that a player can only play for one club at a time; hence, 'registration rights' 'cannot be shared simultaneously among different clubs'. For both FIFA and CAS jurisprudence (CAS 2005/A/878 *Club Guarani v. G. & Club FC St. Gallen AG*), registration rights as defined above have no economic value. They are not a property right which would justify the payment of financial compensation in the event of the transfer of a player to another club. However, others suggest that registration rights in South American countries such as Brazil, Argentina or Paraguay in particular, are valuable since whenever a club and a player are bound by an employment contract, there is an associated pecuniary value. Within this interpretation, the economic rights refer to the financial revenue arising from the transfer of players' registration rights from one club to another, i.e. the assignment of clubs' right to register a player with a national association.

CAS recognises the ownership of economic rights as legally valid and that they derive from the employment contract, instead of registration rights. Thus, according to relevant CAS jurisprudence (CAS 2004/A/635 *RCD Espanyol De Barcelona Sad v. Club Atletico Velez Sarsfield*),

> in professional football a basic legal distinction is to be made between the registration of a player and the economic rights related to a player [...]. A club holding an employment contract with a player may assign, with the player's consent, the contract rights to another club in exchange for a given sum of money or other consideration, and those contract rights are the so called economic rights to the performances of a player. This commercial transaction is legally possible only with regard to players who are under contract, since players who are free from contractual engagements – the so called free agents – may be hired by any club freely, with no economic rights involved [...]. In accordance with the above distinction, while a player registration may not be shared simultaneously among different clubs, a player can only play for one club at a time, the economic rights, being ordinary contract rights, may be partially assigned and thus apportioned among different right holders.

Consequently, the existing case law shows that the apportionment of economic rights – considered as the assignment of contractual rights once the player is transferred from one club to another – is not regarded as contrary to football regulations. Whilst registration rights cannot be fractioned, economic rights can be shared and co-owned by third-parties. CAS, however, qualified its endorsement, saying: 'as long as FIFA does not issue an express prohibition, clubs are allowed to treat those economic rights as assets and commercialise them in ways allowed by States' legal systems'. In this context, although FIFA has expressly banned any form of TPE, it remains to be seen how case law will change. For example, in Spain, the Spanish law admits the existence of economic rights as independent and autonomous rights that are potentially subject to commercial exploitation (Crespo and San Torcuato Caffa, 2014).

TPE can pursue different objectives and be materialised under various forms as arrangements are very diverse and typically undisclosed. Returning to the example of Jorge Mendes' Gestifute in Chapter 6 can provide more detail on TPE. The prospectus of the investment fund 'Quality Sport V Investment LP', registered in the tax haven Jersey, clearly demonstrates the involvement of Gestifute in a TPE (Capitas Sport Limited, 2012).

As illustrated in Figure 7.1, the fund Quality Sport V Investment financed through loan arrangements the Irish securitisation company Quality Football Ireland to acquire economic rights relating to football players whose registration rights are registered with football clubs that are predominantly in Spain, Portugal, Germany, Turkey and Brazil but not in the UK. All the investments were based on the investment reports suggested by the investment advisors, Opto Sport Investment and Gestifute International. The advisors devised, through investment agreements, an investment strategy that supported investors' returns based on a proven track record in brokering football transfers. Previously, both advisors advised the following investment schemes in the names of Quality Sport I Investment LP, Quality Sport II Investment LP, Quality Sport III Investment LP, and Quality Sport IV Investment LP. The amount which was invested

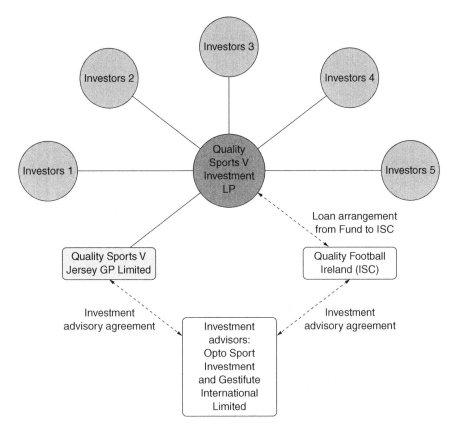

Figure 7.1 Quality Sport V Investment's fund structure (source: adapted from Capitas Sport Limited (2012)).

was €10 million, €13.6 million, €10.9 million and €14.1 million respectively. Opto Sport Investment was managed by Peter Kenyon, who was involved as a former Chelsea CEO in approximately 180 player transfers with a value of €1 billion. In 2009, he joined CAA and set up three funds with similar investment objectives. From 2001 to 2010, Gestifute International was involved in transfers worth, in aggregate, over €500 million.

The fund was managed by the general partner company Quality Sports V, whose shares were split equally between Opto Sport Investment and Gestifute International. The fund expected to partner with three Portuguese clubs, Benfica, Sporting Lisbon and Sporting Braga, and one Spanish club, Atletico Madrid.

The main peculiarity of the fund structure is that both investment advisors were also part of the managing company of the fund and were still active as advisors for other similar investment funds. This created the possibility of potential conflicts of interests at the expense of potential investors, as was promptly highlighted in the investment prospectus.

Nevertheless, as Figure 7.2 simply illustrates, any TPE project in football follows a standard process in order to select investment in players' economic rights.

The formal investment process is as follows:

*   Initial consideration of a player following fundamental, quantitative and qualitative assessment;
*   Enter NDA with the club and request player briefing;
*   Seek player summary from independent source;
*   Send club due diligence enquiries;
*   Standard enquiries of relevant football league and or association;
*   Prepare and report recommendations (including assessing legal positions) regarding player and clubs;
*   Negotiate and agree/sign HOTS with club;
*   Refer to independent valuer and/or insurer;
*   Send long-form investment agreement to club.

This standard process can be modified according to the contractual mechanisms, known as ERPA, that usually involve some clauses between the club and the third parties acquiring the player's economic rights. First, a guarantee period is agreed, during which the player cannot be transferred to another club without the mutual consent of both the club and the investor. This clause protects clubs' interests in order to maintain a certain degree of stability within the team. Second, a minimum value is agreed which would be accepted at the end of the guarantee period in order to sell the player's registration. In this case, the club retains the preferential option to acquire players' registrations. Third, the third party can target deals for an amount equal to or higher than the agreed value in the second half of the year before the final year of a player's contract, although the club still maintains first refusal on the acquisition of the fund's rights. Fourth, as the club uses the players in its activity, the third party receives a variable

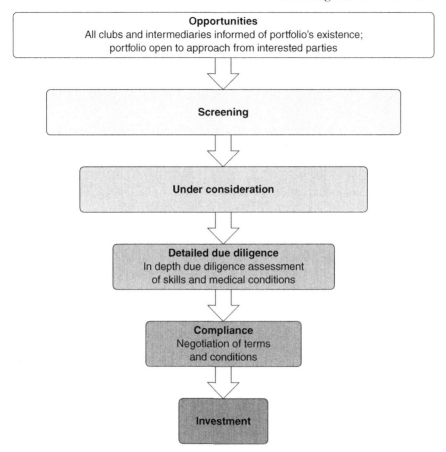

Figure 7.2 TPE investment process.

remuneration related to the investment made in those players and linked to the projected value of the players. Finally, there might be some options in the contract for the club to reacquire the part of player's registration sold to the fund.

Under the investment structure outlined above, three main types of TPE are observed in football: financing TPE, investment TPE and recruitment TPE (KPMG, 2013).

Financing TPE occurs when a club enters into a contractual relationship with a third party in order to generate revenue to finance the club in exchange for a percentage of the economic right of one or several of its players whose registration rights are owned by the club. This type of TPE depends on several factors, such as the investment made by the investors, the potential value of the player and the player's characteristics and performance, as well as the clubs' financial needs. This type of TPE allows clubs to receive the economic liquidity to balance their accounts and to cover external or internal mandatory expenses.

Investing TPE occurs when a club wants to sign a player from another club, but does not have the necessary financial resources to pay the transfer compensation. In this case, the club and the investor interested in financing a part or all of the transfer compensation would enter into a TPE. The percentage owned by the third party will obviously depend on the financial resources of the club at the time of signing the player and thus on the third party investment and financial support provided to the club in this regard. The investor would be entitled to receive a share in the future transfer of the player in relation to the percentage of the economic rights owned through the investment provided. The parties involved, i.e. the club and the investor, are therefore the co-holders of the player's economic rights and agree on the percentage of the player's economic rights that the investor would, from that moment, hold. Any future revenues generated from the player's transfer would be shared accordingly.

In contrast, recruitment TPE appears when a club wants to recruit a young talented player and extends a percentage of his economic rights, and therefore a percentage of any revenues deriving from that in his future transfer, to an agent, a company, a player's relatives, or even the player himself. This TPE is common in South America where intermediaries with sufficient professional capacity and contacts to recruit a player for a particular club may be remunerated with rights to a percentage of transfer fees for current or future compensation.

Not only are agents passive receivers of this benefit, they also take part in the negotiation process related to the redefinition of labour contracts with the club. Negotiating a percentage of future transfers is a way for agents to recover the investment they make in young players and in particular to make this recovery more likely. Without TPE, agents have no guarantee of future returns from a player and considering both the high volatility of the players' representation market and the two year maximum duration of an agent's mandate, there is little protection for agents. When agents represent clubs, they tie the success of selling a player for an amount above his estimated value to the acquisition of a percentage of the residual gain. While the payment may take the form of a commission fee, the agent actually receives a share of the revenue generated by the purchase of the player's economic rights. If agents can access players' economic rights as individual intermediaries, they can also be involved in the purchase and management of players' economic rights through their direct involvement in investment funds or companies as collaborators, advisors or even investors.

7.5 TPEs and their implications for agents

TPE is therefore manifest in various forms. According to CDES and CIES (2014), TPE actors can be separated into two macro categories as illustrated in Figure 7.3. On one side are the natural persons who are individuals who invest directly in TPE contracts and accrue the related benefits. These stakeholders may include football players, intermediaries and football agents, club owners and football directors, as well as individual investors. Alternatively, on the opposite side are legal entities, which include clubs as well as financial investment

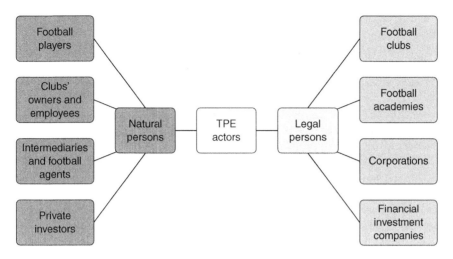

Figure 7.3 TPE actors (source: adapted from CDES and CIES (2014)).

companies, corporations and football academies that are not necessarily affiliated to any football association or clubs.

Despite the presence of high profile individuals such as Jorge Mendes and
Peter Kenyon, most TPE investors, both natural and legal persons, are outsiders
to the football world. This enables agents to provide a dual role, one relatively
official while the other is less transparent. First, agents, as football insiders, are
very often official members of the experts' commission set up by investors in
order to give advice on which players should be targeted. Second, the central
position of agents in transfer deals also grants them the ideal role of ambassador.
Indeed, third parties, although interested in the details and the conclusion of
transfer deals, are not supposed to have an influence. In particular, they are not
physically present around the negotiation table and have in turn to respect the
deal as concluded by the negotiating participants. It is then very tempting to convince an agent to represent the interests of the third party during the negotiation
or at least to communicate the information shared during the discussion. As
clubs have clear incentives to keep third party shares down, agents are the ideal
partner for third parties. The conditions under which agents can conduct such an
emissary role are not always transparent, but the numerous ties between agents
and third party owners of players' economic rights indicate that such relations
exist.

According to Russo (2014), TPE has evolved in three phases, which may
overlap or change order depending on the different national contexts.

An initial phase usually occurs when agents and intermediaries have directly
invested in players' economic rights through open and closed investment funds
and other financial tools. It is an embryonic phase in which trades occur crudely,
based on the acquisition of shares in the economic rights of the player with the

hope of making a profit on future transfers. A second phase occurs when investment funds do not just invest in players' economic rights but contribute funds to be used in various functions within a club that is not able to afford to buy players. In return the investors receive a percentage of future returns from the same players' transfers. In this case, clubs only act as shareholders of transfers. In most cases, the players in question are already controlled by the investment fund, and therefore the clubs mainly act to promote the players on the transfer market. A third phase is when the funds come from private financial institutions that lend money to the clubs for various purposes, from buying players to refinancing clubs' debts. The main consequence of this phase may be the loss of a club's operational autonomy which can lead to the investor taking control or acquiring the club. While the first phase is almost monopolised by agents and intermediaries who are speculative football investors looking for easy returns, the second and the third phases show the involvement of relevant financial institutions and venture capital funds in search of innovative investments. The following case study of Traffic Group epitomises how an agency can operate across all three phases, and in this case has become an influential player in the transfer market over the last decade.

Case study: Traffic Sports

Over the last decade, alongside the commercialisation of football, there has been a steady increase in football investment initiatives in Brazil, and in particular those relating to players' economic rights. Several companies from different industries, such as the Texan HMTF, Supermarket Bretas, Sonda and EMS Pharma, have been involved in TPE supported by intermediaries and agents. In this case study, the focus is on Traffic Group and its strategic expansion into TPE practices (Lemos Neto, 2009). Founded in 1980, the Group has embraced the business of football in its entirety more than any other similar company. Traffic operates as a full service sports marketing company, providing business solutions that add value to its clients' and partners' brands in sports events and other media and entertainment properties, as illustrated in Figure 7.4. In addition, as the broadcast rights holder of the most important competitions in Latin America, the group has expanded beyond continental borders to promote South and Latin American football to consumers around the world.

Additionally, Traffic launched a player representation company to diversify its activities into the management of players' careers (Lemos Neto, 2009). Contrary to the majority of TPE, which normally invests in shares of a player's economic rights through parallel contracts between clubs and themselves, Traffic Football Management had a comprehensive framework which, in principle, allowed the group two different types of investment in players. The first was through its football academy and clubs whereby a first class youth system has been created to help young talent develop into professional players. The second was through the foundation of a privately held company, Cedro SA, which, while being a strictly TPE company, differentiated its model from others by taking into account Traffic's parallel presence in the management of football.

Through Traffic Football Management, the group has managed the career of several players, both as player representatives and through owning their economic rights (Lemos Neto, 2009). In 2000, Traffic Sports Europe was created in Amsterdam. Similarly, in 2002 the group expanded into North America, with the acquisition of 100 per cent of the shares in Inter-Forever Sports, to establish Traffic Sports USA. Besides having television rights to CONCACAF competitions, the American subsidiary became one of the best performing in the group, and in 2006 it founded Miami FC, renamed Fort Lauderdale Strikers in 2011. From a business perspective, competing in the current NASL, the second tier of US professional football, the club has become a training centre for talent from across North America, Central America and the Caribbean. A year previously, in 2005, the group had already expanded its operation into football management founding the club Desportivo Brasil with the aim of discovering and developing football talent to pursue national and international careers in the top Brazilian and international clubs. The group has employed a team of scouts and agents to capture and manage its assets, as well as creating its own fully equipped academy to host and train up to 140 players. The academy of Porto Feliz, designed to serve Desportivo Brasil, was the first of a series of centres from which Traffic monitored the whole process of player training and, incidentally, made sure that nobody else could claim part of any future sale. In November, 2008, Desportivo Brasil announced a partnership with Manchester United to promote the exchange of athletes and coaching staff with the aim of improving training methods and playing friendly matches and international tournaments. In line with their previous operations and strategy, in 2006, after success in Europe, the group strengthened its presence by creating Traffic Portugal. In late 2007 the company signed a cooperation agreement with the club Ituano until March 2009, when the club broke the partnership contract (Maquina do Esporte, 2008). Traffic Group's idea was to merge the two clubs to facilitate the rapid rise of Desportivo Brasil to the first division of the Paulista Championship, as Ituano was in the second division. However, the club board preferred to see Ituano maintain its autonomy and independence (Maquina do Esporte, 2009). Other agreements were established to open new academies in various locations in the states of Parana and Rio Grande do Sul. In July 2009, Traffic Europe bought 74 per cent of the shares of CD Estoril Praia with a view to managing the club. Consequently, the best players from Traffic's academies were transferred to the Portuguese club to compete in a European league. While using lower league clubs for players to gain experience was nothing new in South America – the cases of the agents Juan Figuer and Paco Casal, for example, demonstrate how players' economic right were being transferred to Rentistas and Centro Atletico Fénix, respectively, creating bridge transfers to obtain a greater benefit from future transfers to top South American and European clubs – that was not the case with Traffic (Glüsing, 1997).

Although Traffic invested in players through their own football club, they also operated outside it in attaining the economic rights of players. In 2007, Desportivo Brasil first bought the economic rights of the defender Gustavo and then instantly transferred him to S.E. Palmeiras on loan. By 2008, Traffic created and managed investment funds to directly acquire the partial or total ownership of players' economic rights. Traffic managed a group of 20 shareholders, who each bought a $200,000 share, investing R$40 million in Brazilian players with potential to play in the best Brazilian clubs. The fund Cedro SA was not registered with the CVM and only a limited number of investors were given the opportunity to participate.

The idea of managing an investment fund that was dedicated to acquiring promising players' economic rights in order to speculate on their transfers was not innovative per se. Funds investing in Brazilian players have worked across all kinds of business models. For example, the fund DIS invested in players with great potential, so the initial investment required to get their rights was higher. This implied a greater risk, because it limited the number of players acquired, but it also meant higher profits if their development was as expected. In this sense, Traffic opted for a more conservative strategy: it was not about selecting potential stars, but focussed on several mid-level players. This formula with lower risk and higher liquidity enabled them to attract investors in times of crisis and the fund, Cedro, paid interest bi-annually, after each transfer window, and was settled over three football seasons, the usual period for which Traffic signed its players.

While football has some unique characteristics, the methods used have clear parallels with those of multinationals dealing in raw materials; i.e. controlling the whole process was a necessary condition. Apart from production and control, another important element was the distribution of talent. It is rare that a fund can be established with the necessary infrastructure to be competitive in business. For this reason, a specialist technical department was responsible for the production of videos and reports on the players under the Traffic umbrella to facilitate their transfers.

Cedro provided a ROE of 25 per cent to 30 per cent per annum for the investors and transfers included those of Henrique and Keirrison from S.E. Palmeiras to Barcelona in 2008 for €24 million, generating a 114 per cent return for the fund (Duff and Panja, 2013). Overall, the fund gained 62 per cent profit on the first 21 players that it owned and sold. However, of the 30 players contracted by Cedro, not all made it – one contract expired before the player's economic rights were marketed, for example, meaning the investment was worthless. There are many other risks which are unique to football (Lemos Neto, 2009): a serious injury to a player, for example, can end his career; financial impacts also mean clubs at times are willing to accept or pay much less in a transfer; players' transfer fees can rise due to much greater competition between funds in Brazil. These are some of the reasons, supported by the technical area of the CVM that have prevented retail investors from investing in these funds in Brazil, as the risks associated with these types of investments in football can be only perceived by the qualified investor and, in this kind of investment, it is necessary to separate passion from reason. Another problem to be circumvented by these funds is the competition with individual intermediaries or agents who have learnt to make money with football players. Traffic, for example, had direct contact with clubs to facilitate the inclusion of any promising player in the team and also good relationships with international clubs that provided the best financial proposal to implement a transfer. Competition in this niche market rose sharply after the creation of other funds such as Delcir Sonda and BMG.

After Cedro, Traffic decided not to launch a new investment fund in Brazil, feeling there were not enough players available. Instead, around $100 million was raised for a new fund in partnership with Dubai-based firm CedarBridge which invests in other markets (Calvin, 2013). Quoting Magellan Makhlouf, the CedarBridge managing director, 'the returns are robust because Traffic has an operating team with a proven methodology to buy the right players and connections with football team across the world to sell them at the highest price' (Duff and Panja,

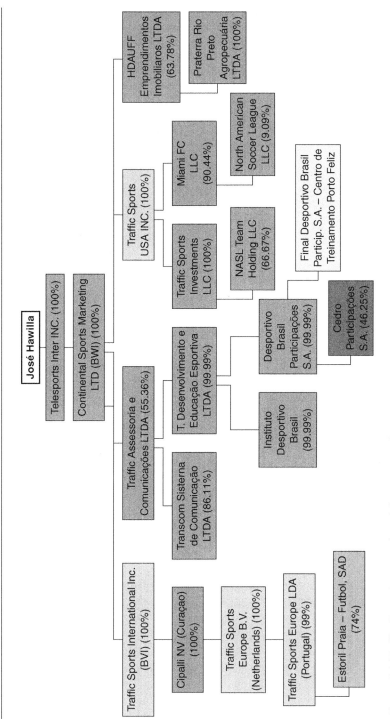

Figure 7.4 Traffic Group (source: adapted from Banco Efisa (2011)).

2013). Despite promising returns initially, Traffic started to reconsider its investment portfolio in football due to the TPE ban introduced by FIFA and ratified by the Brazilian federation, CBF, on 13 January 2015. On 14 April 2014, Traffic sold its training centre, located in Porto Feliz, to the Chinese club Shandong Luneng (Desportivo Brasil, 2014). One year later on 13 April 2015, they also sold off their shares of Estoril Praia SAD including the economic rights of all players to the investment fund Fidelis, owned by a Dubai investment consortium (Correo da Manhã, 2015). Moreover, Traffic has been implicated in the FIFA corruption scandal in which various CONMEBOL and CONCACAF officials, as well as sports marketing executives, are alleged to have been involved in corrupt practices in order to secure the media and marketing rights for FIFA games in the Americas. On 12 December 2014, the owner and founder of Traffic Group, José Hawilla, was indicted and pleaded guilty to charges of racketeering conspiracy, wire fraud conspiracy, money laundering conspiracy, and obstruction of justice (The United States Department of Justice, 2015). Hawilla also agreed to forfeit over $151 million.

7.6 The TPE debate

TPE is the subject of much controversy at present, with the football authorities claiming that it is a destabilising factor in the operation of leagues. The debate surrounding the dangers of TPE is based around the definition of economic rights. Taken to the extreme, the mainstream approach of the NGBs considers that these rights are nothing more than the transfer compensation as stipulated by FIFA regulations. This means that there are no specific rights beyond those deriving from regulations set up by football authorities (Poli, 2015). Under this autarchic perspective, the aims of the transfer market are predominant and are above any jurisdiction except for the law of sporting authorities. In this context, the profit orientation of clubs is the only objective taken into consideration and only if the transfer market activities of the clubs are reinvested within the clubs. In this sense, TPE could jeopardise football's governance, challenge the mechanisms of the transfer system and endanger football competitions, clubs, and players. For this reason, FIFA commissioned two studies in January 2013 and August 2013 respectively, conducted by the CIES and the CDES. The objectives of these studies were to gather data and information available on the TPE as well as on different aspects connected with it. Unfortunately, FIFA did not disclose the findings of the studies, except for their executive summaries, CIES (2013) and CDES and CIES (2014) which briefly illustrate the potential impacts and effects that TPE could have on the world of football at different levels. Following both studies' findings, we can present the main impacts and effects that TPEs can have in the world of football at different levels and contexts.

It is unsurprising that football authorities have sought to stop TPE since the spread of TPE based on investment funds and financial corporations contributes to bypassing the regulations that govern the market of transfers between clubs. For example, TPE is not limited to transfer time windows, and therefore could also contribute to the weakening of certain measures put in place by football authorities to protect the interests of sporting actors and competitions. TPE also calls into question certain principles which underpin the amended transfer regulations, especially contractual stability, solidarity mechanisms and training compensation, since the diffusion of TPE encourages speculation. This leads to players being transferred before their contracts expire, often under pressure from third parties looking to make a profit. Among the top division clubs of 31 major national football championships, the average period that each player remains at his club has reached a record low of 2.3 years (Poli *et al.*, 2015). This instability in contracts favours neither the stability and transparency of competitions, nor the loyalty of supporters and, consequently, the best performing clubs have the most stable squads.

Besides, the profits associated with TPE are not necessarily reinvested in the sector, and solidarity mechanisms and training compensation could be circumvented. As a result of TPE, part of the sum related to a transfer has been exempt from consideration in the calculation of the solidarity payments required by FIFA regulations since 2001. Likewise, payment of training compensation applies only to clubs that have seen the net amount of their transfer payments reduced in this way. Undermining the solidarity principle in this way could be damaging for the entire sector.

The prevalence of financial concerns means that the spread of TPE goes hand in hand with takeover of control of clubs by actors seeking short term profit above all else and speculating on the purchase and sale of economic rights, regardless of sporting concerns. TPE can also drive (or keep) a club in a vicious circle of debt and dependence. While TPE may represent a short term solution for funding a specific transfer, its systematic implementation can, over time, lead to a loss of control over transfer operations and/or sporting policy, and jeopardise the very survival of the club. This is especially true for financially unstable clubs, lured in by third parties whose motives have nothing to do with sport. The consequences are highly worrying, in terms of both player selection and influence by third parties at both club and national level.

The independence of players might also be challenged. Indeed, players, as a result of TPE, may have less and less control over their career development and geographic mobility. TPE agreements based on a principle of maximising short term profit are not necessarily favourable to the long term career development of the player in question. For example, the investor's main objective may be to enter one of the major markets as soon as possible, for reasons of rapid return on their investment. This can deprive the player of playing time. Again, financial and sporting rationales are not always compatible. The same goes for player mobility, with TPE agreements capable of undermining a player's freedom of movement.

TPE could be also considered as a threat to football competitions. It could first undermine the integrity of competitions as a result of the conflict of interest between actors. Third parties are known to hold economic rights in players belonging to teams in direct competition (against each other) at national or international level. This is potentially a major problem with TPE. What makes this all the more serious is that any suspicion of manipulation can tarnish football's image, and dent the trust of those who make football sustainable.

Fairness of competitions might also be compromised, due to both deteriorated balance in international competitions between clubs, and the drive to maximise tax efficiency. TPE has created a distinction between clubs in terms of the acquisition of sporting talent, based on whether or not TPE is regulated in a given country. It can thus improve the competitive balance in domestic competitions by offering an alternative source of funding, but it can also create a distortion between clubs competing in international competitions. Indeed, the widespread use of TPE as an instrument of finance for clubs in many countries is accused of creating disparities on an international level which decrease the level of competitive balance. Indeed, this practice is prohibited by certain national football associations while in others it is permitted and promoted. Although national football associations explicitly forbidding TPE agreements are in the minority, teams from these countries might incur a greater risk of sanctions if they conclude such agreement. Even though these current regulations are there to protect local clubs from the risks outlined above, from a purely financial point of view, teams from these countries might face a competitive disadvantage when it comes to attracting players. Indeed, they might not have the possibility of engaging footballers by offsetting a portion of the transfer costs to third-party investors. Moreover, when TPE agreements are already in place and investors wish to maintain a percentage on future transfers, with the aim of maximising profits, clubs from countries where such practices are forbidden might hold less bargaining power.

Furthermore, another factor related to TPE creates unfair competition in the market for talent among clubs competing, for example, in the same UEFA competitions. Indeed, using the Portuguese clubs as an illustration, the use of TPE allows Portuguese clubs to attract a multitude of players (especially coming from South America), sharing the investments and the risks with third parties. Among this large group of players, the few who succeed will bring sporting victories to the club and ultimately a financial return on investment for both third parties and the club once the transfer is completed. Thus, these clubs exploit TPE opportunities to achieve sporting success and financial health at a low cost and with lower risks, without even mentioning the network which facilitates future transfers. This could be considered as a distortion of fair competition in the market for talent when one compares it with the situation of clubs unable to use TPE, where one bad investment in a player has a direct negative influence on both sporting and financial results.

TPE is clearly an issue that sparks debate, especially since FIFA announced the ban of TPE starting on 1 May 2015. On this matter, it is worth mentioning that it is hard for FIFA, or any other federation, to enforce regulations against private companies and persons out of its reach (Reck, 2012). For this reason, the enforcement of this ban is only possible indirectly, through rules limiting and sanctioning clubs and/or players. Via circular n. 1464 published on December 2014, FIFA determined with Article 18bis that:

No club should enter into a contract which enables the counter club/counter clubs, and viceversa, or any third party to acquire the ability to influence in employment and transfer-related matters its independence, its policies or the performance if its teams.

Where properly structured, any TPO and TPI would hardly breach Article 18bis as it does not explicitly refer to the banning of a third party from having an 'influence' over a club which compromises the club's independence in making decisions (Andrews and Donald, 2012). There has been only one case involving the sole breach of Article 18bis, when the Finnish football association, FAF, for the first time in football history, expelled Tampere United from all competitions during 2011 for having allowed a third party to influence[6] its transfer policy (Pukka, 2011). For this lack, then, FIFA approved article 18ter that explicitly adds that

No club or player shall enter into an agreement with a third party whereby a third party is being entitled to participate, either full or in part, in compensation payable in relation to the future transfer of a player from one club to another, or is being assigned any relation to a future or transfer compensation.

With these articles, neither TPO nor TPI are allowed in any football club, as any third party could influence a club's transfer decisions and have the rights to benefit from them in economic terms. The main aspects of the ban that are debated are related to its relevancy and its enforcement.

Building their rationale on the long list of dangers related to TPE practices, the main argument of the supporters of the ban is based on the effectiveness of such a measure: it is more feasible to put a ban in place than to promote transparency. Furthermore, they argue that a well-managed club must be able to survive without TPE. This is the rationale of the EPL, the LFP and the UEFA. FIFPro joins them in favouring a ban, for it is a threat to players' rights and to football integrity.

Another idea would be to implement restrictive TPE regulations, but with less stringency than a ban. These stakeholders do not believe in the effectiveness of an outright ban, preferring to impose strong constraints on those wanting to become involved in TPE practices. Such a category would favour a series of instruments, both regulatory and economic, which aim to improve the transparency of information, thus limiting the use of TPE. The Spanish League was preparing a set of rules in order to regulate TPE when FIFA decided to implement a ban. The Spanish League supports alternative sources of financing of its clubs which improve their sporting quality.

Other football actors are clearly advocates of TPE but their opinions about the way it should be dealt with somehow diverge. Some are in favour of the implementation of a minimum regulation. Indeed, this category of stakeholders perceives TPE as an essential source of funding for clubs in financial difficulty and believes that regulation is only required to avoid speculation. They call for greater transparency through publicity of the ownership status of every player's economic rights. But others, located almost exclusively in South America, believe that TPE draws attention to the private commercial relationships between clubs and third parties and that it should not be subject to regulation on the part of the football authorities.

However, analysis of the implementation of a ban to TPE by FIFA shows that FIFA's decision used an interventionist regulation to deal with this issue. This should raise questions when compared to the way FIFA lately abandoned the licence system, as FIFA proved unable to effectively enforce it, due to the difficulty of checking and implementing transparency in the agency market. One may thus wonder how FIFA could be more effective in achieving TPE eradication. The FIFA TMS system clearly helps, but as long as it is limited to international transfers, it cannot be sufficient to implement the necessary quality of transparency of information without the support of the national associations. The current tools in the hands of football authorities thus seem pretty weak in terms of enforcing a TPE ban.

7.7 Conclusions

TPE practices have initially developed in leagues with critical market conditions. The worse the financial state of clubs and leagues is, the more clubs rely on TPE to finance their activities. It was no coincidence that TPE first became widespread in South America before later expanding into European markets such as Spain and Portugal. For this reason, TPE has always tended to operate outside the very strict financial controls exercised by the football governing bodies and was initially banned in England, the most competitive and lucrative transfer market.

From an agent's perspective, TPE has become a strategic investment tool for intermediaries to enter into transfer markets and compete directly with football clubs for the acquisition of football talent at all levels. As happens in many industries, agents and intermediaries have acted as venture capital investors who are ready to support clubs in their transfer strategies and opportunistically exploit the recruitment and career development of football players who are seen as strategic resources.

In all its forms, TPE thrives because it originated in response to requests made by club chairmen or sporting directors to finance the recruitment and the transfer of players, particularly when clubs do not generate and obtain the necessary financial resources through their own activity. Therefore, TPE is only a recent expansion of the transfer system, which is widely failing in terms of meeting its original goals of the protection of minors, the training of young players, maintenance of contractual stability and solidarity in the world of football, as well as offering a dispute resolution mechanism (EC, 2001).

Like any regulation implemented by FIFA, as long as football actors (e.g. club executives and players) decide not to actively participate in compliance and enforcement, the effectiveness of the regulations on TPE is likely to be jeopardised. In this context, banning TPE seems to be intellectually relevant but difficult to enforce. In many ways the ban has attempted to treat the effect instead of the cause of the problem. The latest developments indeed show that other financial products linked to financial flows in the transfer system have been developed to substitute for newly banned TPE practices, as in the case of FairPlay Capital (2014). As the TPE ban has not changed or improved the precarious financial conditions encountered by some clubs, alternatives built by ingenious finance companies will still be attractive to them. Additionally, future legal challenges might affect the validity and, consequently, the ability to enforce the ban.

To conclude, TPE is not directly a product of the evolution of the profession and activity of football agents per se, but it is the result of the speculative nature of any market that exchanges products and services, wherein agents and other stakeholders have been able to operate freely in different forms and conditions. It is in this context, that FIFPro has launched its campaign and legal challenge against the current transfer system. In turn, the financial disparity between leagues and clubs in football is one of the primary conditions that led agents to increase their dominant position in the football industry, as clubs compete to sign the best players by any means possible.

Notes

1 Resources are either property-based or knowledge-based. Property-based resources are legally defined property rights held by the firm and other firms are unable to appropriate these rights unless they obtain the owner's permission. Property-based resources are protected by contracts, patents or deeds of ownership. In contrast, knowledge-based resources, such as technical expertise or good relationships with trade unions, are not protected by law, but they may still be difficult for other firms to access.
2 When Michael Owen was looking for a new club, his management even produced a sales brochure similar to that produced by car manufacturers, detailing the highlights of the product being sold.
3 The players involved are not all known but are thought to have included Argentinian player, Enrique Andres Martegani.
4 On 27 April 2007, the club acknowledged having breached Rule B.13 of the EPL's rules by failing to act with the 'utmost good faith' in not disclosing the full nature of the deals. Moreover, the club was found to have breached Rule V.20 by entering into a contractual agreement with a third party who would have the right to exercise control over decisions concerning the future transfer and/or termination of their contracts. West Ham United failed to disclose these details to the EPL, and so breached a rule the purpose of which was to ensure that an outside party does not have the ability to influence team selection and, potentially, the outcome of a match. West Ham United was fined £5.5 million. The independent panel who investigated the case recommended that the EPL terminate Tevez's contract and invalidate his participation with West Ham United due to the third party ownership inherent in it; however, the EPL decided that West Ham United's modification of the contract was satisfactory, the fine was sufficient punishment, and a point deduction was unnecessary.
5 The results are extrapolated from the official documents provided and published by the investment fund as required by law.

6 The agreement was stipulated to facilitate the signings of foreign players by the club. Any profit resulting from the sale of these foreign players had to be split between the club and the third party and, amongst other things, the club had an obligation to sell players on their books to make way for 'third party' players. Finally, in case the players did not play enough, the club would recompense the third party for the opportunity costs occurred.

Bibliography

Allain, P. H. (1999) Brest prêt à chavirer, comme au bon temps. Mis en liquidation il y a six ans, le Stade brestois, qui évolue en amateur, espère retrouiver l'élite due foot. *Liberation* [online]. Available from: www.liberation.fr/sports/1999/08/16/brest-pret-a-chavirer-comme-au-bon-temps-mis-en-liquidation-il-y-a-six-ans-le-stade-brestois-qui-evo_281308 [accessed 20 March 2012].

Amit R., and Schoemaker, P. (1993) Strategic assets and organizational rent. *Strategic Management Journal*. 14(1), pp. 33–46.

Andrews, K. and Donald, I. (2012) Prohibition on third-party ownership: Analysis. *World Sports Law Report*. 10 (2), pp. 14–16.

Banco Efisa (2011) *Traffic Sports Europe, LDA: Prospecto de oferta pública*. Lisbon: Banco Efisa.

Barney, J. B. (1991) Firm resources and sustained competitive advantage. *Journal of Management*. Vol. 17(1), pp. 99–120.

Bourg, J. F and Gouget, J. J. (2010) *Political economy of professional sport*. London: Edward Elgar.

Bower, T. (2007) *Broken dreams: The definitive exposé of British football corruption (updated version)*. London: Pocket Books.

Burgess, W. (2008) The fate of third party ownership of professional footballers' rights: Is a complete prohibition necessary? *Texas Review of Entertainment & Sports Law*. 10(1), pp. 79–101.

Calvin, M. (2013) *The nowhere men. The unknown story of football's true talent spotters*. London: Arrow Books.

Capitas Sport Limited (2012) *Private placement memorandum*. Gibraltar: Capitas Sport Limited.

CDES and CIES (2014) *Research on third-party ownership of players' economic rights – Executive summary*. Limoges: CDES.

CIES (2013) *Third-party ownership of players' economic rights – Executive summary*. Neuchâtel: CIES.

Correo da manhã (2015) Venda da SAD do Estoril provoca medo. *Correo da manhã* [online]. Available from: www.cmjornal.xl.pt/desporto/futebol/detalhe/2015_04_11_venda_da_sad_provoca_medo.html [accessed 22 October 2015].

Cravo, D. and Castro Moreira Sordi, P. (2014) TPO A variety of approaches: Brazil. *Football Legal*. 1, pp. 29–31.

Crespo, J. and San Torcuato Caffa, S. (2014) Before the CAS. *Football Legal*. 1, p. 35.

Desportivo Brasil (2014) Academia Traffic é vendida para time chinês. *Desportivo Brazil* [online]. Available from: www.desportivobrasil.com.br/noticias.php?idn=1258 [accessed 22 October 2015].

Duff, A. and Panja, T. (2013) Football investors get 62% in run around players on transfer bet. *Bloomberg* [online]. Available from: www.bloomberg.com/news/articles/2013-03-06/football-investors-get-62-betting-on-player-transfers [accessed 22 November 2015].

EC (2001) Outcome of discussion between the Commission and FIFA/UEFA on FIFA RSTP. *EC Press release database* [online]. Available from: http://europa.eu/rapid/press-release_IP-01-314_en.htm [accessed 24 March 2013].

FairPlay Capital (2014) The first SICAV in Europe investing in football. *FairPlay Capital* [online]. Available from: www.fairplay-capital.com/wp-content/uploads/2014/03/FairPlayCapital-en_s.pdf [accessed 25 November 2015].

Fantex (2015) Fantex: how it works. *Fantex* [online]. Available from: https://fantex.com/how-it-works [accessed 25 November 2015].

Glüsing, V. (1997) In der Hand der Mafia. *Der Spiegel* [online]. Available from: www.spiegel.de/spiegel/print/d-8799485.html [accessed 12 October 2015].

Hart, S. (2004) Wealthy fans given chance to buy shares in players. *Telegraph* [online]. Available from: www.telegraph.co.uk/sport/football/2387367/Wealthy-fans-given-chance-to-buy-shares-in-players.html [accessed 12 November 2015].

KPMG (2013) *Project TPO*. KPMG Asesores: Madrid.

Leblebidjian, C. (2003) En el fondo ganaron todos. *La Nacion* [online]. Available from: www.lanacion.com.ar/531625-en-el-fondo-ganaron-todos [accessed 30 October 2015].

Lemos Neto, P. (2009) *Third party ownership: A Brazil case study of Traffic Sports*. MSc. Birkbeck University of London.

Maquina do Esporte (2008) Traffic assume gestão do Ituano. *Maquina do Esporte* [online]. Available from: http://maquinadoesporte.uol.com.br/artigo/traffic-assume-gestao-do-ituano_4969.html [accessed 12 October 2015].

Maquina do Esporte (2009) Ituano rompe parceria com a Traffic. *Maquina do Esporte* [online]. Available from: http://maquinadoesporte.uol.com.br/artigo/ituano-rompe-parceria-com-a-traffic_8490.html [accessed 12 October 2015].

Miller, D. and Shamsie, J. (1996) The resource-based view of the firm in two environments: The Hollywood film studios from 1936 to 1965. *Academy of Management Journal*. 39(3), pp. 519–543.

Oei, S. and Ring, D. (2015) Human equity? Regulating the new income share agreements. *Vanderbilt Law Review*. 68(3) pp. 681–760.

Ordine, F. (2002) Il Calcio-mercato. *Treccani* [online]. Available from: www.treccani.it/enciclopedia/calcio-la-storia-del-calcio_(Enciclopedia-dello-Sport)/ [accessed 27 November 2015].

Penrose, E. T. (1959) *The theory of the growth of the firm*. New York: Oxford University Press.

Poli, R. (2010) Understanding globalisation through football: The new international division of labour, migratory channels and transnational trade circuits. *International Review for the Sociology of Sport*. 45(4), pp. 491–506.

Poli, R. (2015) Third-party entitlement to shares of transfer fees: problems and solutions. *Asser International Sports Law* [online]. Available from: www.asser.nl/SportsLaw/Blog/post/blog-symposium-third-party-entitlement-to-shares-of-transfer-fees-problems-and-solutions-by-dr-raffaele-poli-head-of-cies-football-observatory [accessed 24 October 2015].

Poli, R., Besson, R. and Ravenel, L. (2015) Club instability and its consequences. *CIES Football Observatory* [Online]. Available from: www.football-observatory.com/IMG/pdf/mr01_eng.pdf [accessed 27 November 2015].

Pukka, A. (2011) Application of FIFA Article 18bis: Tampere United's case. *World Sports Law Report*. 9(6), pp. 14–16.

Reck, A. (2012) Third party player ownership: current trends in South America and Europe. *EPFL Sports Law Bulletin*. 10, pp. 50–54.

Roberts, D. (2015) Here's why Fantex, the athlete stock exchange, is working. *Fortune* [online]. Available from: http://fortune.com/2015/03/31/athlete-stock-exchange-fantex/ [accessed 15 October 2015].

Russo, P. (2014) *Gol di rapina: il lato oscuro del calcio globale*. Firenze: Edizioni Clichy.

The United States Department of Justice (2015) Nine FIFA officials and five corporate executives indicted for racketeering conspiracy and corruption. *The United States Department of Justice* [online]. Available from: www.justice.gov/opa/pr/nine-fifa-officials-and-five-corporate-executives-indicted-racketeering-conspiracy-and [accessed 15 October 2015].

Vasco, M. A. (2012) Luis Guijarro: El primer representante modern. *AS Color*, N.6, pp. 16–19 July 2012.

8 Future directions and challenges

Overview

This book has given a brief analysis of the major changes in the football market over the recent past and looked at how market interventions have impacted the way in which agents operate. Chapter 1 took a historical perspective, assessing how labour market liberalisation, alongside increases in broadcast rights fees for clubs, gave agents the opportunity to increase wages for players. The removal of quotas on foreign players enhanced the opportunities for intermediaries even further beyond their role in contract negotiation towards talent ID. As transfer fees spiralled and the number of opportunities for local talent to play in some leagues increased, football's governing bodies sought to fix these market failures by introducing regulations such as transfer windows and the UEFA home grown player rule. The ways in which agents have been able to adapt to these conditions have been detailed in Chapters 2, 3 and 4. Chapter 5 looked at how the legal and governance frameworks have developed in response to these issues and the system in place to address future debates. Chapters 6 and 7 then looked at the contemporary landscape, highlighting how the current market structure affords agents a central position in the football network facilitating deals. However, the football governing bodies have a challenge in balancing the principles of the game with the needs of the market. In recent years, various interventions from governing bodies have been contested by other stakeholders creating webs of negotiated power.

This chapter builds on these elements to look at current debates, particularly around the new intermediary regulations and TPE, before looking ahead to other issues which could impact the way that intermediaries act – not least FIFPro's challenge of the transfer system. We then offer an analysis of the current governance system, highlighting difficulties in the regulatory structure before making some initial recommendations on other regulatory systems, which football could learn from.

8.1 The regulations governing intermediaries

After five years of consultation and having faced criticism for not making agents part of the process, FIFA published its RWI in 2014. They came into effect on 1 April 2015. The new system is a marked change from the old regulations, with the previous agents licensing system abandoned completely. Under the new arrangement there is no need to sit an exam and obtain an agents licence. Instead, any natural or legal person can act as an 'intermediary', representing players or clubs in contract or transfer negotiations, subject to certain minimum criteria regarding reputation (FIFA, 2015: Article 4). In a further shift, intermediaries have to register with a national association every time they act in a transaction instead of being licensed for a finite length of time (FIFA, 2015: Article 3).

This shift reflects FIFA's concerns that the majority of agents were acting outwith the rules anyway; however, in some markets, such as England where the old system was thought to be relatively well enforced, there is concern that opening up the industry to anyone will cause problems as they may not be qualified to carry out such a role (De Marco, 2014; Turner, 2014; Couchmans, 2015). While the AFA's view suggests that the intermediaries market is likely to be 'like the wild west' (Riach, 2015), others disagree, seeing the rules in this regard as more far reaching, since anyone who represents either players and/or clubs with a view to negotiating an employment contract or clubs in negotiations with a view to concluding a transfer agreement, is treated as an intermediary irrespective of whether the services provided conform to the traditional agency role (Turner, 2014). As a consequence, it could be argued that this affords regulatory bodies more control over transfers.

As well as the change in definition of the person involved, the burden of responsibility has also shifted under the new rules, as clubs and players are held accountable for the conduct of the people they use as intermediaries and thus face consequences themselves for any breach (FIFA, 2015: Article 9). This intuitively makes sense when either the club or player is complicit in the actions of an intermediary as national associations are able to exert more control over their own members and thus enforce more meaningful sanctions. As a consequence, one can envisage clubs and players undertaking greater due diligence before instructing an intermediary and taking more interest in the intermediary's methods. Nevertheless, it remains to be seen whether in practice this approach works. Chapter 5 cited various examples of wrongdoing where players would not have been fully aware of the actions of their agents and have themselves been victims – in which case it would not seem appropriate to punish the player.

It is this lack of recognition by FIFA of the principal-agent relationship outlined in Chapter 6 that causes most concern for the new regulations. The vast majority of problems relating to agents have occurred through individuals acting in self-interest and the rules pre-2015 sought to address this. When the FIFA rules governing the operation of agents in transfers were introduced in 1994, they required anyone acting as an agent to lodge a bond of 200,000 Swiss francs with FIFA. This is a traditional method used to constrain the likelihood of problems in the principal–agent relationship since, in the case of any wrongdoing, the agent would lose their bond. As we saw in Chapter 5, various complaints were made to the EC on the basis that the FIFA regulations were anticompetitive because they prevented or restricted access to this profession by natural or legal persons possessing the requisite skills and qualifications, specifically by requiring payment of a large and non-interest-bearing deposit. Accordingly, FIFA adopted new provisions whereby the bond system was removed and replaced by the requirement for agents to have liability insurance. However, there was no additional requirement imposed to act as a deterrent against wrong doing. Instead a multiple choice test was introduced to guarantee a minimum standard of knowledge. The agent was also obliged to sign a code of professional conduct setting out the principles of professional integrity, transparency, honesty and the fair management of interests, as well as the requirement to keep accounts. In response to these changes, the EC commented that 'FIFA's aims of extending good practice, raising professional standards and protecting its members from unqualified or unscrupulous agents prevail over competition considerations' (EC, 2002: 2). It is difficult to see how the RWI will protect players and clubs from these same threats.

FIFA also brought to public attention in their 2009 general assembly the fact that the average commission paid by clubs to agents in international transfer deals was 28 per cent of the transaction value. This was criticised as being disproportionate to the level of work done by most agents and, being particularly mindful that many member clubs were struggling financially, FIFA has, under the new system, sought to curb this level of remuneration. Article 7 recommends a cap of 3 per cent of the player's basic gross income or 3 per cent of the transfer fee paid if the intermediary is engaged to act for a club to conclude a transfer agreement. Even though this is a recommendation as opposed to a rule it has still proved to be very contentious. According to De Marco (2014),

> the proposed 3 per cent cap is arguably unlawful under domestic and European competition law. If the national associations club together to effectively fix the price agents can sell their services for the courts may intervene to prevent price-fixing. The AFA has already issued a complaint to the EC.

The concern stems from the likelihood that some players and clubs are expected to refuse to pay any more than the recommended 3 per cent. While this small proportion of a big transfer would still make the intermediary a significant sum, the impact on less high-profile deals may mean it is not worthwhile for an intermediary to work on them, leading to a decrease in the quality of representation services provided to those players who arguably need them most.

While the market rate in the UK is usually between 5–10 per cent, if not higher, the AFA is concerned that a reduction to 3 per cent would put many of its members out of business and also cause people with little skill in negotiation to undercut those who are qualified in this regard. FIFA's new rules require that players and clubs disclose 'full details of any and all agreed remunerations or payments of whatsoever nature … to an intermediary' to their domestic FA. At the end of March each year, national football associations will be required to disclose all intermediaries who have registered in that period and the transactions in which they were involved. The total sums of payments made to intermediaries by all players and clubs within their territory must also be disclosed according to Article 6 (FIFA, 2015). Of course, we have seen in the past that simple disclosure of fees, as already required in the English leagues, may still be underestimating the commissions of intermediaries. It is not unusual to have intermediaries paid through other means and it would not be surprising if a cap in fee level led to payments being driven underground.

In relation to payments, perhaps the biggest difference between the FIFA minimum standards and the rules implemented by national associations lies in the representation of minors; in England, the FA has prohibited intermediaries from entering into agreements with players before the year they turn 16 but FIFA's rules do not forbid such contracts. Under the FIFA (2015) guidelines, no intermediary is allowed to be remunerated for a transfer or contract deal with a player under 18, but they can still act as the young player's representative without a fee. It is not difficult to envisage a situation where any money owed to an agent for work with a young player will be backdated until the player in question turns 18. This may be compounded by the removal of regulations on the length of contract between players and intermediaries, with no maximum time suggested. Additionally, changes in rules around transfers of players will also mean that clubs seek to sign players at ever younger ages. It is therefore anticipated that the rule on this will probably be tightened by FIFA in due course. If this does not happen, and individual domestic associations bring in their own rules, it will be difficult to maintain a level playing field, and younger and younger players may be pushed to move abroad where they can benefit from strong representation. As FIFA has delegated responsibilities to the national associations, it is not competent to hear disputes regarding intermediaries and indeed provides no dispute resolution forum. This raises an issue for national associations who either need to bring registered intermediaries under their own jurisdiction and provide a dispute resolution forum themselves, or must accept that disputes between intermediaries and clubs or players concerning fees would have to be resolved in the national courts.

Already, widespread differences have emerged between national adoptions of the new system of working with intermediaries. France, for example, has decided to deal only with licensed agents in a system akin to the old method, whereas the English FA has adopted the FIFA regulations and is shifting away from regulating agents (Skysports, 2015). It is not difficult to see why the differences between two countries which have tended to be fairly well run in relation to agents in the past raise questions over how the rules may be interpreted in countries which have historically been more problematic. In areas where national associations have traditionally held little regulatory sway, such as Africa and South America, the effects of the change in approach are likely to be even more pronounced, with concern that corruption could be increased, not decreased, when barriers to entry are removed.

It is difficult to argue with FIFA's assertion that it was unable to control agents and that the industry had clear problems under the old system; however, it is questionable whether moving away from direct regulation will help this. In fact, one might think that FIFA should have imposed more strict regulations on agents. Various NGBs had managed to strike a balance in their domestic regulations where their operations were not unduly restricted by regulation, but players and clubs were afforded some level of protection from unscrupulous behaviour. In England, the FA was thought to have established an effective way to monitor the actions of agents and stopped unlicensed agents from representing players or clubs in transfers. There are concerns that the new regulations make the industry under less well run national governing bodies even worse, while also restricting the ability of well run NGBs to act.

8.2 TPE on football players

The issues surrounding intermediaries have largely centred on their activities in transferring players – particularly relating to payments. This issue is complicated further when a club does not wholly own the rights to a player who is to be transferred. Having established that TPE is more prevalent in some countries than others, it is worth recapping the impact in those markets. In South America, there are four potential times for economic rights to a player to be assigned to a third party:

1   When a player signs his first contract, a right of 10–20 per cent is transferred to the person who introduced the youth – this may be the player's family, an agent, a former player or a scout. This can help small clubs to attract good young players as they would be unable to compete with other forms of inducement in signing the best talent.
2   When a club is in need of capital for reasons other than transferring players. Under these circumstances economic rights to a player may be sold to a third party to provide funds.
3   When a club wants to sign a player whose contractual rights they cannot afford, a company may already own, or be willing to buy, the player's rights from the selling club to bring them to the buying club. Under these circumstances the player usually signs a one year deal for the new club to act as a showcase, with an option for the club to purchase the player's rights at the end of the season.
4   When a player discusses contract renewal his club may assign the player a proportion of his own economic rights so he benefits from each future transfer, usually 10–20 per cent. This is usually used when a club needs to increase the value of a player's contract in order to keep him, but cannot afford to increase his wages.

Addressing the impact of the ban on each of these separately, the first point is likely to mean that the clubs with the biggest recruitment department and the most resources will secure the best talent. Intermediaries will still play a big role in this as they are even more important in providing benefits to the player's family, even before they sign a professional contract. While in the current market it is not acceptable for agents to offer inducements to young players or their families, we know that this practice is not uncommon. It could happen more often if a valuable source of income for parents of talented young players is cut off. In this case, the intermediary is likely to invest in the families of the best talent in order to represent them, with a view to future benefits accruing when the player turns professional. This is reflective of the behaviour of agents in many markets around the world where TPE is not ingrained.

Looking at point two, if clubs are facing difficulties in generating capital, their most obvious option would be to sell players. Under TPE the club could sell some of the economic rights to a player while still retaining the player's services. If this option is removed, it is likely that, in future, players would be transferred to other clubs. Intermediaries could again be involved in making sure that clubs can move players on when they need to.

As clubs seek to find new ways to be able to afford to sign a player, point three above becomes the biggest concern in banning TPE. Bridge transfers, whereby a TPE effectively buys a club which can then hold the registration of a player who is then loaned out to another club, are expected to become more common. In this case the new club holds the same role as the TPE, but with arguably more restriction – the third party benefits also from retaining a proportion of the player's future transfer fees, or placing the player under a very long term contract with a huge buy out fee and loaning the player to various different clubs across the duration of that contract. A consortium headed by the agent Pini Zahavi, who has close links to Chelsea FC, invested €8.5 million to buy a 90 per cent stake in Belgian club Royal Mouscron-Peruwelz (Kanti, 2015). Though few details have been revealed, the club will be used as 'an incubator for young Chelsea players, and in order to get around attempts by UEFA to clamp down on third party ownership of players by agents and investors' (Griver, 2015).

Point four is an interesting issue. In South America it is normal for players to be assigned ownership of part of their own economic rights. Under the current rules it is unclear whether this would still be allowed.

Looking more closely at the reasons for TPE, it is easy to see that in some ways the ban simply shifts the balance of power from third parties to richer clubs, making it impossible for smaller clubs to retain their best talent (Reck, 2015). In the case of Cristiano Ronaldo potentially being transferred for €1.2 million when he was 16 years old, his club, Sporting Lisbon, was only able to afford to refuse a transfer because they could rely on TPE. Similarly, Santos was only able to hold on to Neymar as long as it did because of external funds. Without TPE, these clubs would have been forced to cash in on their best talent early, thus weakening both their squads and their future revenues. According to FIFA TMS (2015), South American players account for approximately 25 per cent of all the international transfers worldwide and it is expected that this figure will increase once the ban is in place as South American clubs can no longer afford to refuse offers for their best players from clubs in richer leagues. Poli (2015) however, describes how as the number of players with TPE has increased, so too has the number of transfers. If we argue that TPE induces players to transfer more often, then it is likely that the ban will lead to fewer players moving and doing so less often and there could be a slowing of wage inflation.

While it is difficult to predict the future of the transfer market with any certainty, one can envisage that, with less liquidity in the market, intermediaries would theoretically play an even bigger role in providing a matching service with the relevance of their networks coming to the fore.

8.2.1 Legal challenges against the ban

The ban on TPE is being challenged in various forums. In February 2015 a complaint was brought to the EC by the Spanish and Portuguese Leagues, LFP and LFLP, who argue that the ban violates the rules of competition set out by the TFEU, as well as the fundamental freedoms of establishment, services, labour and capital movements (LFP, 2015). They state that the decision restricts the economic freedoms of clubs, players and third parties without any justification or proportionality. This restriction on free competition infringes Articles 101 and 102 of the TFEU that respectively deal with the prohibition of anti-competitive agreements and the prohibition of FIFA abusing its dominant position, as well as violating other fundamental EU liberties.[1]

One of the various arguments raised by the Spanish and Portuguese leagues is that TPE helps to balance leagues by enabling the small to medium clubs to sign higher quality players. If those small to medium clubs now have to fund their own investment in playing talent, there is a much greater chance of a boom or bust cycle occurring whereby the rich clubs become richer and the poor clubs struggle. The impact therefore could potentially be that of a decrease in competitive balance both within and between leagues. The Spanish legal challenge also argues that the quality of leagues in countries that rely on TPE arrangements will decrease as the best players move to clubs in the richest leagues. Again, this is likely to be a vicious circle with the rich becoming richer. While this is an interesting perspective, it is questionable whether allowing TPE is necessary to improve clubs' financial stability. Instead, more strict financial controls could be introduced, like those in Germany and France, in other nations.

In July 2015 the Spanish competition authority, CNMC, gave its opinion on the matter, agreeing that banning TPE would be detrimental to the football sector as well as to competition for clubs and players. According to CNMC (2015), the ban violates the regulatory principles laid down by the Spanish authorities and the EC. In considering whether the ban is proportionate to achievement of its objectives, the CNMC argues that regulating the potential conflicts of interests and enforcing greater transparency could potentially achieve those same objectives in a less disruptive way.

However, while this opinion is certainly an important consideration, in the first challenge to reach court, a different outcome resulted. Maltese Investment fund Doyen Sports and Belgian club Seraing United brought a case in front of the CFI in Brussels against the Belgium football association, RBFA, FIFA and

UEFA. FIFPro also intervened to give the players' perspective. The basis of the case was that the club had signed an agreement with Doyen Sports in January 2015 whereby Doyen and Seraing United would collaborate to select at least two players in each summer transfer window to be recruited by Seraing United via TPE. In return, Doyen would contribute €300,000 for the 2015/2016 season to Seraing United's budget and own 30 per cent of the rights of the players it picked (Duval, 2015). In the summer 2015 transfer window this arrangement facilitated the recruitment of Ferraz Pereira, whose transfer led to the present dispute. In their registration of the player through the FIFA TMS, Seraing United indicated that Ferraz Pereira was recruited via investment from a third party. Consequently, the RBFA blocked the player's registration and the release of an ITC by FIFA was not granted.

Doyen and Seraing United requested that the judge stopped the football authorities from imposing the TPE ban, arguing that it contravened EU competition law (Articles 101 and 102 TFEU) and the rights of free movement within the EU (Articles 63, 56 and 45 TFEU). In his ruling, the judge recognised that FIFA has a dominant position on the market for the services of players' agents, following the ECJ judgement in Piau, and questioned whether this dominant position had been abused. Key to this is whether or not the ban is legitimate and proportionate to its objectives. In this case, the following objectives were cited by FIFA and FIFPro as underlying the ban:[2]

- TPE is usually conducted by investment firms, whose shareholders are unclear;
- The firms involved could have conflicting interests as they conclude contracts with various clubs who may compete against each other in footballing competitions;
- The contracts themselves are not registered and therefore there is no transparency;
- The contracts can be transferred between various parties very easily so it is difficult to keep track;
- It is more beneficial for investors if players transfer quickly as they will get rewards more quickly and can ensure that a transfer fee must be paid (as opposed to a player being able to leave on a free transfer at the end of his contract). This would be contrary to the contractual stability for players and clubs which FIFA hopes to achieve.

The court agreed with FIFA and FIFPro that TPE raises conflicts of interest, potentially increasing the risk of match fixing and other manipulations, and that this is unmanageable in an environment which already lacks transparency. Consequently, banning TPE was judged to be important for the sport. Looking back at previous efforts to regulate in this area, the court noted that FIFA's attempt via Article 18 bis of the FIFA RSTP had been ineffective. Legal commentators suggest that this hints that a complete ban could be necessary (Duval, 2015). As such, the Court found that the TPE ban could be deemed proportionate to achievement of its legitimate objectives and therefore rejected the request of Doyen and Seraing United to rule against FIFA. Shortly after the ruling, FIFA banned the club from signing players for two years and fined it 150,000 Swiss francs over the matter.

While this first court ruling does not bode well for overturning the ban on TPE, it is unclear whether this verdict is the last. We eagerly await the findings of the EC. If a challenge to the ban is to be successful, it has to be built on thorough arguments which clearly demonstrate the availability of a less restrictive system to tackle the problems which may arise through TPE. It is interesting to note that in the discussion of conflicts of interest and impacting competition in the market, loan signings could also fall into this category. However, these are considered as a benefit, not a problem, for the football industry. As clubs and intermediaries seek to find ways around the TPE ban, loan signings might play an even more important role.

It is difficult to speculate on the long term future of TPE. While many parties are seeking ways to circumvent the ban, in contrast to other rulings, it seems that UEFA in particular is keen to enforce sanctions against those clubs acting against it and, as such, a decrease in the number of South American and African players entering European leagues is possible as their transfers will face much closer scrutiny. However, in regions that are less concerned about the enforcement of the ruling, many contracts continue in the same vein, even if they are conducted in secret, particularly in domestic transfers. Similarly, new methods of funding are likely to come to the fore.

While it is often argued that TPE makes money leave the game, it must be understood that this is no different to any football stakeholder earning significant sums of money from the game – there is no guarantee that they reinvest their profits in football. As soon as football became a business, this was likely to happen and we must balance the benefits of football becoming a global entertainment spectacle with the fact that people can and do profit from it.

8.3 The youth market

TPE and transfers of youth players often go hand in hand, with intermediaries providing funding which enables these players to move to clubs where their footballing skill can be nurtured and paid for. In removing TPE as an option for young players, it remains to be seen whether there will be an improvement in the issues which have occurred relating to child trafficking (Caceres, 2007; McDougall, 2008; FIFPro, 2015a).

Chapter 6 outlined the centrality of agents and intermediaries in networks involved in transferring players to clubs around the globe. Of note is the number of minors involved in this process. FIFA made an amendment to its statutes in March 2015 to lower the age limit for international transfers to include players aged ten and above (FIFPro, 2015c). Before the change was introduced, clubs only needed to go through the official process of applying for an ITC if their target was at least 12 years old. This change in statute was brought about by the increase in the number of transfers of children under ten years old. While little has been made of the issue so far, it is expected to be higher on both the political and football agendas in the years ahead. Foot Solidaire, a French NGO, estimates that 15,000 teenage footballers are moved out of just ten West African countries every year – many of them underage, with agents receiving between $3,000 and $10,000 for each child they send to a potentially fictitious trial at an imagined club (Piers, 2015).

The change in regulation has been welcomed across the world, but concerns have also been raised that the younger the age where official papers need to be lodged, the younger the children are who will be imported to circumvent the rules. This sort of practice led FIFA to suspend Barcelona from transfer activity for one year (Domènech, 2015). Alerted to the problem by the TMS, FIFA investigated the club's dealings for youth team players signed between 2009 and 2013 (Whittall, 2014). The acquisitions of ten players were found to be in breach of Article 19 RSTP that prevents minors from being exploited by unscrupulous clubs and agents. The club has since announced that their relationship with the players in question has now been ended. As agents and intermediaries play such an important role in the careers of footballers, young players and their families need to be able to access information about the different options they have. Transparency around what a player can and should expect from an agent can help with this. While the new rules on intermediaries are a step in this direction suggesting a maximum commission payable to agents,[3] in reality intermediaries often get paid in different ways. With more clarity around where money flows in a transfer, players at all levels could make better choices about how they are represented. All football stakeholders, such as unions, leagues and clubs, have a role in helping to educate young players in particular. However, as discussed in Chapter 3, various conflicts of interest arise when stakeholders act with their own agenda.

8.4 Challenges to the transfer system as a whole

While the challenges above all have an impact on the operation of one element of the transfer process, perhaps the most far reaching debate at present is whether or not the whole transfer system needs to change. FIFPro announced in December 2013 that it would challenge the system, stating 'Football players are workers and only when they are able to enjoy the rights enshrined in law and enjoyed by all other workers, will FIFPro be satisfied' (FIFPro, 2013). The challenge was formally launched in September 2015 when FIFPro lodged a complaint with the Competition Directorate of the EC.

When the EC recognised, post Bosman, that football needed to be treated differently to some other businesses, it insisted that the transfer system had to take into account the needs and rights of players as workers. Specifically, a limit of a maximum five year contract length was enforced with a three year protected period within which a breach of contract could only be allowed if there was just cause or sporting just cause; otherwise, a unilateral breach in contract, where a player wanted to move clubs, would mean that the club had to be compensated. In the case of a transfer occurring for a player under the age of 23, a fee must also be paid to any club that the player was registered with between the ages of 12 and 21 as training compensation – thought of as a form of solidarity payment. Finally, transfer windows were introduced.

These restrictions were justified in order to maintain contractual stability, develop young players, improve competitive balance and maintain solidarity. FIFPro recognises that these are all valid goals but questions whether or not they are actually being achieved in the current market. In support of the challenge, FIFPro conducted an economic analysis of the situation which has been lodged with the complaint, which specifically considers whether these points have been met, whether there is a less restrictive alternative which could achieve the desired outcome, and whether the restriction is proportionate to the achievement of its aim (Szymanski, 2015).

Addressing each aim separately, the analysis argues that the current transfer system is not achieving its stated aims. Contractual stability has not been achieved since the football system, with promotion and relegation, is inherently unstable and this has only been exacerbated as the gap between divisions increases. The length of a player's contract does not address the source of this instability. While the aim of promoting youth participation is not disputed, the analysis argues that the method of doing it is neither proportionate nor the least restrictive alternative, even if it were to achieve its intended goal, which it arguably does not. Competitive balance has been a big issue which governing bodies consistently seek to address. However, various interventions have in fact favoured the richer clubs. Szymanski (2015) argues that this is also the case with the transfer system. Finally, the intention of maintaining solidarity through the transfer system is also questioned, given the inefficiency of the system whereby only a very small proportion of fees do in fact trickle down.

The basis of FIFPro's argument is that the transfer system is not a proportionate or least restrictive way to achieve its stated aims. In fact, it can be thought to be anticompetitive on the basis that 'the transfer regulations prevent clubs from fairly competing on the market to acquire sporting talent, harming the interests of players, small and medium sized professional teams and their supporters' (FIFPro, 2015b); thus, it violates European law. FIFPro therefore argues that if players were able to move freely between clubs without high transfer fees, clubs outside of the elite would be more likely to hire these players, potentially on shorter contracts, and become more competitive.

Should the EC decide that there is need for investigation, it must be considered whether there are alternative ways to promote balance within the leagues. As Pinsent Masons (2015) points out, the EC has already commissioned a report on transfers in 2013, which states that competitive balance must be addressed and that one potential route would be to cap the transfer fees that can be paid for players as well as introducing a 'fair play levy' on transfer fees beyond a certain amount as a way of ensuring wealth redistribution among clubs (KEA and CDES, 2013). However, it is questionable whether a limit on fees would solve any of the competition issues as the same richer clubs would still be able to afford to pay the best players the highest salaries and the distribution of talent would therefore be unchanged. Furthermore, the vast majority of transfers take place when a player and his agent are able to benefit from a transfer – enforcing a more restrictive contractual system would therefore potentially leave players worse off as clubs currently cannot force a player to leave when he is under contract.

In this very early phase of the challenge it is very difficult to predict the outcome. While FIFPro's arguments are clear, whether or not the EC will agree that a different system would be better placed to achieve the set objectives remains unclear. It is likely that the EC will investigate the complaint and a case could potentially reach the ECJ for a ruling on the compatibility of the FIFA RSTP regime with EU law. If this does occur, and the courts find in favour of the complainant, we could see the removal of transfer windows as well as transfer fees, thus creating a much more fluid market where agents will have an even bigger role to play in connecting the right players and clubs at the right time.

8.5 The various routes of governance

As the football industry has become increasingly commercial, the gap between the haves and the have nots is more and more transparent both within and between leagues and countries. This scenario has led to many people, not least intermediaries, involved in the industry becoming increasingly entrepreneurial in the way they operate, forming alliances and developing ways to create new revenue streams. It is often this innovative thinking that changes the way the market operates, which in turn often leads to regulation. All of the challenges previously discussed have come about as a consequence of these changes.

Taking a theoretical stance, there is always discussion over whether markets should be free or whether regulation is necessary. The agents industry is no different and FIFA's decision to introduce a licensing system in 1994 responded to the historical actions of some individuals. Additionally, agents who were operating in the late 80s to early 90s themselves sought legitimacy through recognition from governing bodies. The operation of the existing regulatory system cannot be understood without bearing in mind the past, as well as more contemporary policy deliberations which have helped to shape the conditions of action within which these developments have occurred.

Nevertheless, governing bodies have a difficult path to negotiate as dominant clubs refuse to adopt certain regulations and regularly lobby FIFA and UEFA. The funding and revenue systems in place help to reproduce asymmetries of power and control over time. The incentives in place favour the high achievers, rewarding each higher league place with additional funds, making it difficult to achieve in future and therefore to attain power. However, this is not to say that clubs' behaviour is or has been totally determined, rather that the context in which they operate is conditioned by antecedent social structures in which current discursive interaction takes place (Lewis, 2000). In the case of intermediaries, the shift away from regulation by FIFA to devolve powers to the national football associations could potentially lead to conflicting interests which make the negotiation and enforcement of regulations even more difficult. While, traditionally, FIFA imposed a top down governance system, that is no longer the case and the power of certain continental federations and clubs has led to rules being negotiated instead. Even before the decision was taken to get rid of the licensing system, FIFA had been the least keen of all governing bodies to enforce its own rules. It is suggested that this was due to external pressure from other stakeholders. Similar problems exist at continental level where it is notable that the only clubs to be sanctioned by UEFA on breaches of FFP are Manchester City and Paris Saint-Germain – both clubs which have not traditionally been in the European elite, but whose billionaire owners have unsettled the old guard. Likewise, at the domestic level different objectives are pursued by different parties. The banning of TPE is a good example of this wherein the main international footballing bodies are united over the need to ban but various NGBs are against it.

Agents too have become more powerful with their networks and the overlaps in the services offered, at times creating conflicts of interest but also affording agents power over a number of stakeholders. They have unionised at continental level in Europe and also domestically and are currently refusing to accept some of the new regulations. While it is clear that agents and intermediaries are central to the operation of the football market, they are very rarely, if ever, given a place at the negotiating table. Leading agent Jonathan Barnett questions whether the governing bodies understand how intermediaries operate and thus their efficacy in creating rules, stating (James, 2015):

> I think what frustrates me is the lack of understanding of what a proper agency does, by FIFA and the FA … I think it's absolutely ridiculous that they come up with rules when nobody knows what they're talking about. I don't understand why the FA haven't sat down with agents … to find out what we actually do for a living, because they haven't got a clue.

As such, there is a very real threat that if the governing bodies do not comply with their demands or at least compromise on a number of key issues, then they, and lawyers involved in representing players, could challenge the system in court as a restraint of trade. Additionally, there is a threat that regulations such as the home grown players ruling would also be challenged. The fear that the whole governance structure would be undermined if agents were to win such battles has endowed them with power.

Issues have been raised over the different levels of enforcement across member states and the organisational and administrative acuity of FIFA as the overarching regulator has been questioned by clubs, agents and NGBs. Clearly the issue of providing a regulatory framework which is enforceable across a wide variety of circumstances and contexts is a difficult task, exacerbated by the influence of different stakeholders and the fact that all leagues, nations and clubs are attempting to gain a competitive advantage over their rivals. It is beneficial for all to have the best players – the clubs want them for commercial and playing success; the leagues want their competition to show off the best players and also generate commercial revenues; the governing bodies also need to generate revenue and to satisfy the leagues which are influenced by the member clubs. It is therefore almost impossible to keep all stakeholders happy as power is negotiated. The leagues cannot afford to alienate member clubs who could potentially form breakaway leagues – as happened with the English PL – and this situation makes it very difficult to enforce or change existing regulations.

Though monitoring has been suggested to reduce the opportunity for agent opportunism, as outlined in Chapter 5, the monitoring system in place in football is not administered by the principal, as would be the case in a normal principal-agent relationship. This shifts the dynamic so that the governing body then becomes the agent of the player and the same problems of self-interest and opportunism apply. We have seen throughout this book that the monitoring of agents' activities in particular, and transfers more generally, has been ineffective and the governing bodies do not behave uniformly in enforcing punishment for breaches of regulations. As was the case with the old agents' regulations, if they are not being enforced, there is no incentive for players, clubs or intermediaries to comply. It is also likely that, if some associations enforce rules while others do not, there could be a migration of the best talent to those with the weakest rules. The mere introduction of regulations does not always lead to the intended outcome since individuals exercise free will and adopt practices which, though mediated by rules, do not necessarily conform to them. However, in the context of the principal-agent relationship, this does not suggest that we should abandon the system altogether; instead, the aim should be to enforce a more efficient system of monitoring. Given all of the discussion up to this point, enforcing a worldwide system is both very difficult and potentially too costly for FIFA to do itself; there are therefore a number of options:

1 Self-regulation

The EFAA and the English AFA have already taken steps to develop their own system for regulation of football agents and it is expected to be supported by the leading European football federations. Such a model of self-regulation would be in accordance with European law, given the decision of the ECJ in T-193/02, *Piau v. Commission of the European Communities*. Seen as an interesting option for agents, self-regulation is often born out of public concern about a particular industry when it is felt that the industry as a whole would benefit from improving standards. One of the biggest problems with regulation by FIFA and some football associations has been in reacting quickly to a changing environment. As self-regulatory bodies are entrenched in the industry which they regulate, they have the opportunity to anticipate and recognise areas of concern more quickly.

While self-regulation can be manifest through various routes, it is envisaged by the authors that an agents' body could be both a representative and a regulatory body, governed by a council similar to other self-regulatory bodies, such as the Law Society, the representative body for solicitors in England and Wales. In the case of the Law Society, it has responsibility for setting the rules of conduct and standards for the profession as well as enforcing compliance, as set out in the Society's comprehensive guide to the professional conduct of solicitors. Anyone who does not have a practicing certificate and who is therefore not a member of the Law Society is unable to act as a solicitor. If any practicing solicitor is acting in breach of the rules, the Law Society will investigate and, when appropriate, enforce sanctions.

The self-regulatory organisation of the advertising industry, ASA, provides another useful example since it was originally completely unregulated and reaching massive and growing audiences (IFC, 2004). While statutory regulation was introduced for TV adverts, it was agreed that this system would be too slow for the fast moving press world and the Committee of Advertising Practice, CAP, was formed, representing 19 trade associations. While it faced criticism for its lack of action in the early years, it is now thought to be very effective. The ASA takes seriously its responsibility to be known and invests much effort in promotion of its role and in public information.

Self-regulation works best when it has a code of practice which has been compiled by the industry, giving it a vested interest in functioning well, but which is administered separately by an independent body. In the examples given, since the code is owned by the industry, it is rare for adjudications to be challenged. However, there are inherent challenges with systems of self-regulation. From an economic perspective and returning to the principal-agent rationale, power to regulate should only be devolved from central control to a third party if control can be maintained over the aims of the independent body. In the case of agents self-regulating, it is questionable whether the governing body, FIFA, would share the same objectives as the agents themselves.

2 Independent global regulation

Over the last decade football's biggest challenge has probably been that the general public have lost confidence in its ability to regulate itself. The need to re-establish this confidence is paramount. Revelations about corruption running through the heart of FIFA have undermined any steps that may have been taken by NGBs. Introducing a degree of independence to the regulatory function may help the new regime in this regard, potentially by creating a fully independent, worldwide regulator with the power to enforce meaningful sanctions. Policy coordination in some other areas of sports may provide some guidance.

The World anti-doping agency, WADA, is one such example, having been formed to restrict the illegal use of drugs in sport. However, as in the football industry, different groups, such as NGBs, with divergent interests are involved and they have often appeared to demonstrate a win-at-all-costs mentality, preferring to raise the profile of their sport by breaking records even if that is achieved illegally, so long as they continue to believe that their sport is advancing. And also similarly, while agents are able to exploit loopholes in regulations before they are closed, third parties have managed to develop new ways of using illegal substances which are not detected through regular tests. In this way, similar problems exist where methods of circumventing regulations are often covert and methods of policing must constantly evolve. Again, problems of different cultural approaches and boundaries between what is and is not acceptable are noticeable. Yet WADA, as an independent enforcement agency, oversees the industry.

WADA was established in 1999 'to promote and coordinate anti-doping in sport internationally' (UNESCO, 2005: 3) and the world anti-doping code followed in 2003 to provide the framework for all rules, policies and regulations concerning anti-doping. The Copenhagen Declaration on Doping in Sport, a non-binding agreement which recognises and supports the Code, is signed by the relevant NGBs, committing parties to the development of a legally binding and enforceable agreement and obliging member states to implement the code in their jurisdiction. As governments are not bound by a non-governmental document, the anti-doping convention was created under the auspices of UNESCO (Vermeersch, 2006). The international convention provides governments with a legal framework for worldwide harmonisation of anti-doping policy (WADA, 2005). Though independent, each country signs up to a form of self-regulation, with the agreement that if a country does not comply, sanctions will be very onerous. However, even with such efforts, there are limitations to the efficacy of the policy thus far. The absence of criminal sanctions and harmonisation efforts still seems evident, though the legal basis for such sanctions is still in its infancy, and it is hoped that political will and support will allow a much more efficient system in future, with member states willing and prepared to follow through their commitments to concerted action.

3 Regulation locally with redress to courts or FIFA

The third option is the route which has currently been chosen for the majority of regulatory processes in football. However, the challenges currently facing the world football governing body make it very difficult for the general public to put their trust in the existing system. As FIFA is overhauled, it will be interesting to see whether there is an impact on the processes and rules currently in place.

8.6 Conclusions

While various regulatory changes, including home grown player rules and squad size limits, have impacted on the way agents can conduct their business, they have managed to adapt to these changes, adopting different methods of working. Nevertheless, there is concern that each time regulations are made tighter in one element of the football landscape, there is a knock on effect in another. As shown throughout this book, it is the nature of football agents as entrepreneurs that allows them to keep changing and reacting to the industry in which they work.

The internationalisation of the game also continues apace and intermediaries have been crucial actors in the transfer networks that enable players to move around the world; however, the removal of FIFA regulation and the push towards local enforcement sit uneasily with this internationalisation. Given the divergent interests of the stakeholders involved, the task of bringing order is an arduous one. The various interested parties enjoy a difficult relationship, with divisions existing between the power of different clubs based primarily on their commercial success and their resulting ability to compete for players. Those clubs competing on an international stage would appear generally more reluctant to accept the authority of the federations, particularly in the day to day running of the game. Although, in public, the relationship between the federations is often one of mutual support, this frequently disguises an underlying tension, with each expressing general concern about the ability of the others to actively enforce their regulations. The lack of a unified policy and governance structure makes it even more difficult to monitor effectively the level of competence of both the national and international governing bodies to effectively regulate, and thereby enhance trust, with current weaknesses in the monitoring of compliance compounding the level of fragmentation between the stakeholders involved. The continuing tensions between parties have led to the development of a number of parallel policy debates in distinct forums which need to be unified in order to progress.

As the global governing body, FIFA has for a long time grappled with the cultural and national differences between its members, while at the same time promoting the game. Its role in regulating, policing, licensing and controlling agent practices is just one such example. Football now sits in an entertainment space and, as such, must continuously evolve in order to keep pace with its competitors commercially – which in future will include not only other sports, but also various other activities and passions which consumers may choose to pursue in place of football in terms of using their time and money. The technological advances reached over the last decade also make the football market a very different place to what it was even at the end of the twentieth century, one in which players have an even greater opportunity to be seen and intermediaries can develop networks and trade routes in a much more expedient manner. These changes make it almost impossible to predict what will happen next and any system in place must be flexible enough to adapt to future changes. In order to do this, self-regulation may be an efficient option.

While some actions of agents may not be within the rules, the win at all costs mentality adopted by clubs means that the majority are still willing to deal with those that breach regulations and these practices have become industry norms. Though the new regulations should go some way towards constraining the actions of parties involved in transfers, which are under the direct control of national associations, this only happens if governing bodies enforce the rules and impose punitive sanctions on offenders. Conversely, the same problems will endure. The main problem of the regulatory system in place before 2015 was that there are too many complicated rules which were inconsistently enforced. While the new rules remove some of the complications, they have introduced others and problems inherent to conflicts of interest are likely to remain.

Notes

1 The legal defence of the LFP and the LFLP is being put together by a large team of lawyers headed by Jean-Louis Dupont of Bosman fame.
2 The court decided that it did not have jurisdiction over UEFA.
3 This is not to say that the maximum level recommended by FIFA is necessarily appropriate.

Bibliography

Caceres, J. (2007) The dubious business of financial investors. *The German Times for Europe* [online]. Available from: www.german-times.com/index.php?option=com_con tent&task=view&id=1131&Itemid=68 [accessed 24 October 2015].

CNMC (2015) *Informe sobre la prohibicion de la propriedad de los derechos económicos de los jugadores de fútbol por parte de terceros.* Madrid: CNMC.

Couchmans (2015) Commentary on the regulation. *Football Intermediary* [online]. Available from: http://footballintermediary.co.uk/regulations/commentary-on-the-regulations/ #commentary-on-the-regulations [accessed 24 October 2015].

De Marco, N. (2014) The end of the licensed football agents. *Sports Law Bulletin* [online]. Available from: http://sportslawbulletin.org/2014/10/21/the-end-of-the-licensed-football-agent/ [accessed 24 October 2015].

Domènech, O. (2015) La FIFA echa a Patrice de La Masia. *Mundo Deportivo* [online]. Available from: www.mundodeportivo.com/20150906/201569939762/la-fifa-echa-a-patrice-de-la-masia.html [accessed 22 November 2015].

Duval, A. (2015) EU Law is not enough: Why FIFA's TPO ban survived its first challenge before the Brussels Court. *Asser International Sports Law Blog* [online]. Available from: www.asser.nl/SportsLaw/Blog/post/eu-law-is-not-enough-why-FIFA-s-tpo-ban-survived-before-the-brussels-court1 [accessed 29 November 2015].

EC (2002) Commission closes investigations into FIFA rules on players' agents. *EU* [online]. Available at: http://europa.eu/rapid/press-release_IP-02-585_en.htm?locale=en [accessed 20 November 2015].

FIFA (2015) *Regulations on working with intermediaries.* Zurich: FIFA.

FIFA TMS (2015) *Global transfer market report 2015.* Zurich: FIFA.

FIFPro (2013) FIFPro announces legal challenge to transfer system. *FIFPro* [online]. Available from: www.fifpro.org/en/news/fifpro-announces-legal-challenge-to-transfer-system [accessed 25 October 2015].

FIFPro (2015a) Trafficking football players in Portugal. *FIFPro* [online]. Available from: www.fifpro.org/en/news/trafficking-football-players-in-portugal [accessed 24 October 2015].

FIFPro (2015b) FIFPro legal action against FIFA transfer system. *FIFPro* [online]. Available from; www.fifpro.org/en/news/fifpro-takes-legal-action-against-fifa-transfer-system [accessed 24 October 2015].

FIFPro (2015c) FIFPro and FIFA improve protection of minors. *FIFPro* [online]. Available from; www.fifpro.org/en/news/fifpro-and-fifa-improve-protection-of-minors [accessed 24 October 2015].

Griver, S. (2015), Zahavi purchases Royal Mouscron. *The Jewish Chronicle* [online]. Available from: www.thejc.com/sport/sport-news/139369/zahavi-purchases-royal-mouscron. [accessed 28 November 2015].

IFC (2004) The Independent Football Commission Report on Self Regulation. *IFC* [online]. Available from: www.theifc.co.uk/publications/documents/SelfRegulation Report.pdf [accessed 24 October 2015].

James, S. (2015) Jonathan Barnett: 'Bale and Ronaldo are complete opposites, but there's no hatred'. *Guardian* [online]. Available from: www.theguardian.com/football/2015/ oct/12/football-gareth-bale-ronaldo-real-madrid-joe-hart-ashley-cole-jonathan-barnett [accessed 25 January 2015].

Kanti, S. (2015) Zahavi steps in with €8.5 m cash and Chelsea 'links' to save Belgium's Mouscron. *Inside World Football* [online]. Available from: www.insideworldfootball. com/world-football/europe/17356-zahavi-steps-in-with-8-5m-cash-and-chelsea-links- to-save-belgium-s-mouscron [accessed 6 December 2015].

KEA and CDES (2013) *The economic and legal aspects of transfers of players.* Brussels: Sport EC.

Lewis, P. (2000) Realism, Causality and the Problem of Social Structure. *Journal for the Theory of Social Behaviour.* 30(3) pp. 249–268.

LFP (2015) Las ligas española y portuguesa denuncian ante la Comisión Europea la pro- hibición de los TPO de la FIFA. *LFP* [online]. Available from: www.laliga.es/noticias/ las-ligas-espanola-y-portuguesa-denuncian-ante-la-comision-europea-la-prohibicion- de-los-tpo-de-la-fifa [accessed 15 November 2015].

McDougall, D. (2008) The scandal of Africa's trafficked players. *Guardian* [online]. Avail- able from: www.theguardian.com/football/2008/jan/06/newsstory.sport4 [accessed 24 October 2015].

Piers, E. (2015) Can FIFA end child trafficking from Asia to Africa? *BBC* [online]. Available from: www.bbc.co.uk/news/world-africa-33602171 [accessed 24 October 2015].

Pinsent Masons (2015) Research and case law hint at how FIFPro's challenge to football transfer system might develop. *Out-law* [online]: Available from: www.out-law.com/ en/articles/2015/september/research-and-case-law-hint-at-how-fifpros-challenge-to- football-transfer-system-might-develop/ [accessed 25 October 2015].

Poli, R. (2015) Third-party entitlement to shares of transfer fees: Problems and solutions. *Asser International Sports Law* [online]. Available from: www.asser.nl/SportsLaw/ Blog/post/blog-symposium-third-party-entitlement-to-shares-of-transfer-fees- problems-and-solutions-by-dr-raffaele-poli-head-of-cies-football-observatory [accessed on 24 October 2015].

Reck, A. (2015) The impact of the TPO ban on South American football. *Asser Inter- national Sports Law* [online]. Available from: www.asser.nl/SportsLaw/Blog/post/the- impact-of-the-tpo-ban-on-south-american-football-by-ariel-n-reck [accessed on 24 October 2015].

Riach, J. (2015) Football agents fear 'wild west' as FIFA reforms seek to cap fees. *Guardian* [online]. Available from: www.theguardian.com/football/2015/mar/31/ football-agents-fifa-reforms [accessed 24 October 2015].

Skysports (2015) 'Intermediaries' chief in talks with the FA over FIFA reforms. *Sky- sports* [Online]. Available from: www.skysports.com/football/news/11095/9784302/ intermediaries-chief-in-talks-with-the-fa-over-FIFA-reforms [accessed 24 October 2015].

Szymanski, S. (2015) The economic arguments supporting a competition law challenge to the transfer system. *FIFPro* [online]. Available from: www.fifpro.org/attachments/ article/6242/Embargoed%20Stefan%20Szymanski%20Transfer%20System%20 Analysis.pdf [accessed 24 November 2015].

Turner, R. (2014) Player contracts: FIFA's proposed player agent reforms: analysis. *Bird&Bird* [online]. Available from: www.twobirds.com/en/news/articles/2014/uk/player-contracts-fifas-proposed-player-agent-reforms [accessed 24 October 2015].

UNESCO (2005), International Convention Against Doping In Sport. *UNESCO* [online]. Available from: http://unesdoc.unesco.org/images/0014/001425/142594m.pdf#page=2 [accessed 28 November 2015].

Vermeersch, A. (2006) The European Union and the fight against doping in sport: On the field or on the sidelines? *Entertainment & Sports Law* [online]. 4(1). Available from: www2.warwick.ac.uk/fac/soc/law/elj/eslj/issues/volume4/number1/vermeersch/ [accessed 24 October 2015].

WADA (2005) WADA welcomes adoption of International Convention against doping in sport by UNESCO. *WADA* [online]. Available from: www.wada-ama.org/en/media/news/2005-10/wada-welcomes-adoption-of-international-convention-against-doping-in-sport-by [accessed on 28 November 2015].

Whittall, R. (2014) Analysis: Barcelona hit with year-long transfer ban by FIFA. *Thescore* [online]. Available from: www.thescore.com/liga/news/469842 [accessed 22 November 2015].

9   Conclusions

This book has provided an overview of the football agents industry and how their role of intermediation has become so critical within the labour market. The regulatory interventions from both football governing bodies and national and international public authorities have contributed to creating a role for agents that has responded to previous market failure and also, at times, by limiting agents' activities, these interventions have pushed them to become more entrepreneurial in their operations.

We suggest that the role of an agent is case specific. Though there are commonalities in some of their roles, such as providing a matching service for clubs and players, brokering deals and negotiating players' contracts, the scope of their job tends to be determined by the specific needs and contract situation of the player. For a superstar player, the agent – or more likely the agency he is represented by – would tend to be a specialist in marketing and commercial aspects as well as contract negotiation. Although the majority of players do not need this level of special assistance, agents will still have a role in helping to provide them with the opportunity to progress their football careers. With a good knowledge of the market, an intermediary can transfer information between stakeholders and, when representing a player, this knowledge can help to negotiate a salary level which reflects the worth of the player to the club. Good agents offer a valuable service and have become a necessary part of the industry.

However, incident of malpractice have also been identified. Agents consulted in the process of writing this book themselves expressed concerns that they are often made a scapegoat for anything which goes wrong in the industry. Nevertheless, they also acknowledged that some elements of rule breaking exist and not all agents always act in the interest of their clients. The FIFA PAR, first introduced in 1994 then redrafted in 2000 and again in 2008, was thought to be largely ineffective and this perception led to FIFA stepping away from regulating the profession of agents altogether, instead delegating the responsibility of supervising 'intermediaries' to national associations in 2015. While various structural changes to the market place have impacted the role of intermediaries, the basic relationship between players and their representatives is still based on the principal-agent model and an agent earns the majority of his or her income when a player signs a new contract. Consequently, while it may be advantageous for a particular player to remain at a club, this decision might not be in the best interest of the agent. Scholars such as Holt *et al.* (2006) and Magee (2002) have shown that the biggest criticism clubs have of agents is that, at times, they seek to unsettle players who are currently under contract to clubs with the aim of generating transfers, guaranteeing another commission fee from contract negotiations without necessarily putting the player's interest first. While this has always been a concern, and was previously addressed in various drafts of regulations, a lack of enforcement of the regulations which were in place has suggested that the whole governance system has been 'a joke'. It is difficult to see how the new rules governing intermediaries will improve this situation given that the intermediaries may have no relationship at all with football's governing bodies.

Whether or not the removal of any governance structure is a good move remains to be seen; however, without strong authorities who are willing to enforce the rules, intermediaries – such as large FSAs and their business associates – are likely to become more powerful and challenge the decisions of the authorities on all issues. While individual NGBs may decide on their own level of regulation, meaning that for some markets there will be stricter rules than in others, essentially the new regulations on intermediaries have created a vacuum at the international level with no one really completely in control of activity within the representation industry. The decision of FIFA to effectively give up on trying to regulate an industry which has been always problematic seems somewhat symptomatic of the inability of the main world football governing body to control this sport. Football is without doubt a contested terrain in which various stakeholders have their own agendas. FIFA's proposed solution is to make the transfer market more efficient and at the same time try and stop money flowing out of the game. Agents have always faced claims that they are able to earn disproportionate sums of money for doing relatively little. In reality, it is the clubs and players who decide whether an agent is deserving of their level of commission and the frequency of huge sums being paid suggests that these people are willing and able to pay.

In order to improve transparency and integrity in transfers, FIFA has introduced two new systems: the TMS and the GPX. The GPX, in many ways, plays the same role as many scouting companies who collect and collate the details of players, documenting their characteristics and performance records. It is intended to provide an online resource through which stakeholders can gain detailed information about players. This in turn overlaps with the role that agents have typically occupied in working with clubs, and it remains to be seen whether it can do the job of an agent. Typically, agents have been able to provide clubs with a comparative advantage over their rivals in both having access to knowledge before anyone else but also in being able to directly appeal to players through trusted relationships with them when a club wants a particular player to sign for them. It is when agents are able to finalise these potentially difficult transfers that they really make their money and it is difficult to see why the introduction of an online database would limit that. Similarly, from a player's perspective, with clubs having easy access to information about many similar players around the world, it is not difficult to imagine that the transfer market will become more competitive. Again this will make an agent even more important for those players who need help to find a new club at the end of their contracts.

Even if the introduction of the TMS and GPX do have a role to play, we cannot forget that football is a global industry wherein clubs and countries work together but also compete against each other. As such, there will always be incentives for some stakeholders to overrule the system. In the case of NGBs there is not always an incentive for them to disclose misconduct or to effectively police their own leagues and competitions. Similarly, FIFA's dual role in attempting both to control the governance of football and to meet commercial objectives, particularly related to global competitions such as the World Cup, has proved difficult, if not impossible, to balance. In essence, business objectives have dominated while there has been little thought about whether or not the means to the end of becoming the biggest sports business have overshadowed any ethical considerations. There has in the process been a total failure of any internal regulation at the heart of FIFA and the same could be said for the rela-tionship between FIFA and its members, where decisions have been made for the wrong reasons and corruption has been inherent. FIFA at present is in dis-array. At the time of writing FIFA officials have been accused of corruption, particularly relating to decisions concerning which countries should host World Cup Tournaments, and the end of the Blatter era reveals the lack of future leader-ship and direction of the main football governing body. It is therefore not too surprising that challenges to the decisions made by FIFA are emerging. FIFPro's challenge against the transfer system is well timed to capitalise on lack of leader-ship. Agents too may be able to capitalise on a total restructure of the govern-ance system to force through their own objectives.

If FIFPro wins its case, it will be unclear whether a new system is to be intro-duced or restrictions removed altogether, creating a similar market to any other occupation where players would be free to move, having worked a specified notice period, should they find another job. It is anticipated that this would be a step too far for football and that the specificity of sport means that some restric-tions will remain to maintain the competitive balance and credibility of competi-tions. Whether or not a transfer market still exists in future, it is likely that agents will still have a role to play in the labour market for players. Given the sums of money involved in being successful, football clubs will always seek to contract the best talent and players will always want to play, no matter what the process is to secure a contract for either side. Agents have adapted in response to various regulatory changes and their entrepreneurial outlook tends to suggest that they will always find a role.

While it is clear that public perception of the governance of football is at an all-time low, and deservedly so, it is less obvious why the public perception of agents is typically bad. We have seen throughout this book that various attempts at reforming the agents industry have failed, leaving the perception of agents, if perhaps not true of the majority, as participants in an industry that is rolling in cash and ripping off clubs, stealing money from the game. Clearly this is not always the case, and agents still fill a useful role in the transfer market. The public perception in Europe in particular is largely negative. Typically, concerns are expressed that money paid to agents is leaving the game. However, it must be recognised that the same could be said for any football stakeholder – the majority of players, managers and chairmen are very well remunerated and reinvest little if any of their pay into the game itself. Perhaps then a key role for agents' unions could be in educating the public about the good that agents do. That said, in the current context, it is expected that there are more pressing issues for them to deal with.

Bibliography

Holt, M., Michie, J. and Oughton, C. (2006) *The role and regulations of agents in football*. London: The Sport Nexus.

Magee, J. (2002) Shifting balances of power in the new football economy. In: Sugden, J. and Tomlinson, A. (eds) *Power games: A critical sociology of sport*. London: Routledge: 216–239.

Index

Printed in Great Britain
by Amazon